CISTERCIAN STUDIES SERIE

MW00989727

David N. Bell

Many Mansions

An Introduction to the Development and Diversity
of Medieval Theology, West and East

Cover. The Virgin Mary is venerated by both Orthodox and Roman Christians alike. Crowned to indicate her status as Queen of Heaven, she stands on an altar above the orb of the earth. Below her are the abbot of the great benedictine abbey of Saint Vaast in Arras in northern France (right) and Saint Stephen Harding, third abbot of the 'New Monastery' of Cîteaux in Burgundy (left). Each offers to Mary a model of his abbey, thereby invoking her protection, but the representations are symbolic, not literal, for Cîteaux had not yet been built. During a visit to Saint Vaast in 1124, Abbot Stephen had commissioned this book from the monk-scribe Osbert, shown kneeling at the bottom. The manuscript was in the library at Cîteaux until the Revolution and is now, with most of Cîteaux's surviving books, in the municipal library of Dijon (France).

Saint Jerome's Commentary on Jeremiah, ca. 1125.
Dijon, Bibliothèque municipale ms. 130, f° 104.
Photo: CNRS (IRHT).

CISTERCIAN STUDIES SERIES: NUMBER ONE HUNDRED FORTY-SIX

Many Mansions

An Introduction
to the
Development and Diversity
of Medieval Theology
West and East

by

David N. Bell

Illustrations selected and described by
Terryl N. Kinder

Cistercian Publications
Kalamazoo, Michigan - Spencer, Massachusetts

Drawings and cover design by Alice Duthie-Clark
Photographs not otherwise credited by Terryl N. Kinder

Cistercian Publications
Editorial Offices
The Institute of Cistercian Studies
Western Michigan University
Kalamazoo, Michigan 49008-5415

The work of Cistercian Publications is made possible in part
by support from Western Michigan University to
The Institute of Cistercian Studies.

ISBN 13: 978-0-87907-546-0
ISBN 10: 0-87907-546-5

Typesetting by Photo-Composition Service, Grand Rapids

Printed in the United States of America

TABLE OF CONTENTS

INTRODUCTION

THE CORRECT TITLE of this book should be something like 'A brief introduction to selected themes of medieval church doctrine as they were developed in the latin west and the byzantine east from about the eighth century to the fourteenth'. But while such a title may be accurate, it is not very catchy. It is, however, important, for it specifies what this book is, and what it is not.

As to what it is, it is a companion volume to an earlier study of mine, published in 1989, which attempted to trace, as simply as possible, the development of the major theological doctrines of the christian tradition from their earliest beginnings in the first century to the period following the Council of Chalcedon in 451.[1] This present volume takes up the same basic themes—the Trinity, the Incarnation, the Sacraments, Eschatology—and continues the story, again as simply as possible, to about the year 1400. The two books were designed to be used in an introductory university course, lasting a single semester, dealing with the

---

1. D. N. Bell, A Cloud of Witnesses: An Introductory History of the Development of Christian Doctrine, CS 109 (Kalamazoo, 1989).

history of christian doctrine from the period of the early church through the Middle Ages.

My reason for writing the book was straightforward: I had no alternative. Introductory texts dealing with medieval christian *philosophy* are abundant (though few, in my opinion, are introductory enough), but when it came to finding an elementary introduction to christian *theology*, the situation was lamentably different. The second and third volumes of Jaroslav Pelikan's *The Christian Tradition: A History of the Development of Doctrine*,[2] are splendid studies, and, with their wealth of references, are of immense benefit to the scholar, but they were not appropriate for the course I had to teach. Furthermore, I also wanted a single text-book, not too long, which dealt with both western and eastern christian theology; and my friends and colleagues were united in their agreement that no such book existed, and that, in all probability, it could not be written. They may be right, but my own view is that impossibilities exist only to be surmounted. There is always a way.

In including the Orthodox east, however, I found it necessary to be selective. There is obviously no room in a book of this nature for a comprehensive examination of Orthodox doctrine, and I have therefore limited myself to Byzantium. There are no Orthodox Slavs in these pages, and the non-Chalcedonian churches appear only in passing. I have tried to present what might be termed 'basic medieval Orthodoxy', and those who wish for further detail will have little difficulty in finding it elsewhere.[3]

---

2. J. Pelikan, *The Christian Tradition: A History of the Development of Doctrine*, Volume 2 *The Spirit of Eastern Christendom (600–1700)* (Chicago/London, 1974), and Volume 3 *The Growth of Medieval Theology (600–1300)* (1978).

3. The best account in English of byzantine theology is J. Meyendorff, *Byzantine Theology: Historical Trends and Doctrinal Themes* (New York, 1974). For Russian Orthodoxy, see the bibliography to Meyendorff's article, 'Russian Orthodox Church', in the *Dictionary of the Middle Ages*, ed. J. R. Strayer (New York, 1982) 10:591–7 (but reliable works in English on medieval russian theology are very limited). For the ideas of the non-Chalcedonian churches,

So much for what this book is. What it is not is perhaps more important, not least for my own protection. Firstly, it is not designed for specialists or scholars. It is intended primarily for people who know nothing of medieval theology and who, for various reasons, would like to remedy that situation. As a consequence, the usual scholarly apparatus of footnotes, either informative or apologetic, has been reduced to a minimum; a number of complicated doctrines and controversies have been greatly simplified; and I have exercised stringent selection as to whom and what should be included in my discussion. That there will be some who will neither like nor approve my choice is, of course, inevitable.

Secondly, this is not a history of the medieval church (though an historical framework is obviously essential), and it is not a study of medieval philosophy, medieval spirituality, or medieval religion. That it overlaps all four of these areas is only to be expected, but they are not here my primary concern. Medieval theology is not the same as medieval philosophy, and although the two were certainly not separate disciplines, they did differ in focus and emphasis. 'Most histories of medieval doctrine', writes Jaroslav Pelikan, 'have been histories of Christian thought, or even histories of philosophical thought, rather than histories of what the church believed, taught, and confessed on the basis of the word of God.'[4] For us, he continues, the word theology 'tends to mean what individual theologians do and how they develop their systems, but I am employing it almost as a synonym for "church doctrine" '.[5] In this present study, I am employing it in precisely the same way.

The situation with regard to medieval spirituality and the practice of religion is very similar. One cannot avoid a discussion of some aspects of spirituality, for virtually all eastern theologians

---

see the excellent study by A. S. Atiya, *History of Eastern Christianity* (Notre Dame, 1968).

4. Pelikan, *Growth of Medieval Theology*, vii.

5. *Ibid.*

and most western theologians before the rise of scholasticism were agreed that the study of theology found its culmination in spiritual experience. The Venerable Bede defined theology simply as 'the contemplation of God'.[6] But to trace the history of the medieval christian spiritual tradition in east and west is not my intention in these pages. Nor is my concern with the day-to-day practice of religion in the Middle Ages. This is an interesting and important subject which is receiving much attention these days, though the accounts published so far have been restricted to the latin west. In some areas, such as a discussion of the western doctrine of purgatory, it cannot be avoided, but its appearance here is incidental, not primary.

This leads me to say a word or two about the place of women in this present study. It will not escape the reader that women are notable by their absence. The reason for this is not any chauvinism on my part, but simply a reflection of the fact that in the development of theology as we have defined it, western women played a minimal role, and eastern women no role at all. In the areas of medieval spirituality, medieval visionary literature, and medieval religion and devotion, the situation is radically different, and the profound influence of women in these spheres has only recently begun to be appreciated. But this present book is not primarily a study of religion, visions, or spirituality.

In short, what I have tried to do is to sketch an outline, and no more than an outline, of the development of 'church doctrine' in medieval times, to trace the course of the major controversies, to point out some differences of approach between east and west, and to introduce the reader to a number of fascinating and sometimes flamboyant personalities.

In making this attempt I have been greatly assisted by Dr E. Rozanne Elder, the Director of the Institute of Cistercian Studies and the Editorial Director of Cistercian Publications. She read through my manuscript with an eagle eye, saved me from a variety of embarrassing errors, and contributed a vast

---

6. Bede, *In Lucae evangelium expositio* III.x; PL 92:471D.

number of immensely useful suggestions. Most of these I have been more than happy to include, and I take great pleasure in acknowledging the invaluable assistance of someone who, for many years, has been both friend and colleague.

The illustrations to the volume were selected by Dr Terryl N. Kinder, a specialist in cistercian art and architecture, who persuaded me that if one were going to have illustrations at all, they should be not merely decorative, but instructive. She therefore took the time not only to choose the illustrations (and, in some cases, to photograph them), but also to write the accompanying captions. I am much indebted to Dr Kinder for her generous assistance, and should this book prove helpful or practical, both she and Dr Elder must share much of the credit.

D. N. B.

A NOTE ON THE ILLVSTRATIONS

Terryl N. Kinder

SOME SUBJECTS LEND themselves more readily to visual imagery than others, and theology is no exception. Whatever the topic, all representational art is an artifice: it is a two- or three-dimensional illustration of an event, object, or idea that exists or existed 'out there' somewhere—perhaps in Scripture or just in the mind of the interpreter. It must therefore be created by someone, out of available materials and technology, in recognizable visual form.

In transforming abstract theological concepts into images, medieval artists had much the same difficulty as would we. It is obviously easier to depict Mary the God-bearer or to illustrate the torments of hell than it is to represent the divine nature of Christ. For this reason, the distribution of images in this book is as uneven as are the surviving examples. Sometimes the artistic problems were just as dramatic and difficult as the theological controversies which were raging at the same time. But an investigation of this fascinating topic lies outside these notes.

It is well to remember that medieval art was not primarily the individual expression of a particular artist, as is the case today. In the Middle Ages, 'art' was a trade, like barrel-making or stone-cutting, and the artist was essentially a craftsman. He or she (for women practised some of these crafts) worked to commission: they might be hired to fill a large hole in the wall of a church with a stained-glass window; to copy and illustrate a book for a monastery, cathedral, or private patron; or to design an impenetrable castle. When a specific theological message was intended, the craftsperson would have followed the counsel of theological advisors. Sometimes even the colors to be used were specified in the contract. Individual expression might be exercised in the style or the composition or the details, but not in the content of the message to be delivered.

The objects illustrated in this book were chosen for their iconography (a word derived from 'icon' = image, and 'graphy' = writing), that is, their subject matter. Iconography is only one aspect of art, but it is the one most easily understood. Medieval images frequently illustrate stories, and since the majority of people at the time were illiterate, the narrative (and moralizing) aspect is stressed. When certain things were exaggerated and drawn out of proportion, this was not because the artist was unable to do it better: it was done to draw attention to a particular and important element. The hand of God coming out of the sky not infrequently has several extra finger joints; this is not an accident, but a message: 'God directs this scene, and don't you forget it!'

Other aspects of art play important, if sometimes less obvious, roles: medium and scale, for example, are significant. An ivory carving of a Crucifixion has an impact very different from that of a life-size frieze on the facade of the building or a tiny colored miniature in a manuscript. Proportion, perspective, and the relationship to the viewer are likewise important, for the effect that a piece of sculpture or a painting has on us may depend on where we are standing when we look at it, where it was originally located, and the conditions under which we view it (the light, the time of day or year).

Color also played a prominent part, since medieval painters could use color to suggest, in very subtle ways, ideas that could not be addressed directly. A good example is the gold background frequently used in byzantine icons and mosaics. This obviously expresses dazzling preciousness and shimmering richness in a cavernous church illuminated by candles, but it also has another function. It is a glimpse of the light of heaven, a foretaste of the glory of the world to come, and it creates a sense of otherworldliness that helps the viewer grasp and, in a sense, 'feel' the nature of an event which, like the Transfiguration, would normally be beyond physical comprehension. So far as we know, no eyewitness of the Transfiguration recorded an image of his experience. Yet the events, however remarkable, began in a world we know and which we can depict: Jesus took three disciples, Peter, James, and John, up a mountain to pray. So far there is no problem: a simple line separating heaven and earth serves to orient the viewer, and we can all recognize a mountain. But when Moses and Elijah appear, the artist runs into trouble: not only has he never seen Moses and Elijah, but he also has the unenviable task of depicting a Jesus transformed in prayer when 'the appearance of his countenance was altered, and his raiment became dazzling white' (Lk 9:29). Depicting Jesus on his knees in a white cloak scarcely begins to transmit the impact of the event. And while it does not solve all the problems—the artist had to call forth other things from his arsenal of trade secrets—having a radiant background of gleaming gold transforms the earthly mountain into a realm outside our daily experience: a realm where anything can happen, and apparently did. In this way, the artist creates two worlds—one terrestrial, the other celestial—to tell a story which itself takes place in two worlds (see ill. VIII-1, 3, IX-4). If we look at this from the limited point of view of logic and consistency, we will be unable to appreciate its sheer brilliance as a multi-level narrative that transcends words.

The variety of objects chosen for this book illustrates how certain theological points were treated for public instruction, and how a single theme could develop and evolve. It also offers a sampling of different media, regions, and styles, and it may usefully remind us of the ways in which art and theology were (and are) intimately intertwined. Theology helped determine the form of art; art was visual publicity for theology; theology interpreted Scripture; art interpreted theology and could itself create theological controversy. Theology was interwoven with art (and, indeed, with much else, as this book frequently reminds us). It might also be remembered that every object created was the product of the theology and taste of the time, the technical and financial means available, and the creative spirit of the person producing it. And every viewer of every object at any time—ourselves included—receives a reverberation of the original multifaceted impulse, amplified and continued through all the thoughts, experiences, expectations, edification, insight, and delight we exchange with it.

T. N. K.

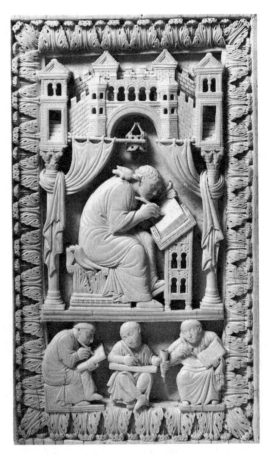

I-1 This luxury book cover, an ivory panel measuring 8 x 4⅜ inches, was carved by one of the most important artists of the Ottonian period (second half of the tenth century). Pope Gregory the Great is hunched over his manuscript in industrious solitude, with the dove of the Holy Spirit dictating into his ear. Of the three scribes below, the varied postures, bent heads, writing tools and unflappable attention give Gregory's authorship an air of urgency and authority. The architecture evokes the Lateran Palace in Rome, residence of the popes from the fourth century until 1309.

Gregory the Great and his Scribes, 960–980.
Metz Master. Vienna, Kunsthistorisches Museum, Inv. no 8399.
Photo: Kunsthistorisches Museum, Vienna.

1

Developments in the West

FEW PEOPLE have difficulty in locating their head or their feet, but defining the 'middle' is much more difficult. Some would regard it as no more than the area immediately around the navel; others might include the whole body from the neck to the shins. Defining the 'Middle Ages' is no less difficult. Some might prefer to confine themselves to western Europe and deal only with the three centuries from 1050 to 1350; others would like to include the entire range of eastern and western history from the death of Augustine of Hippo to the invention of printing. The first alternative is too narrow; the second is too broad. Our interest, however, does not lie in the philosophical definition of 'middle', nor are we primarily concerned with the complexities of political history and intrigue. We are concerned with the theological ideas of a number of remarkable individuals who appear like stars on the greek and latin skies from about the eighth century to the fourteenth, and those dates, therefore, will represent the limits of our investigation. Nevertheless, a certain amount of background information is necessary if we are to appreciate better the position and impact of these personalities, and in this first chapter we shall outline very briefly some of the major developments in european history, especially european intellectual history, from the sixth century onwards. There are five mile-stones to mark our way: (i) the pontificate of Gregory the Great from 590 to 604; (ii) the Carolingian Renaissance of the late eighth and ninth centuries; (iii) the papal reform movements of the eleventh century; (iv) the renaissance of the twelfth century; and (v) the rise of scholasticism and the universities in the thirteenth century. All these are essentially western or latin phenomena; what happened in the greek east we shall consider in our next chapter.

1. The Pontificate of Gregory the Great

Born in Rome about 540, Gregory belonged to a rich and influential family. But rather than simply following in the footsteps of his senator father, Gregory, after inheriting the family fortune, sold much of the property, converted the family mansion into a monastery, made vast contributions to the relief of the poor, and founded six other monasteries on family estates in Sicily. He was an honest, humble and devout man, but (unfortunately for him) he was also immensely talented, and that talent was not to go unrecognized. In the 570s Pope Pelagius II appointed him one of the seven deacons of Rome, and a few years later sent him as *apocrisiarius*, or papal ambassador, to the greek court at Constantinople. He remained there for some seven years (though he never learned Greek) and then returned to Rome to become abbot of one of the monasteries he himself had founded. Here he stayed for about five years until, in 590, Pelagius II died and

Gregory, the obvious, but most reluctant, candidate, assumed the office.

Gregory had no desire to be pope, but once the position had been thrust upon him, he devoted himself wholeheartedly to fulfilling its duties and responsibilities. At the time of his accession, the situation in Italy was appalling. There had been floods, famine, plague, and pestilence; there was widespread poverty and starvation; civil government had collapsed and there was no political stability. Gregory was prepared to spend both time and money in redressing this unfortunate situation, and although he could not succeed in solving all the problems, his efforts were marked with considerable success.

Part of his success lay in establishing the papacy as a major temporal power with jurisdiction over all Christians, eastern and western, clergy and laity, and in extending this power as widely as possible. Gregory, therefore, was a staunch advocate of missionary activity, and it was during his pontificate that England was converted to roman Christianity and the power and influence of the roman church in northern Europe greatly strengthened. But it was not a quest for self-aggrandisement that inspired Gregory in these activities. He regarded himself as the shepherd of his christian flock, and if this flock were to benefit from his administration, it was essential to have some sort of stability, some sort of security, and some sort of centralized authority.

Gregory, however, was not only an administrator. He was also a writer and a very sound theologian. Two of his works are of special importance. First, we have in the *Regula pastoralis* (*Pastoral Care*) a clear and concise manual of conduct for his bishops (and in later centuries for parish priests as well) which lays great stress on their role as pastors. This, as we have seen, was something dear to the heart of Gregory and was a simple reflection of the life and work of the Good Shepherd, Christ, himself. The *Pastoral Care* presents us with a picture of the ideal pastor: devout, humble, learned, charitable, honest, concerned, and one who would teach by his example, not just by his words. To a large extent, Gregory himself fitted the picture; many of his successors did not.

A much longer work was Gregory's *Moralia in librum Job* (*Morals on the Book of Job*). This is a vast (and sometimes rambling) commentary in which Gregory slowly works his way through all forty-two chapters of the Old Testament book, explaining and interpreting the successive verses in a variety of different ways. Sometimes he dwells on the literal or historical meaning of the text. Sometimes he uses a verse as a sort of intellectual springboard and soars upwards into the ethereal realms of mystical theology, those sublime regions which deal with the relationship of the soul to God and the ascent of the mind to divine contemplation. But most often he concentrates on the moral sense of scripture, on what it teaches us about living the christian life and following in the footsteps of Christ. The treatise is an impressive piece of work and was immensely popular in the Middle Ages. Together with the *Pastoral Care*, it was standard reading in western monasteries, and since most of the theologians we shall meet were trained in monasteries, there is not one of them who was unfamiliar with Gregory's ideas.

Another area in which Gregory played an important role was in transmitting the ideas of Augustine of Hippo to the Middle Ages. Medieval western theology is firmly rooted in the doctrines of Augustine, but not always in the doctrines of Augustine as he himself explained them. In his *Morals on the Book of Job*, Gregory presents a somewhat amended version of Augustine's ideas. He is not afraid to simplify them, or to change them if he finds it necessary. He tidies up loose ends; he sometimes alters the emphasis; and, in general, presents the doctrines of Augustine in a more systematic, synthesized, and comprehensible way than did Augustine himself. He also has more to say than does Augustine on the life of asceticism and prayer, and his ideas on these matters, clearly expressed in lucid and straightforward Latin, are central to the development of medieval spirituality in the west.

After Gregory's death in 604, no strong leader was to appear for about a century. The north of Italy had already been lost to the Lombards, a germanic people who had established themselves there between 568 and 572, and none of the popes possessed the power to win back the disputed territory. The papacy, therefore, was forced to seek support from a secular ruler, and the ruler it found was the leader of the up-and-coming frankish dynasty, Pepin III. With the agreement of Pope Zacharias, who governed the church from 741 to 752, the merovingian king then on the throne was deposed and forced to enter a monastery, and Pepin was elected in his place. This happened in 751. But our interest lies not in Pepin, but in his brilliant son Charlemagne, who conquered the Lombards in 772, united Europe for the first time since the days of the legions, took for himself the title of Holy Roman Emperor, and instigated the Carolingian Renaissance.

2. The Carolingian Renaissance

Charlemagne—the name means Charles the Great—was born about 742 and was elected sole ruler of the Franks in 771. He was about thirty years old. For the next several decades he occupied himself in extending his dominions throughout as much of Europe as he could conquer, annex, or control; and so successful was he that by the time of his death in 814 the greatest part of western christian Europe from the Tiber to the Elbe to the Pyrenees was carolingian.

Charlemagne was a man consumed by the idea of empire and a man who saw himself as roman as any Roman before him. And so, just as the old Roman Empire had once dominated and united the whole civilized world, so too would that of Charlemagne. His empire, however, his new Roman Empire, would be not pagan, but christian and holy. During the 790s his dreams and vision were slowly realized, and when Pope Leo III was violently driven out of Rome in 799 by his political rivals, Charlemagne was the obvious person to look to for protection and help. He himself had already declared to the pontiff his intention to defend and strengthen the church, and after hearing Leo's appeal, Charlemagne provided the pope with a powerful escort and arranged for his return to Rome and his reestablishment on the throne of Peter.

Next year, Charlemagne himself went to Rome to investigate the charges that had been levied against Leo, and after the pope had cleared himself, he crowned Charlemagne as the new Roman Emperor in Saint Peter's basilica on Christmas Day in the year 800. It is one of the most famous and dramatic events of the Middle Ages, but it was not well received in the greek east. The emperor in Constantinople took a very dim view of the imperial pretensions of someone he considered no more than a barbarian upstart, and neither he nor his ministers were eager to recognize Charlemagne's authority. The consequences of that, however, are something we must leave for discussion until our next chapter.

The new emperor did not settle in Rome. Unlike other germanic chieftains who travelled around their territories, staying only for a short time in one place before moving on to the next, Charlemagne had already established a permanent capital at Aachen (also known as Aix-la-Chapelle) in what is now Germany, and from this administrative and bureaucratic centre he ruled his vast empire. But Charlemagne was well aware that if he were to govern such an empire effectively, he required not only a strong central administrative authority, but an effective means of imposing this authority whenever and wherever required. To do this he appointed *missi dominici*, 'those sent by the ruler', royal legates who would travel throughout his empire and ensure that Charlemagne's intentions were being carried out. But the *missi* were not enough in themselves: Charlemagne also needed intelligent and loyal deputies stationed in all the major centres, and—most important of all—he required standardized laws, lawcodes, and customs to ensure that all people in all places knew what was expected of them.

At the basis of all this lay the need for education. Charlemagne himself was deeply interested in learning, especially theological learning. He spoke Latin fluently, he understood Greek, and he had been thoroughly trained in grammar, rhetoric, dialectic, and mathematics. He realized that if his rule were to be exercised sensibly and competently, his *missi* and other deputies likewise needed to be educated. One cannot govern effectively by means of illiterate and half-witted civil servants.

Charlemagne's vision, however, did not end here. His own love of learning inspired him to wish the same for everyone with any talent, and in 787, three years before his coronation, he commanded that all the monasteries and cathedrals in his realm should be centres of study, and that those who had the ability to teach should do so. There was even a school in the Royal Palace where grammar, rhetoric, and logic were taught to members of the court, children of the high nobility (daughters as well as sons), and other interested parties, including Charlemagne.

The overseer of this astonishing educational reform was an Englishman, Alcuin of York (c.735–804). He had met Charlemagne in 781 and had been appointed his tutor in theology and education. It was he who organized a library in the palace, and after being appointed abbot of Tours in 796, he established there the model for all other monastic and cathedral schools. The fact that these schools were to be set up in monasteries and cathedrals not only illustrates the intimate linkage between education and religion in Charlemagne's days, but also reminds us that Charlemagne saw himself not just as a political ruler, but as an ecclesiastical authority as well.

Charlemagne's new empire was not only roman but christian, and he himself had no doubt that he was the God-sent, God-anointed defender of the faith. He was quite prepared to issue decrees on ecclesiastical matters, including church discipline and doctrine, and he obviously expected to be obeyed. One of his prime objectives, therefore, was to ensure not only standardization of law and custom throughout his dominions, but also standardization in ecclesiastical discipline, doctrine, and liturgy. To accomplish that required the circulation of standardized texts of scripture, liturgy, and the fathers of the church—Augustine of Hippo, for example, or Gregory the Great—and that meant the wholesale copying of manuscripts.

Charlemagne's schools, therefore, were intended not only for the promotion of learning, but also for the dissemination of information. They were the printing-presses of the ninth century. And to assist in the long and laborious task of copying the manuscripts, Alcuin and his colleagues devised a new, clear, easy,

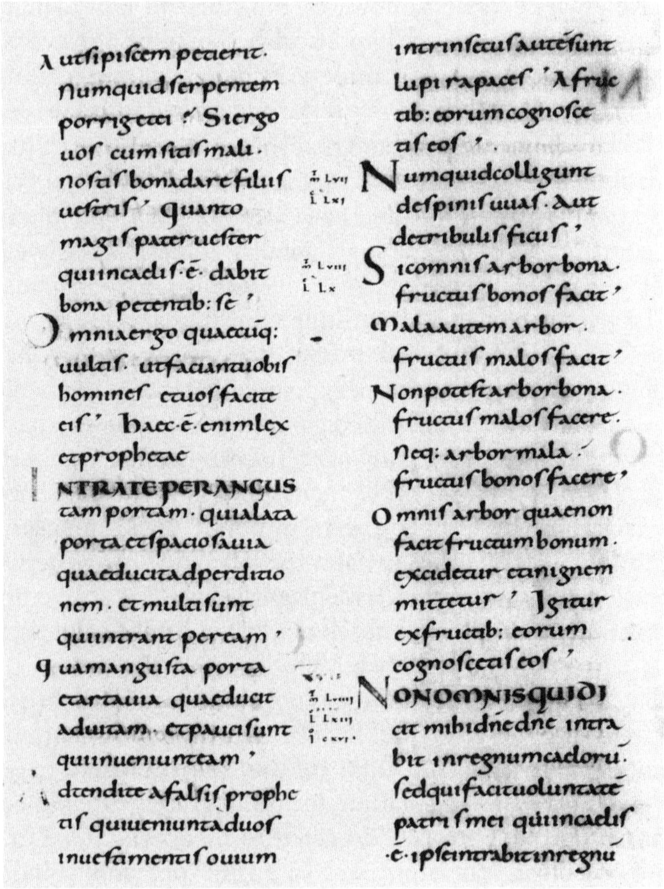

A ut si piscem petierit.
Numquid serpentem
porriget ei? Si ergo
uos cum sitis mali.
nostis bona dare filiis
uestris, quanto
magis pater uester
qui in caelis ē. dabit
bona petentib: se.
Omnia ergo quaecumq:
uultis. ut faciant uobis
homines et uos facite
eis. haec ē. enim lex
et prophetae
INTRATE PER ANGUS
TAM PORTAM. quia lata
porta et spatiosa uia
quae ducit ad perditio
nem. et multi sunt
qui intrant per eam.
Quam angusta porta
et arta uia quae ducit
ad uitam. et pauci sunt
qui inueniunt eam.
Attendite a falsis prophe
tis qui ueniunt ad uos
in uestimentis ouium
intrinsecus autem sunt
lupi rapaces. A fruc
tib: eorum cognosce
tis eos.
Numquid colligunt
de spinis uuas. aut
de tribulis ficus.
Sic omnis arbor bona.
fructus bonos facit.
Mala autem arbor.
fructus malos facit.
Non potest arbor bona.
fructus malos facere.
Neq: arbor mala.
fructus bonos facere.
Omnis arbor quae non
facit fructum bonum.
exciditur et in ignem
mittitur. Igitur
ex fructib: eorum
cognoscetis eos.
NON OMNIS QUI DI
cit mihi dne dne intra
bit in regnum caeloru
sed qui facit uoluntate
patris mei qui in caelis
ē. ipse intrabit in regnu

I-2 Carolingian (or Caroline) minuscule is a clear and easy-to-read script devised at the end of the eighth century by those (principally Alcuin of York) who oversaw Charlemagne's educational reforms. The script is the basis of our modern type, and most of the letters have the same form as those used today. Exceptions are the long 's' (which resembles an 'f') and the 't' (which looks like a 'c' with a line on top). The manuscript illustrated here contains the four gospels and was written by a scribe named Sigilaus between 849 and 851. The first line reads *Aut si piscem petierit* (Matt 7:10).

The Lothair Gospels, 849-851.
Paris, Bibliothèque nationale, ms lat 266, f° 32.
Photo: Bibliothèque nationale, Paris

standard writing-system which we now refer to as 'carolingian minuscule'. There were certainly plenty of other scripts in circulation, but some of them were difficult to write, and among others there was wide variation in the forms of the letters and in commonly used abbreviations. Alcuin took the best of a number of systems and devised the eminently readable script which is the basis of our modern lower-case lettering. The type-face that you see in this book is a direct descendant of the Carolingian Renaissance.

Legal reforms, liturgical reforms, reforms in church discipline, the quest for unity, the copying of texts (both religious and secular), the provision of a basic education, the development of a script that was easy to write and read: these were the aims and achievements of the Carolingian Renaissance. They must not, of course, be overestimated. Education was essentially restricted to grammar and rhetoric; theology (with some notable exceptions[1]) was little more than a reiteration of the ideas of the established fathers; mathematics served only to calculate the dates of the feasts of the church. Even during the lifetime of Charlemagne not every cathedral and monastery provided a school, and after his death the cathedral schools faded away until their revival in the eleventh century. Equally, we must not underestimate Charlemagne's achievement. The monastic schools did survive, and in the dark years of the two centuries following the death of Charlemagne, what little light there was came from these centres. The Carolingian Renaissance might have lacked originality, but had it not been for the vision of Charlemagne, european culture, especially literary culture, might have fizzled out in the declining years of the eighth century.

It was inevitable that after the demise of someone as powerful and charismatic as Charlemagne, things could not continue as they were. All but one of his sons had died before him—a fortunate occurrence, since Charlemagne had intended to divide

1. One of the most notable was John Scot Eriugena, whom we shall discuss in Chapter XVII.

I-3 Beneventan minuscule was developed in southern Italy around the middle of the eighth century, and was still in use there in the fourteenth century (its name comes from the former Duchy of Benevento). Characteristics include the 'a' (resembling 'oc'), the high-shouldered 'r', and the use of ligatures: et, fi, ri, ti, st. This folio comes from the first of two manuscripts which make up the volume. The very top line reads: *ab apostolis audierunt verbum veritatem et subversi*, and is part of a prologue to the First Letter to the Corinthians which normally introduced the Letter in copies of the Vulgate. The Letter itself begins with the initial P, illuminated with geometric and floral ornament: *Paulus vocatus apostolus Ihesu Christi per / voluntatem Dei, et Sosthenes frater.*

Composite manuscript of the Pauline Epistles, ninth century.
Paris, Bibliothèque nationale, ms lat 335 f° 31.
Photo: Bibliothèque nationale, Paris.

the empire among them—and although the sole survivor, Louis the Pious (778–840) did what he could, he was too weak and indecisive to keep the empire united. It is true that he continued his father's educational reforms, but Louis the Pious, as his name implies, was more interested in religion than politics, and his reign was characterized by ever more serious political struggles, especially with his sons. After Louis's death they split up the empire between them, and thereby reintroduced the regionalism and factionalism which are the inevitable concomitants of such a process. We shall meet Louis the Pious again in another context in Chapter III.

By the mid-ninth century, therefore, Charlemagne's empire had begun to disintegrate, and the situation was exacerbated by the wide-spread depredations of the Vikings and, to a lesser extent, the attacks of the Muslims and the Hungarians. Nor was the degeneration confined to political matters: european morality also sank to a low ebb, and nowhere was this more evident than in the depressing situation of the papacy.

3. *The Papacy and Reform in the Eleventh Century*

The ninth and tenth centuries were dark indeed for the history of the bishops of Rome. The lives of many of the popes will not bear close scrutiny and their deaths were often violent. Hadrian III was probably murdered; Stephen VI (VII) and Leo V were strangled; Benedict IV may have been assassinated; John X was suffocated; and Stephen VIII died of his injuries after being tortured. As for Pope Formosus, an educated and, for the time, exemplary pontiff, nine months after his death his successor had his body exhumed, arrayed in pontifical vestments, put on trial, condemned, mutilated, and flung into the Tiber. Most of the popes, in fact, were little more than dispensable pawns in a complicated and bloody game of chess being played by certain of the noble italian families. Perhaps the lowest point came in the pontificate of John XII. The political manoeuverings of his father had assured him of the position, and when he became pope in

955, he was barely eighteen. He was known to be a womanizer and a debaucher and many said that he had turned the Lateran Palace into a brothel. As a hard-nosed politician and intriguer he was fairly effective, but within a decade his sins had caught up with him: when he was about twenty-eight he suffered a stroke while in bed with a married woman and died a week later.

Churchmen were not ignorant of the fact that their church had become corrupt. The problem was the lack of any candidate for the papacy who was sufficiently strong and sufficiently concerned to do something about it. There were attempts, that is true, but it was not until the pontificate of Leo IX (1049–54) that these attempts really bore fruit.

Leo was not an Italian, but a member of a noble family from Alsace and a cousin of the Holy Roman Emperor, Henry III. He was educated at Toul and, in due course, his abilities were recognized by his elevation to the bishopric of Toul. Even as bishop his concern for moral reform was apparent, and his skills in negotiation were exercised in the field of international politics. When Pope Damasus II died from malaria in 1048, Leo, with the influential support of the Emperor, was elected pope. He proved to be a diplomatic and high-minded reformer who was deeply concerned about two of the greatest problems faced by the church of his time: simony (the buying and selling of ecclesiastical office)[2] and clerical unchastity. But although he exercised all his skill and put forth all his power to eradicate these vices, they were far too deeply ingrained in medieval thought and society to be easily removed. It was Leo who was pope in 1054 at the time of the Great Schism (a matter we shall discuss in the next chapter), and the separation of the eastern and western churches caused him great distress. When he died in 1054 he was a broken and disappointed man, but one nevertheless who had restored the papacy to a higher, brighter, and more respected position than it had enjoyed for more than two hundred years.

2. The word derives from the name of Simon Magus, the magician of Acts 8:9–24, who tried to buy from Saint Peter the power to confer the Holy Spirit.

We may see in his reign a true foreshadowing of the much more dramatic reforms which were to be introduced twenty years and five pontificates later by Gregory VII.

Gregory was a Tuscan who had come to Rome as a child. When of the proper age, he took the habit in a monastery which may have had associations with Cluny (we will deal with Cluny in Chapter III), but was soon recalled to Rome by Leo IX who clearly recognized his abilities. He was one of Leo's bright young men and was undoubtedly imbued by him with the spirit of reform. He was elected to the papacy in 1073 and took the name Gregory out of reverence for the first pope of that name. Like Gregory I, Gregory VII was also brilliant, gifted, authoritarian, devout, perhaps a little fanatical, and a very sound theologian. And like Gregory I, he was also a staunch advocate of the idea that the pope was the shepherd of all Christians, both lay and cleric. Simony—the greatest scourge of the early medieval church—and clerical unchastity occupied his attention as they had occupied the attention of Leo IX, and he was determined to establish the papacy as a strong and respected centralized authority in Europe. His efforts were not always rewarded, and his attempts at imposing the papal will on lay rulers inevitably led to prolonged and unfortunate conflict. But despite the fact that he did not live to see all his reforms come to fruition, the ideas and ideals which possessed him were taken up by his successors and established the direction that the western church would take over the succeeding centuries.

4. The Renaissance of the Twelfth Century

When Gregory VII died in 1085, the abbot of the benedictine monastery of Bec in Normandy was a man in his early fifties named Anselm. He had been born in Italy in about 1033 and had moved to France in his early twenties. In 1059 he entered Bec, where he soon gained a reputation for learning, teaching, and spiritual direction, and on the death of its founder-abbot in 1078, Anselm was elected as his successor. He had close relationships with the english church and the english crown, and when the archbishop of Canterbury—another monk of Bec—died in 1089, the english clergy made it clear that they wanted Anselm to be his successor. Anselm himself was willing to accept the office, but conflicts between him and William Rufus, the english king, on the relative authority of church and state delayed his consecration for four years. Indeed, the question of how far papal power extended—and of how far the power of the pope's archbishop extended—was to be a problem in England for many more years. Like Gregory VII and Leo IX, Anselm of Canterbury was also a reformer, but as theologian and philosopher he far outshone most of his predecessors and all of his contemporaries.

For Anselm, our God-given gift of human reason was to be used in demonstrating and defending the faith of the church. Former theologians had, in general, been content to quote the scriptures and the old established authorities—Augustine, for example, or Jerome, or Gregory the Great—but this was not sufficient for the archbishop of Canterbury. Reason must not be used to question the faith, that is true, but it may—indeed, it should—be used to explain it. The faith of the church tells us that God exists. We do not question that. But by the use of human reason, said Anselm, we can prove logically that God exists, and that is a great step forward.

Anselm represents the first trickle of a flood which was soon to break over the whole of western Europe. It was a flood which is often referred to as the 'renaissance of the twelfth century,' though it had its beginnings in the last decades of the eleventh. There had, in fact, been numerous renaissances before it—the Carolingian Renaissance is the most obvious—but the renaissance of the twelfth century differed both in degree and in kind from its predecessors. It was based on reason as well as authority, and it recognized, though within severe limits, the positive value of human logic and the autonomy of the human mind. Authors who had hitherto been unknown or ignored in the west were now cultivated. Law and legal studies came into their own. Science and medicine which, for centuries, had been hidebound by the theories and ideas of classical authors, began to break free from these constrictions. And the old cathedral schools, the schools that had been founded by Charlemagne and which had faded away in the course of the ninth century, were re-founded and re-planted in the fertile soil of France. There they blossomed and flourished and, in due course, transformed the intellectual life of western Europe.

Until about the middle of the twelfth century western scholars and theologians knew only the works of latin writers and a few greek texts—primarily logical works of Aristotle and Porphyry—that had been transmitted to them in latin translation. But from the 1130s we begin to see the impact of islamic Spain. The Muslims had conquered that country in the eighth century and had established there a civilization remarkable for its learning, culture, architecture, literature, theology, mysticism, and general sophistication. As part of this cultural flowering, the Muslims had translated into Arabic huge amounts of greek literature—especially the works of Aristotle—and it was these aristotelian treatises which, in the second half of the twelfth century, burst upon the gaze of an astonished Europe. They were like a new sun, and for the next two centuries they bathed the west in the brilliant but dangerous light of aristotelian day.

Aristotle wrote on almost everything. He discussed physics, astronomy, astrology, meteorology, zoology, biology, physiology, geology, logic, metaphysics, ethics, politics, sociology, and theology. We now know that much of what he said was totally wrong, but that was not the opinion of the bedazzled people of the twelfth century. Unfortunately, however, the scientific ideas of Aristotle soon brought him into conflict with God. In 1070 storms and floods had been caused by the will of an indignant deity; in 1170 they were the result of meteorology and the position of the planets. God's domain was being invaded by aristotelian science and it would not be long before God himself was invaded by aristotelian logic. Obviously, the church had to do something about it, and what it did and how successful it was in doing it is something we shall discuss in its proper place.

Suffice it to say that after the renaissance of the twelfth century, western Europe was never the same again; and all the

problems, disputes, and controversies which the modern christian churches are experiencing can, to some extent, be traced to
the events of this remarkable period.

5. Scholasticism and the Universities

The word 'scholasticism' comes from the Latin word *schola* or
'school', and it refers to the methods of thinking and speaking
which were the legacy of the medieval schools. Which schools?
Not so much the monastic schools, which still tended to stay
close to the facts of the faith and the fathers of the church, but
the cathedral schools and, a little later, the universities.
The schools taught three main subjects: grammar, logic, and
rhetoric. Grammar enabled students to write and speak correctly;
logic taught them how to present a reasoned argument; rhetoric
provided them with the techniques they needed to win their case.
This group of three subjects, the *trivium*, had been established
in the time of Charlemagne, and in the dark centuries which
followed his death and the death of his son, Louis the Pious, they
had been kept alive in the monasteries. But with the reestablishment of the cathedral schools in the late eleventh century, they
were fanned to new flame and applied to the service of the faith.
God has revealed certain truths to us, but (as Anselm had said) it
is our duty to use our trained reason to examine, analyze, define,
and demonstrate these truths so that we may attain a deeper and
better understanding of them.
Scholasticism therefore demands great clarity and precision
in thinking, speaking, and writing. It requires us to define our
terms and to progress stage by logical stage to an inevitable and
necessary conclusion. First of all, we state our thesis as precisely as
possible. Secondly, we martial the opposing arguments and state
the antithesis. Thirdly, we examine both points of view and derive
a resolution, the synthesis, which then becomes the new thesis,
and the whole process begins again. Good scholasticism can be an
extremely useful and revealing tool: a razor-sharp scalpel to open
up the mysteries of salvation. Bad scholasticism—and there was

I-4 The College of Huban (or Hubant) was founded in Paris in 1346 by Jean de Hubant, counsellor to the king of France, who established scholarships for six young students from his native region in central France. Better known as Ave Maria College, it existed until the French Revolution and part of the buildings still stand. This is one of six remarkable painted folios included in a collection of legal acts on the foundation and administration of the college made in 1387. Some of the drawings illustrate rules requiring the students to perform various religious and domestic duties and charitable acts. The bottom band, for example, shows them approaching the Virgin and Child for devotions. The college also supported ten poor women and ten poor men, who are shown in the top two bands, engaged in various labors.

Student Life in the Middle Ages.
From the *Statutes of Huban College*, 1346–1541 (paintings 1387).
Paris, Archives nationales, AE II 408.
Photo: Service Photographique des Archives nationales, Paris.

a great deal of it—serves only as an antidote to insomnia. Two of the best and most influential scholastics were Bonaventure (1221–74) and Thomas Aquinas (c.1225–74), and we shall meet both of them in Chapter V.

The techniques of scholasticism were not limited to theology and philosophy. They were also applied elsewhere, especially in the realm of law, both canon law (the law of the church) and civil law (the law of the kingdom). Indeed, the precision, logic, and clarity of the scholastic approach seemed ideally suited for dealing with legal questions, but law was not taught in the schools. Nor was medicine. The translation of arabic works in the twelfth century had included a great deal of medical material, and there is no doubt that for all its failings, arabic medicine was far in advance of anything the christian west could offer. And in addition to all this, once human reason had been acknowledged as a legitimate tool, it tended to rebel against the bounds within which it had been confined by the church and desired to extend itself into uncharted areas. A need developed, therefore, to accommodate those scholars who were interested in subjects other than those taught in the schools and for bright young men who wished to enlarge the boundaries of human knowledge and reason.

Hence, in the course of the twelfth century, we see the establishment of the universities of Salerno and Bologna, and we will not here examine the tricky question of which preceded which. Salerno specialized in medicine and Bologna in law, both canon and civil. Shortly thereafter, in about 1200, came the university of Paris, specializing in theology and philosophy, and, following the Parisian model, Oxford and Cambridge in England. Other institutions followed rapidly: Padua in Italy, Prague in Czechoslovakia, Montpellier in France (which would soon take over from Salerno as the foremost medical school in Europe), Coimbra in Portugal, and Valladolid and Salamanca in Spain. From this time onwards the universities dominated the intellectual life of Europe. The most important theologians and philosophers all received a university education, and from Alexander III[3] onwards, most of the medieval popes were hard-headed lawyers trained at Bologna.

With the rise of the universities in the thirteenth century we will draw to an end this brief account of the intellectual history of Europe. We shall meet all the people and all the developments again in later chapters, and the fact that certain major events seem to have been excluded—the crusades, for example—does not mean that they are not important. It means that they are not important for our immediate purposes. In any case, we shall have cause to discuss the crusades in the course of Chapter II. For the moment it is time to take our leave of Europe and the latin west and see what had been happening during these centuries in Constantinople and the greek east.

3. Alexander III was pope from 1159 to 1181.

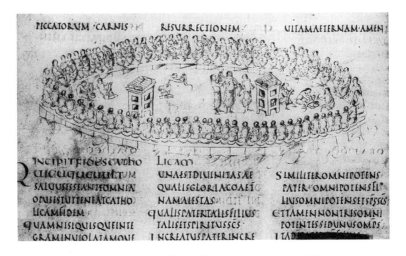

II-1 The Utrecht Psalter (named from the university where it is kept today) was made and illustrated in Hautvilliers, in the Champagne region of northeastern France, between 820 and 830. The Psalter uses an older style of roman capitals, not the more modern carolingian minuscule, and the pages are lavishly decorated with lively, spontaneous pen-and-ink sketches illustrating the individual psalms. This one show the unnamed ninth-century artist's idea of a Council of the Church: nearly eighty participants are seated in a circle listening or conversing among themselves; three are speaking from the floor, while six seated scribes are taking notes on parchment rolls, dipping their quill pens into their inkpots.

Utrecht Psalter, 820–830
Utrecht, University Library, ms 32, f° 90v.
Photo: University Library, Utrecht.

11

Developments in the East: The Road to Schism

IN THIS SECOND chapter we shall consider a number of major developments that took place in the greek east from the Council of Chalcedon onwards, and we will concentrate on those that relate to the final breach between the eastern and western churches. Some of the material has already been covered in *A Cloud of Witnesses*, the companion volume to this present book, and rather than repeating all that information here, it will sometimes be more convenient to refer back to the earlier study. In this second chapter, just as in that which preceded it, there are five convenient mile-stones to mark our way: (i) the aftermath of the Council of Chalcedon in 451; (ii) the iconoclastic crisis

of the eighth century; (iii) the schism of Photius the Great and
Nicholas I in the ninth century; (iv) the so-called Great Schism
of 1054; and (v) what happened after that.

1. Christological Controversy after Chalcedon

During the first half of the fifth century, the eastern christian
world had been rent apart by a complex and vicious controversy
that centred on the person of Christ. The question was not
whether Jesus of Nazareth was God and man—that was accepted
by both parties—but how the Godhead and the manhood were
related and what words should be used to describe the relationship. Was Christ God *and* man, or God *with* man, or God *in*
man, or just the God-man? Was the manhood united with the
Godhead or conjoined with the Godhead? Was the humanity
absorbed by the divinity or the divinity by the humanity? And if
not, how could the two natures be distinct, yet not separate? Or
how could both be present in one body, yet not confused?[1]

Such difficult theological questions rapidly became entangled
in political and ecclesiastical rivalries, and by 451 the christian
east was in turmoil. The eastern emperor at the time, Marcian,
together with Pulcheria, his more intelligent wife, did what the
eastern church always did in times of crisis: they called a council,
the Council of Chalcedon, the greatest council of the early
church. More than five hundred bishops attended, and after long
and animated discussion, the Council issued the *Chalcedonian
Definition of the Faith,* a most important document which stated
that Christ was

> made known in two natures without confusion, without
> change, without division, without separation; the difference
> of the natures being in no way removed because of the union,
> but rather the specific property of each of the two natures
> being preserved, and coming together in one person and one

1. See *Cloud* Chapter IX.

subsistence, not parted or divided into two persons, but one
and the same Son and only-begotten God the Word, Lord
Jesus Christ.[2]

For Constantinople and the christian west, this was a clear and
unambiguous statement, but it was not so for the Christians in
Egypt. The problem lay with the word 'nature', *physis* in Greek.
Physis did indeed mean 'nature', as in the 'nature' of the Godhead
or the 'nature' of the manhood, and that is what the fathers at
Chalcedon intended it to mean. But, unfortunately, it could also
be interpreted as 'person,' and if it were taken in this sense, the
Chalcedonian Definition had stated that Christ was two people!
Constantinople and the latin west took *physis* to mean 'nature'
and therefore had no trouble in accepting the *Chalcedonian
Definition*; the egyptian christians took it to mean 'person' and
therefore rejected the Council and all that it stood for. For them,
Christ was *one physis*, *one* person, and they therefore came to be
known as Monophysites. Their opponents are usually referred to
as Chalcedonians.[3]
Between these two groups there was no love lost, and after Chalcedon the antagonism between Alexandria and Constantinople became increasingly bitter and vicious. None of the
attempts at ending the hostilities and misunderstandings succeeded, and some led only to further difficulties and yet more
violence.
In 482, for example, Zeno, the eastern emperor, and Acacius,
the patriarch of Constantinople, issued a document which tried
to avoid the problem of the meaning of *physis* by omitting the
word altogether. Christ was declared to be 'one, not two', and
people could fill in the blanks as they pleased. The document
also implied that although it was most probable that the fathers
at Chalcedon had been correct in what they said, this was not

2. *Cloud* 122.
3. See *Cloud* 129–32.

absolutely certain, and just to be on the safe side, the chalcedonian reference to 'two *natures*' should be avoided.[4]

When news of this document reached the west, Pope Felix III was infuriated. Firstly, he had not been consulted on the matter, and as a good Chalcedonian (as were all westerners) he was not prepared to concede that the fathers at Chalcedon might have erred in any way at all. In 484, therefore, he excommunicated the patriarch of Constantinople, and the patriarch replied by removing the name of the pope from the diptychs. The diptychs were the lists of names of christians, both living and dead, who were considered fully orthodox and for whom special prayers were said in the course of the Divine Liturgy. To have one's name removed from the list, therefore, was to imply that one was not orthodox, and it was a convenient, if passive, way of implying that patriarch and pope were no longer in communion. Thus was born the so-called Acacian Schism which lasted from 484 to 518. It was the first schism between the eastern and western churches. It was not the last.

Another attempt at resolving the conflict between the Chalcedonians and Monophysites ended even more disastrously. In 624 the eastern emperor held consultations with monophysite leaders on what could be done about the problem, and they suggested that it might be possible to admit that in Christ there were indeed two natures, but that these two natures always operated together in harmony. In other words, there were two natures, but one single 'operation' or 'activity'. This suggestion was then sent off to the patriarch of Constantinople, who accepted it, and also to Pope Honorius I in Rome, who likewise accepted it, but who, in his reply, added the unfortunate comment that what one was really saying was that in Christ there were two natures but only one *will*. Both emperor and patriarch thought that this was an even better solution to the problem, and in 638 the emperor issued a proclamation stating that in the future there should be no further mention of 'operations' or 'activities', but that in

4. See *Cloud* 132–3.

Christ there were two natures united in a single will. This was the beginning of Monotheletism, and the interested reader will find details of the matter in A *Cloud of Witnesses*.[5]

Monotheletism was always wrong—it denied any effective role to Christ's human will—and theologians both eastern and western objected to it. But the emperor was not pleased with their dissent and wreaked violent retribution. In the east his antagonism led to the mutilation and subsequent death (in 662) of one of the most brilliant of the greek theologians, Maximus the Confessor. In the west it led to the astonishing episode of the arrest of Pope Martin I. He was seized, smuggled out of Rome, taken to Constantinople, flogged, imprisoned, and finally banished to the Crimea, where he died from starvation and mistreatment in 655.

The voices of Maximus, Martin, and their colleagues did not go unheard, but it was politics rather than theology that brought an end to Monotheletism. When a later emperor, Constantine IV, saw that the doctrine of one will had lost its usefulness in reconciling Monophysites and Chalcedonians, he decided that there was no longer any point in antagonizing the west by maintaining it as imperial policy. He therefore wrote to Pope Agatho (an intelligent and impressive pontiff) suggesting a council to discuss the matter, and in 680–681, the Sixth Ecumenical Council was held in Constantinople. But despite the fact that Monotheletism was rightly condemned, there was still to be no peace in the eastern church. In little more than forty years, it would be rent apart by another protracted and violent controversy, this time over the use of icons.

2. The Iconoclastic Controversy

Icon or *eikōn* is simply the greek word for 'image', but in the eastern church three-dimensional images—statues—are very

5. See *Cloud* 134–8.

rare. An icon is normally a two-dimensional representation of Christ, Mary, an angel, or a saint which may be painted on a portable wooden panel or on the walls of a church as a fresco. Icons could also be executed in mosaic.

A full account of the theology of the Iconoclastic Controversy must be left for Chapter XIV, but it will do no harm to summarize the main historical developments here. According to eastern christian tradition, the first icons were icons of Mary and were painted by Saint Luke (some of these survive, though the reality does not correspond to the tradition), but the use of religious painting in Christianity was slow to develop. The earliest christians preferred to symbolize Christ rather then portray him, and it was not until the later fourth century that pictorial representations of Christ and Mary became common. Even then there were objections to 'graven images'.

The veneration of icons probably began not with depictions of religious figures, but with representations of the emperor. A painting of the emperor was an extension of the imperial presence, and to bow to the painting, or burn incense before it, was no different from bowing or burning incense to the emperor himself. How much more, then, should we bow before a representation of the Emperor of emperors, the King of kings? By the second half of the sixth century, veneration of religious icons had come to play a major role in eastern christian devotion, but it was all too easy for people to slide from the veneration of icons into straightforward idolatry. We know from contemporary reports that by the seventh century some christians thought that all they needed to do to achieve salvation was to go into a church and kiss the icons. The Divine Liturgy was unimportant.

It was against this background that Leo III the Isaurian, in 726, launched his campaign against the use of icons. But although the hands were the hands of the emperor, the voice was that of certain of his bishops, especially those in Asia Minor. There is no doubt that these bishops were genuinely concerned, and it is also clear that they had sound support from many of their colleagues. But by the 720s the use of icons in popular piety was virtually universal in the christian east, and its staunchest supporters were not the educated clergy, but the monks and the working classes. Given the fact that the greek east was perpetually on a short fuse, it will come as no surprise to learn that Leo's first measures against the icons resulted in widespread and violent rioting.

To help him in his cause the emperor appealed both to the bishop of Rome and the patriarch of Constantinople. The pope was Gregory II, a politically astute and theologically sound pontiff, and the greatest pope of the eighth century; the patriarch was Germanus of Constantinople, a well-educated priest of noble family, deeply devoted to the Mother of God (seven of his homilies on Mary have survived), and the focal point of resistance to iconoclasm in the east. Both uncompromisingly rejected the emperor's overtures.

Leo, however, was not dismayed and continued his policy unabated. His son, Constantine V (741–775), did more. In some ways he was a sort of eighth-century proto-puritan who objected not only to the veneration of icons, but also to the veneration of relics and the intercession of the saints. The fact that he was also a very good theologian was offset by his being a monophysite, which did not help him in his negotiations with chalcedonian Constantinople, and by his inordinate savagery in persecuting the iconophilic monks.

Resistance to the imperial policies was not only physical, however, but also theological. In the midst of all the violence, there was need for a reasonable and logical voice that might appeal to the educated clergy and laity and persuade them that, despite the obvious dangers, the value of icons far outweighed their perils. Such a voice was heard from John of Damascus and, after John's death, from Theodore of Studios and Nicephorus of Constantinople, and we shall examine their arguments in Chapter XIV.

Under Constantine's son, Leo IV, persecution began to die away, and after his death his wife, the Empress Irene, brought the first phase of the controversy to an end in 780. Seven years later, the united efforts of empress, patriarch, and pope brought about the Second Council of Nicaea in 787 which wholly condemned iconoclasm and asserted that the veneration of both images and relics was right, proper, and necessary for christian devotion.

That, however, was not quite the end of the story, for in 814, primarily as a consequence of the retention of iconoclastic views by the byzantine army, the controversy broke out anew. Icons were again removed from churches; monks again were martyred; and Nicephorus, the iconophile patriarch of Constantinople, abandoned by his bishops, was deposed and exiled to the monastery whence he came. Once again, both sides put forth their theological arguments, but it was death rather than debate that ended the controversy. After the demise of the last iconoclast patriarch and the last iconoclast emperor, the latter's widow, the Empress Theodora, was able to put an end to persecution in 842. The restoration of the icons and the triumph of those who supported their use is still celebrated in the eastern Orthodox church on the first Sunday in Lent.

Throughout the hundred and twenty years of the controversy, the papacy had supported the use of the holy icons. But among secular rulers, and especially the most important secular ruler of the late eighth and early ninth century, Charlemagne, that was not the case. By his time most westerners could not understand Greek (Charlemagne was an exception), and when he received a copy of the Acts of the Second Council of Nicaea, it was a copy that had been translated into Latin. Unfortunately, it had been badly translated, and it appeared to say that adoration of icons should be equal to that given to the Holy Trinity itself. Charlemagne was not too troubled by this. He did not like the Greeks, for as we saw in the last chapter, the eastern emperor had been unwilling to acknowledge his claim to imperial authority in the west; and whereas the emperor in Constantinople considered Charlemagne a barbarian upstart, Charlemagne viewed the emperor as an arrogant élitist who refused to recognize reality when he saw it. Charlemagne, therefore, was quite happy to have theological reasons to support his political ambitions. So despite the fact that the western popes and a number of the eastern patriarchs had supported the same cause and were coexisting more harmoniously than had been the case for a very long time, the political animosity between east and west remained virtually unchanged and came to a head in the ninth century with the schism of Photius the Great and Nicholas I. The west refers to this event as the Photian Schism; the east as the Schism of Nicholas.

3. The Schism of Photius and Nicholas

The real origins of this schism lay far back in history, back in the first half of the fourth century in the time of Constantine I. Before Constantine, the Mediterranean world had been much more of a unity. For the most part, its inhabitants acknowledged the same emperor, obeyed much the same laws, and shared much the same culture. Greek-Latin bilingualism was fairly common, and even if you were not bilingual, you could get by in Greek in most corners of the mediterranean world.

During the course of the fourth century, this unity began to fall apart. Part of the problem was the very size of the empire. It was like too little icing spread too thinly on a cake that was too large: it began to crack at the edges and split in the middle. And then, in the first decade of the fifth century, the western half of the Empire had been subjected to a series of invasions by various barbarian tribes, and as a consequence of this, entered upon a long period of political and economic instability. In a world in which there was no security and in which all values had collapsed, the roman popes, whether they liked it or not, had been forced to assume secular as well as ecclesiastical power. Some, like Gregory I, deserve the highest praise for their sound and far-sighted government; others, as we have seen, were weak and unreliable. But whatever their individual talents, the institution of the papacy stood like a rock in a political quicksand and offered hope and security to a hopeless and insecure population.

Other barbarian incursions in the late sixth and seventh centuries contributed further to the mutual isolation of east and west, but by this time the two halves of the once united empire were separated not only politically and economically, but culturally, socially, and linguistically. From about 500, very few Greeks knew Latin, fewer Latins knew Greek, and neither side was much interested in doing anything about their mutual ignorance. There had already been one schism—the Acacian schism—and we have just seen that Charlemagne had no interest in aligning himself with the greek east, nor the greek east with the upstart west.

Against this background of mutual distrust and ignorance we must now introduce the two protagonists in the events which are to follow: Photius the Great, patriarch of Constantinople, and Nicholas I, bishop of Rome. Photius came from a noble family and had been very well educated—in time, he would become the most learned scholar of his generation—but his earlier training had been as a secular statesman rather than as an ecclesiastic. Nicholas was an energetic and forceful pontiff who had inherited from Leo I and Gregory I an absolute conviction that the pope was the vicar of Christ, God's representative on earth, and thereby had dominion over the whole of christendom, east and west alike.

The affair began in 858. It seems that Ignatius, the patriarch of Constantinople at the time, had been too outspoken in denouncing the dissolute lifestyle of the emperor, Michael III, who was not called Michael the Drunkard for nothing. Michael responded to this by deposing Ignatius and appointing Photius as his successor; but since Photius was at the time a layman, he had to be rushed through the various stages of ordination with unusual haste. Then, after his consecration, Photius sent an official letter to Pope Nicholas informing him of his appointment.

Nicholas was scandalized that a layman should have been elevated so precipitously to such an exalted position and he refused to recognize Photius. But since he was also an astute politician, he saw a way to profit from the situation. At this time large areas in the far south of Italy were nominally under byzantine control, so in 861 Nicholas sent legates to Constantinople to say that in exchange for the return of certain of these territories, he would overlook the irregularities and recognize Photius. The emperor, of course, had not the slightest intention of relinquishing any territory whatever, but to show their goodwill, he and Photius suggested to the legates that they be the main arbitrators between Photius and Ignatius at a synod that would be called to consider the matter.

The legates accepted the offer (though they should first have consulted with Rome), took part in the synod, agreed (probably under pressure from the easterners) to the deposition of Ignatius, recognized the appointment of Photius, returned to Rome, and informed the pope. Nicholas was furious. So far as he was concerned, the vicar of Christ had full authority over the whole church, and he alone had the power to make and break patriarchs. He therefore accused his legates of exceeding their powers (which they had), declared the deposition of Ignatius null and void, and excommunicated Photius at a synod held at the Lateran in August 863.

The pope's actions infuriated the emperor and the eastern bishops. They were quite prepared to see in Rome a primacy of honour, but not a primacy of jurisdiction.[6] In any council or synod Rome might certainly take the first seat and act as spokesman, but no more than that. The bishop of Rome was *primus inter pares*, 'first among equals', and had no right to interfere in the affairs of another patriarchate. The situation was rapidly becoming critical, and was soon to be made worse by events in Bulgaria.

At this time, pagan Bulgaria was being evangelized by the greek church and had, in any case, a long history of looking to Constantinople rather than Rome for religious advice. But although the bulgarian ruler, Boris, was eager to accept Christianity, he also wanted to maintain his independence, both politically and ecclesiastically, and the eastern church made it quite clear to him that this was impossible. Boris therefore began to play politics. He wrote to Pope Nicholas to see if he could get a better deal from him, and the pope was only too delighted to provide him with missionary bishops (the greeks had provided

6. See *Cloud* 174.

mere archimandrites, clerics of a much lowlier status) and anti-eastern advice.

Photius, naturally, objected to this and in 867 circulated a letter stating that the latin church had no business in Bulgaria and that, in any case, the latin missionaries were teaching heresy. What they were teaching was the double procession of the Holy Spirit, a problem we shall consider in some detail in Chapter X. Later in the same year, Photius held a synod at Constantinople and excommunicated Nicholas, but the pope died in November 867 before news of the excommunication could reach him.

The subsequent history of this unfortunate affair need not detain us. Later in 867, as a consequence of murder and political manipulation, Photius was deposed and Ignatius reinstated. Then, after the death of Ignatius in 877, Photius was restored, but only for eight years. In 886 he was deposed again and so disappears from the stage of history. He retired to a monastery where he died towards the end of the century.

We should note, however, that at the time of Photius's first deposition in 867, communion between east and west had been restored—Photius, after all, was no longer patriarch and Nicholas was dead—and this communion was to continue throughout his second period as patriarch. The new pope, John VIII, was more diplomatic than his predecessor and Photius behaved with more circumspection than had earlier been the case. But although Photius himself died in full communion with Rome, the damage had been done, and the clash between Nicholas and Photius was an unfortunate prefigurement of the way things would develop in the future.

4. The Great Schism of 1054

Over the next two centuries, relations between east and west further deteriorated. By the early 900s pope and patriarch were once again at odds, and Patriarch Nicholas I (the same name as the roman adversary of Photius) removed the name of Pope Anastasius III from the diptychs. It was not the first time this had been done: Acacius had done the same to Felix III back in the

Like theology, architectural preferences for church design in East and West evolved differently. A longitudinal (basilica) plan was favoured in the West, the form being that of a latin cross in which the stem is longer that the three upper arms (✝). In the East a centralized plan was more common, whether circular, octagonal or shaped like a greek cross with four equal arms (✜).

II-2 The present church of Saint Peter in Vatican City was built over the site of a much earlier church now called Old Saint Peter's, whose construction was begun after the Edicts of Toleration (311-313). Old Saint Peter's was an especially grand example of the western basilica type; the nave had clerestory windows allowing direct light and double aisles to hold worshippers and pilgrims, transepts gave added space for processions (and for viewing Saint Peter's tomb), a small semi-circular apse (not visible here) enclosed the altar, and a wide narthex preceded the nave.

Old Saint Peter's, Rome, begun c. 320.
Re-drawn by Alice Duthie-Clark, after K. J. Conant's reconstruction.

fifth century. It is true that a hundred years later there would be a temporary reconciliation when the pope's name was once again included,[7] but it was not to last. The name of John's successor,

7. The pope in question was John XVIII, bishop of Rome from 1003 to 1009.

II-3 The celebrated monastery of Daphni is located six miles west of Athens. The church was built on a centralized plan, known as the greek cross-octagon or cross-in-square. Monastic congregations in the Middle Byzantine period were small (frequently fewer than twelve monks); hence the churches were small, yet it was the monastic church that defined the form for religious buildings in the East. The design is compact, the dome rising above the four short cross-arms to allow direct light into the central space. The apse (*hierateion*), as in all christian churches, faced east, and was normally flanked by the *prothesis* (sacristy) to the north and the *diakonicon* (vestry) to the south. The *naos* (nave) faced west and was no longer than the other three arms of the cross; it was preceded by a vaulted narthex.

Church of the Dormition, c. 1080. Daphni, Greece.
Re-drawn by Alice Duthie-Clark.

Sergius IV, did not appear, and no pope has been listed in the diptychs for the last thousand years.

A further separation of the churches came in the following century and centred upon what may seem to be a minor point of liturgical usage: whether to use leavened or unleavened bread in the eucharist. Leavened bread was used by the Greeks; unleavened by the Latins. The theological arguments advanced by both sides were unimpressive and ineffective. Nor were they of much importance, for by this time the question of the azymes—*azymos* is the greek word for 'unleavened'—was simply the tip of a very large iceberg. The controversy over the azymes symbolized centuries of mutual ignorance, prejudice, hostility, and dislike.

By the early eleventh century large greek communities had been established in southern Italy, and the eastern emperors and patriarchs had long claimed that these areas fell under the jurisdiction of Constantinople. Others, however, had different ideas. In 1020 an anti-byzantine revolt broke out in southern Italy—the details need not concern us—and the leader of the revolt had hired norman mercenaries to assist him. The revolt failed, but the Normans appear to have liked both the place and the climate and had invited their friends and relations in northern France to come and join them. This they did, and a powerful norman dynasty was established in the south of Italy. As it prospered and expanded, it gradually encompassed more and more of the greek communities, and since the Normans were western latin christians, the areas they controlled now came under the ecclesiastical jurisdiction of the pope. The pope was Leo IX—we met him in Chapter I—and Leo was one of the first great reformers. Since part of his reform policy required liturgical uniformity, he gave his support to the Normans (whom he neither liked nor trusted) when they demanded that greek christians in norman territory follow western latin usage.

At this time the patriarch of Constantinople was Michael Cerularius (more accurately, Keroularios), a retired bureaucrat who had been ordained late in life. He was a sound administrator and, like Leo, something of a reformer, but he was not a good theologian and he was violently anti-latin. His reaction to the events in Italy was predictable: if greek christians were being forced to follow latin usage, then latin christians in Constantinople would follow greek usage. Michael, too, wanted liturgical uniformity, and the situation in Italy provided him with a good excuse to enforce it.

When the latin churches in Constantinople refused to conform to greek liturgical customs, Michael closed them down. He then had one of his bishops write a letter, designed to reach the pope, which contained a fierce attack on a number of western liturgical practices, of which the use of unleavened bread in the eucharist was by far the most important. An equally ferocious reply to this letter was prepared by the pope's private secretary, Cardinal Humbert, an authoritarian and stubborn prelate with a violent temper, and Humbert not only argued for the use of unleavened bread in the eucharist, but also for the total jurisdiction of Rome over the whole christian world and the full acceptance by the greek east of a roman primacy of jurisdiction.

The reaction of the patriarch can be imagined. East and west were once again headed for confrontation. Both the eastern emperor and the pope recognized the gravity of the situation and both wished to avoid the inevitable outcome. Leo, therefore, sent a deputation to Constantinople to try to achieve some sort of conciliation, but he put in charge of the deputation the worst possible man for the job: the hot-headed Cardinal Humbert. If the pope and the emperor had met, something might have been salvaged; but with Humbert and Cerularius, there was no real hope. The attempts at reconciliation were doomed from the start and the papal mission was a total failure.

On 16 July 1054, just before the afternoon liturgy in the great church of the Holy Wisdom in Constantinople, Humbert walked up to the altar and placed upon it a Bull that excommunicated Michael and all his supporters. Leo himself was dead by this time—he had died three months earlier, a sad and broken man—but Humbert was still acting in his name. On 24 July, the patriarch replied by excommunicating Humbert and his colleagues, and according to historical tradition, it was this year—1054, the year of the Great Schism—which marked the final separation of the greek and latin churches. The tradition is incorrect.

5. After 1054

Humbert had excommunicated the eastern patriarch, not the eastern church; Michael had excommunicated Humbert, not the papacy. In other words, the mutual excommunications were personal rather than institutional, and over the next few years they were gradually forgotten. Far more serious were the disastrous effects of the Crusades.

In 1071 the Turks had captured Jerusalem, and Jerusalem was part of the eastern empire. The attempt of the eastern emperor at retaking the city was an embarrassing failure, and the east appealed to Pope Gregory VII (whom we met in Chapter I) for assistance. Gregory was eager to help but was too involved with western imperial politics to do so, and it was Urban II who launched the First Crusade in 1096. For the west it was a triumph—Antioch was captured in 1098 and Jerusalem retaken in 1099—but the succeeding crusades were far less impressive. The Second Crusade (1147–9) was a failure (many of the crusaders never even reached Palestine); the Third (1188–92) achieved a partial success when Richard I of England negotiated a three-year truce with the only gentleman of the whole depressing period, the cultivated and courteous Saladin; the Fourth Crusade (1202–4) was a disaster.

The crusaders were on their way to Egypt when their leader was approached by the eastern emperor—or, more precisely, by Alexius, the son of the eastern emperor—who had recently lost his throne to a usurper. Would the crusaders turn aside and restore him and his father to their rightful place? If they did he, Alexius, would provide them with both money and military aid, and would grant trade-concessions to the Venetians from whom the crusaders had leased their ships. Most of the crusaders agreed to this (the pope deplored it, but had no power to stop it), and Alexius was accordingly restored as emperor of Byzantium.

Alexius then found that he could neither pay his debts nor keep his promises, for the treasuries of Constantinople were almost empty. The crusaders were not at all pleased with this and their response was simple: what they could not be given, they would take by force, and on 6 April 1204 they stormed the city. They captured it within a day, and the soldiers were then told that for the next three days, the city was theirs to pillage. The results were appalling. Men were mutilated and murdered; women were raped; children were put to the sword; the libraries of Constantinople were burned; french prostitutes who had accompanied the army caroused in the church of the Holy Wisdom and one of them was seated on the patriarch's throne; the iconostasis was destroyed and the altar broken; every church in the city was desecrated; everything of value was stolen.

It was this terrible event, an event that the east never forgot and never forgave, which really represents the final separation of east and west. There were, it is true, a few sporadic attempts in later centuries to heal the breach—the council of Lyons in 1274 and the Council of Florence in 1438–98[8]—but the agreements they produced were worth no more than the parchment on which they were written. By this time, west and east were firmly entrenched in their own separate ways. Both were content to remain in a state of mutual ignorance, and neither side had any real interest in changing its perspective. In any case, the east had its own problems: while the west was grappling with the challenge of scholasticism, the east found itself rent apart by the Hesychast Controversy (which we will examine in Chapter IX), and by the end of the Middle Ages, the long and slow process of separation had finally ended with the establishment of two different worlds. The seamless cloak of Christ had been rent apart, and despite the statements by Pope Paul VI and Patriarch Athenagoras I on 7 December 1965 that both sides deplored the mutual anathemas of 1054, rent apart it remains.

8. These Councils are discussed in Chapter X below.

III-1 The byzantine emperor John VI Cantacuzenus as both emperor and monk (see Chaper IX). John reigned from 1347 to 1354, then abdicated, took the monastic habit and a monastic name (Ioasaph), and remained a monk until his death in 1383. On the right he is shown wearing the distinctive habit of a medieval byzantine monk: a long black tunic, the black cloak which was worn over it (the *mandyas*), with the *koukoullion* or cowl covering his head. In his hand he carries a scroll that says, 'Great is the God of the Christians'.

John VI Cantacuzenus. Theological Works, 1370–1375.
Paris, Bibliothèque nationale, ms gr 1242, f° 123v.
Photo: Bibliothèque nationale, Paris.

III

Monks and Monasticism

IN THE LAST two chapters we have been primarily concerned with presenting an outline of some of the major historical and intellectual developments which took place in east and west during the Middle Ages. It is now time to turn our attention to a medieval institution—a religious, social, intellectual, educational, and political institution—which is one of the characteristic features of medieval christianity. We are speaking of medieval monasticism. It must be remembered, however, that this brief account is not intended to serve as a comprehensive history of the monastic movement: its purpose is merely to set forth a certain amount of information which may assist us in coming to a better understanding of the chapters which follow.

First of all, let us do away with any attempt at comparing modern monasticism with its medieval counterpart. In the modern world, monasticism is very much a peripheral pursuit. There *are* monks and nuns, certainly, but apart from those who serve in the various teaching Orders, they are unlikely to cross our paths. Becoming a monk or nun is not high on the list of modern job priorities, and the desire to enter a contemplative Order is a very rare vocation.

The situation in the Middle Ages was radically different. Religious houses were to be found everywhere; monks and nuns were commonplace; and entry into the religious life was a regular and convenient alternative to life in the world. A recent gazetteer lists more than 850 religious houses in England alone;[1] in France they were as thick upon the ground as autumn leaves in Vallombrosa; in the greek east, at the time of the iconoclastic controversy, the number of monks had reached an estimated hundred thousand. In other words, we are talking about a very numerous, very widespread, and very powerful institution.

It is customary to begin the story in Egypt during the third century when a young man named Antony (c.250–356) heard a reading from the gospel according to Matthew: 'If you want to be perfect, go, sell your possessions and give to the poor, and you will have treasure in heaven' (Mt 19:21). Antony took the words of Christ at face value, gave away what he had, retreated to the solitude of the egyptian desert, and devoted himself to a life of prayer and asceticism. He was not the first to seek the solitary life, but he was certainly the most famous. Why? Because an account of his life and his struggles was composed by no less a person than Athanasius the Great, archbishop of Alexandria and one of the greatest lights of the fourth-century church.[2] With the immense authority of Athanasius behind it, the *Life of Antony*

1. Roy Midmer, *English Mediaeval Monasteries 1066–1540* (Athens, GA, 1979). Midmer excludes alien priories, hospitals, and the houses of the Templars and Hospitallers. To include them would double this number.
2. See *Cloud* 67–71.

was widely read and achieved great popularity and influence—
such influence, indeed, that even a single reading might produce
miracles. According to Augustine of Hippo, when two pagan roman legionaries read the book, they were immediately converted
to Christianity, received baptism, and went off into the desert to
follow in Antony's footsteps.

Antony, however, was a hermit (the term derives from *erēmos*,
the greek word for 'desert' or 'solitude'), and was not much interested in community life. His was an austere and individualistic
spirituality, and although he was prepared to assist others in
achieving some sort of communal way of living, it was not his own
choice. Nevertheless, the way of the hermit—the eremitic path—
is not for all. It is hard and unforgiving and can all too easily lead
to delusion and despair. Less heroic, or less determined, souls
found they needed behind them the support of a community
with an established rule and a spiritual father to whom they
could go for advice when difficulties and temptations arose.

According to long tradition, the founder of the communal
life was also an Egyptian, a young man named Pachomius. Born
about 290 in Upper Egypt, he served as a conscript in a roman
legion, but after his release from the army he was converted to
Christianity. He then spent some three years as the disciple of
a hermit, and after that, in about 320, he built a monastery at
Tabennisi near Thebes. His reputation for sanctity attracted large
numbers of monks and Tabennisi grew rapidly both in size and
importance. Other foundations soon followed and by the time
of his death in 346, there were eleven pachomian monasteries in
Egypt: nine for men and (in a discreet location across the Nile)
two for women.

Pachomian monasteries were truly coenobitic[3] and were often
very large. Within an enclosing wall there was a church, refectory,
guest-house, and infirmary, and a series of simple houses for
the monks. Each house lodged about twenty monks under the
direction of a prior, and the whole complex could house up to

---

3. The term derives from *coenobium*, the latin word for 'community'.

a thousand. Such a monastery would have been very similar
to the legionary barracks which Pachomius had known in his
days as a soldier. Pachomian monks worshipped together and ate
together, and all were bound by total obedience to the will of their
superior. They also worked. Manual labour was an important
part of the pachomian system, not only because the products—
baskets, mats, ropes, and linen cloth—could be sold to support
the monastery, but also because continual manual work was a
sovereign remedy against boredom and the insidious attacks of
the devil. Pachomius laid the foundation for the famous dictum
of Benedict: idleness is the enemy of the soul.

During the second half of the fourth century monasticism
became wildly popular, not only in Egypt but also in Syria and
Palestine. Monasteries sprang up everywhere, in the cities as well
as in the deserts, and the trickle that had begun with Antony
became a flood. Some adopted the life because they saw in
it the only way to keep the commandments of Christ in all
their perfection and rigor. Some sought to achieve a spiritual
martyrdom, the conquest of their own selves, for since the Edicts
of Toleration[4] and the reign of Constantine, physical martyrdom
was difficult to achieve. Some, more practical, merely desired to
escape starvation and poverty. Some wished to avoid the growing
corruption and worldliness of a church that was rapidly becoming
part of the state, and which seemed to them all too willing
to compromise its religious principles for the sake of political
advantage. Many undoubtedly went because so many others had
gone: it was the thing to do, the band-wagon of the late fourth
century.

Whatever the reason, the numbers of monks and monasteries
increased enormously and the local bishops became more and
more nervous. The loyalty of monks was first and foremost to
their abbot, not to their bishop, and if abbot and bishop had
different views, either ecclesiastically or politically, the situation
could become very strained. An abbot who was not averse to

4. See *Cloud* 15.

political action and who could draw upon a large, loyal, and obedient force of several hundred monks was clearly a power to be reckoned with. One bishop who was aware of this problem and who was deeply concerned about it was the eldest of the Cappadocian Fathers, Basil the Great.[5] He had been well educated in Caesarea, Constantinople, and Athens, and was known and respected for his learning and holiness. He had always been drawn to the ascetic life, and in 357–58 he visited a number of monastic communities in Palestine and Egypt, including the pachomian monasteries. The latter impressed him immensely. When he returned to Cappadocia he lived the eremitic life for some years before deciding that the coenobitic system was preferable, and he then established a community at Caesarea. It was during this period—sometime between 358 and 364—that he produced his two important monastic works, the Longer Rule and the Shorter Rule.

These Rules are not rules in any strict systematic sense. They are rather a series of questions and answers on a variety of ascetic and spiritual topics, but the principles they enunciate have remained the standard for eastern monasticism and have had a profound effect on monasticism in the west. Basil advocates the *coenobium*, the community, but not the huge institutions of Pachomius. A small, workable group is what is needed for the development of a true community spirit, for only in a community can one practise the christian virtues of mercy, charity, and love of one's neighbour. It is true that the ascetic life, the life of poverty and chastity, is the most effective way to God, but true asceticism must be balanced asceticism. Basil had no time for the extreme and occasionally absurd mortifications practised by many of the desert hermits, especially those in Syria.

Like Pachomius, Basil insisted on the importance of hard work and, again like Pachomius, he stressed the importance of obedience. But for Basil, obedience was owed not just to the abbot of the monastery, but also to the local bishop. Basil, in

5. See *Cloud* 71.

other words, was not only interested in establishing disciplined and useful communities, but in ensuring that those communities occupied a proper place within the structure of the church. This, we might add, was not always a good thing. Within thirty years of Basil's death, his successor to the see of Caesarea was using the local monks as ecclesiastical storm-troopers to promote his own ideas, and for centuries afterwards the monasteries all too often provided bishops with disciplined supporters bound by unquestioning and often unthinking obedience.

Basil's two Rules were later modified and adapted, but in their essence they remained the standard for eastern monasticism. The *minutiae* of daily life certainly differed from monastery to monastery—the Rules were never intended to furnish detailed instructions for the day-to-day running of a community—but since their principles were so widely and generally accepted, eastern monasticism never had reason to divide and subdivide into the multitudinous Orders which characterize monasticism in the west. For the most part, Orthodox monasticism remained (and still remains) one Order, professing obedience to one rule, and wearing one distinctive habit. Byzantine monks and nuns wore a black tunic of cotton or wool which covered the whole body from neck to ankle. Over this they wore the *analabos* or scapular, and both tunic and scapular were covered by a long black cloak—the *mandyas*—which was fastened at the neck and below the waist. On their feet they wore light-weight black shoes and on their heads the *koukoullion* or cowl.[6] It is a reflection of the importance of Basil's rules that westerners often refer to Orthodox monks as Basilians, though not all Orthodox agree with the designation.

So far we have been speaking of monasticism in the eastern christian world, and we must now turn our attention to the west.

---

6. The habit has changed somewhat over the centuries. Modern Orthodox monks wear a long black robe called the *rason*, and since the seventeenth century, a black felt hat, rather like a top-hat without a brim, called the *kamelavkion* or *kalimavki*.

The ideas and ideals of monasticism were transmitted to the west in a variety of ways, not all of which are fully understood, and it is fortunate that for our present purposes we need give only the briefest summary. One of the first to inform the west of eastern asceticism was Athanasius the Great, the biographer of Antony. During his exiles from Alexandria as a consequence of the Arian disputes[7], he spent some years in Trier and Rome where he established lasting and useful contacts with the western church. Next came the saintly but acerbic Jerome (342–420) who, after a period of discipleship in the Syrian desert, went to Rome and became a major propagandist for the monastic ideal. His teachings proved especially successful among the widows and unmarried women of the roman aristocracy. Monasticism in what is now France owes its inception to Martin of Tours (c.316–387) who was trained in the north of Italy and founded the first french monastery at Ligugé near Poitiers, and Martin was followed by John Cassian, one of the most important monastic writers and a vital link between Egypt and the latin west.

Born in Romania c.366, Cassian spent ten years in a monastery in Bethlehem, made extensive visits to Egypt, lived for a time in Constantinople and Rome, and eventually (about 415) made his way to Marseilles. Here he established two monasteries, one for men and one for women, and here he remained until his death in about 435. During his sojourn in Egypt, Cassian had toured the major monastic communities, both eremitic and coenobitic, and had accumulated a mass of information on all aspects of the ascetic life. Some twenty-five years later, after he had settled at Marseilles, he wrote down his memoirs in his *Conferences*. These are a record of his conversations with the various egyptian abbots and they remain one of our most important sources of fourth-century egyptian spiritual teaching.

The west, however, was not merely a recipient, but also a contributor to the development of monasticism. In the second half of the fourth century, Eusebius, bishop of Vercelli (midway

7. See *Cloud* 69.

between Turin and Milan in the north of Italy), introduced the principles of the monastic life to his diocesan clergy and organized a small community of priests dedicated to the ascetic ideal. This merging of clerical life and monastic life was a uniquely western phenomenon, and the ideas of Eusebius were supported by Augustine of Hippo, who established a rule for these monastic clerics, the *Rule of Saint Augustine*. The origins of this Rule are obscure, and modern scholarship has confused rather than clarified the issue. That its essential principles derive from Augustine himself is not in doubt, but whether it was originally written for nuns and then adapted for monks (the older view), or vice versa, remains the subject of scholarly controversy. Whatever its origins, it was this Rule that was adopted by the Canons Regular in the eleventh century and its real importance dates from that time. That, however, is something we shall discuss later in this chapter.

By the end of the fifth century, then, the roots of monasticism were firmly entrenched both in Italy and France, but there was no uniformity in daily practice and no one rule was considered authoritative. The break-through came in the next century when an italian abbot named Benedict compiled a rule which became the most important document in the history of western monasticism, just as Benedict himself became one of the best-known monks. Like Antony before him, Benedict had the inestimable advantage of a famous biographer. Just as the life of Antony had been written by Athanasius, one of the greatest archbishops of Alexandria, the life of Benedict was composed by one of the greatest bishops of Rome: Gregory the Great. Gregory's work, which proved immensely popular, provides us with all that we know about Benedict and his life, but it is difficult to know whether Gregory's account reflects the fame of Benedict, or whether it created it.

According to Gregory, Benedict was born in central Italy in a period marked by successive waves of barbarian marauders. He was sent to Rome for his education, but the licentiousness of the city appalled him, and c.500 he retired to a cave at Subiaco, thirty-two miles east of Rome, where he spent three years as a hermit.

During this period and in the years that followed numerous disciples made their way to the spot and Benedict organized them into twelve small communities, each consisting of twelve monks and an abbot, just as Christ's community had consisted of Christ and the twelve apostles. About 525 (the date is uncertain) he moved from Subiaco to Monte Cassino, a hilltop midway between Rome and Naples, and there established a monastery which he administered until his death sometime between 546 and 550.

Benedict's true claim to fame, however, lies not in his life but in his Rule, though even here we must be careful not to overemphasize his contribution. He used a number of earlier sources in its composition—Cassian, Basil, Caesarius of Arles—but the most important of these was a document generally referred to as *The Rule of the Master*. The identity of 'the Master' is unknown, but he was probably an italian abbot who was writing about forty years before Benedict, and it is obvious that Benedict greatly admired his work. He had no hesitation in paraphrasing it, adapting it, or, in some cases, simply taking over large lumps of material and copying them out without change. On the other hand, his approach to the Master was not uncritical, and there is no doubt that Benedict's version of the Rule was a noticeable improvement. It is better written, better organized, more humane, more democratic, and more compassionate towards human frailty.

First and foremost, the Rule demands that the aspirant have a true intention to forsake the ways of the world and follow in the footsteps of Christ. It also demands stability (a monk was supposed to live and die in his monastery and leave it only on important monastic business), and absolute obedience to the abbot. One is reminded of Pachomius and Basil. Indeed, the abbot stands in the place of Christ, and the monk should obey the abbot as he would obey Christ. Poverty is not explicitly mentioned, but since private ownership is forbidden and all possessions are to be held in common, it is obviously implied. Nor does the Rule specifically mention chastity, though it is certainly presupposed.

The most important part of the monk's life is the performance of the *opus Dei*, 'the work of God', by which Benedict meant the seven liturgical offices, along with the night-office, that punctuate the monastic day. Outside of these offices, a monk is either working, reading, eating, or sleeping. At no time is he idle, for, as we noted above, idleness is the enemy of the soul. During the summer, there were about seven hours set aside for manual labour and three hours for reading, and since seven hours of hard work demands considerable effort, the food in the monastery had to be sustaining. The main meal, says Benedict, should comprise two cooked dishes with any fruits and vegetables that were in season, but at the abbot's discretion, any monk engaged in particularly strenuous labour could be given more—though never to excess. As for drink, each monk was apportioned about half-a-pint of wine per day, 'but as for those to whom God gives the ability to abstain', says our author, 'let them know that they will have their own reward'.[8]

Between the time of Gregory the Great and the era of Charlemagne, benedictine monasticism and the benedictine Rule gradually became more and more popular, especially in what is now Austria, Germany, France, and the British Isles. It was not, however, the only form of monasticism, and other varieties, often closer to the older eastern models, sometimes offered strong resistance to the benedictine advance. That they failed while the Benedictines triumphed was less the result of theology than a consequence of politics.

As we saw in Chapter I, the reign of Charlemagne was dominated by his desire for a united empire: an empire united under one ruler with one set of laws and one uniform liturgy. It will come as no surprise, therefore, to learn that Charlemagne would also have liked uniformity in monastic observance. He himself did not live to see this, and it was achieved by his son, Louis the Pious. It is also true that by the ninth century, monastic fervour had declined, monks had become lax, discipline had

---

8. *The Rule of Saint Benedict (Regula S. Benedicti)* 40:4.

slackened, and the regular daily routine of the seven offices had fallen into desuetude. Louis therefore looked for someone to carry out a necessary unification and reformation of the monastic communities, and he found that person in Benedict of Aniane.

This second Benedict was born c.750 to an aristocratic family in southern France. As a young man he was a member of Charlemagne's court, and while on an expedition to Italy, he had a narrow escape from drowning. He became convinced that his deliverance was a result of the direct intervention of the Almighty, and he therefore determined to leave the world and seek the cloister. In 773 or 774 he entered the monastery of Saint-Seine near Dijon, and a few years later founded his own community on his own property at Aniane in Languedoc. The new abbey was placed under the direct supervision of Charlemagne and its rule was the Rule of Saint Benedict. For the second Benedict, we might add, this was a compromise. His fiercely ascetic spirit considered Benedict's Rule too lax for the true aspirant to evangelical perfection, and his own inclination was towards the severity of the desert. But his contemporaries, he thought, were incapable of such ascetic devotion, and the Rule of Saint Benedict was, if not perfect, at least a sound and workable alternative.

This devout and dedicated monk was chosen by Louis the Pious to effect the reformation of monasticism in his empire, and Louis therefore summoned him to the imperial court at Aachen and had a new abbey constructed for him just a few miles away. Benedict threw himself whole-heartedly into his new task, and in 816 and 817, at two synods held at Aachen, proclaimed, on the authority of the Emperor, that from that time forward there would be but one rule for all monasteries under his jurisdiction. Which rule? The Rule of Saint Benedict of course, the Rule with which the second Benedict was most familiar and which had been the standard for his own monastery at Aniane. But it is important to note that by this time certain changes had taken place in the interpretation of the benedictine Rule, and in ninth-century France it was not kept in quite the same way as it had been in sixth-century Italy.

The major change that had occurred was an increase in the amount of time devoted to the liturgy and a corresponding decrease in the time given to manual labour. Many monks at this period came from noble families, and nobly-born monks did not expect to work with their hands. For most people, too, it was axiomatic that the more you prayed, the more you got from God, and by the ninth century, additional psalms, musical elaboration, time-consuming processions, and daily masses had all but destroyed the old benedictine balance between work and prayer. Monks now spent most of their day in choir. Furthermore, just as the liturgy had become more elaborate, the setting of the liturgy had likewise become more elaborate. Nothing was too glorious for God. Churches, vestments, and church furniture were becoming ever more ornate, and this would reach its culmination, as we shall see, in the great church at Cluny.

Benedict died in 821 and Louis the Pious in 840, and as we have seen, Charlemagne's empire began to disintegrate. So too did Benedict's reforms. Wealthy landowners who had founded abbeys felt free to intervene in their day-to-day operation, and just as they appointed priests to the churches they built and bishops to the dioceses they controlled, so they appointed abbots to what, in their view, were their own monasteries. During the same period political stability was destroyed by the incursions of the Northmen, and as far as they were concerned, monasteries were simply unguarded repositories of riches, ripe for plunder and pillage. If their inhabitants were female, all the better. By the end of the ninth century, therefore, the situation was worse than it had been before Benedict's reforms—so much so that when a young man named Odo, together with a friend, decided to become monks and travelled through France seeking a monastery where the Rule of Saint Benedict was kept, they failed to find one. Odo gave up and returned home, but his friend continued their quest and eventually found such a monastery at Baume-les-Messieurs, five miles north-east of Lons-le-Saunier at the foot of the Jura mountains. The name of the abbot was Berno, and abbot and monks followed the Rule of Saint Benedict according

III-2 The habit of western christian monks varied according to their Order, but all had in common the tonsure, or distinctive shaved pate. Benedictines wore the black habit shown here—a long tunic with wide sleeves and a hood—and were called 'Black Monks'. Cistercians, by contrast, were called 'White Monks' because their cowl was light in color (see Abbot Stephen Harding on the cover). It was, in fact, made of undyed wool, so the precise shade depended on the color of the local sheep. Canons Regular wore a long over-tunic of fine white linen with tight-fitting sleeves, and Dominicans had a similar garment covered with a long black scapular. The Franciscans initially wore a grey habit but soon changed to a brown robe with knotted belt.

The Dialogues of Gregory the Great, thirteenth-century.
Tours, Bibliothèque municipale, ms 327, f° 49.
Photo: CNRS (IRHT).

to the interpretation of Benedict of Aniane. Odo immediately came to join his friend, and both of them took the habit.

Some years later the local landowner, Duke William the Pious of Aquitaine, decided to found a monastery, and he came to Berno for advice on a suitable location. Berno selected a beautiful and luxuriant valley on the duke's land, and after considerable discussion and some hesitation (for it was the duke's favourite hunting ground), William agreed to donate the place for his new foundation. The name of the valley was Cluny (it lies close to Mâcon in Burgundy) and the year was 909.

William appointed Berno first abbot of the new monastery, but stipulated that from that time forward no lord, whether civil or ecclesiastical, should ever again interfere in the internal affairs of the community, and that henceforth it would elect its own abbot, just as the Rule of Saint Benedict had specified. Both he and Berno demanded from the monks the highest standard of monastic discipline, and so too did Berno's successors: Odo (the young man we met above), Aymardus, Maiolus, Odilo, Hugh, Pontius, and Peter the Venerable. The abbey insisted on the strict observance of the benedictine Rule (interpreted, of course, in the spirit of Benedict of Aniane), and unlike many other abbeys of the time, it practised what it preached. Almost without exception, the abbots of Cluny were intelligent and learned men, spiritual yet practical (they paid great attention to sound economics), powerful yet humble (they regularly refused high ecclesiastical office), and widely admired and respected. Hugh of Cluny, who was abbot from 1049 to 1109, was one of the most trusted men in Europe, and, as advisor to no less than nine popes, dominated ecclesiastical affairs for nearly fifty years. During his abbacy hundreds of cluniac houses sprang up all over Europe, others voluntarily allied themselves with the Order, and at Cluny itself, on 25 October 1095, Pope Urban II (a former monk of the abbey) came in person to consecrate the new high altar of what would be one of the largest and most magnificent churches in Christendom.

There was, however, a worm in the cluniac apple. Despite the example it provided for reform in the church, despite the remarkable qualities of its abbots, despite its strict observance and high standards, Cluny was in some ways the antithesis of the desert ideal. Over the years it had attracted lavish donations; its church was a monument to magnificence; its liturgy was long, elaborate and glorious; and its powerful abbots were deeply involved with the world outside the cloister. One writer of the time goes further and accuses the Cluniacs of gluttony, of drinking too much, of wearing furs and extravagant clothing, of staying in the monastic infirmary when they were not really ill, of having negligent superiors, of riding in state, of possessing an abundance of gold and silver images and, in general, of throwing the simplicity of the desert out of the window and of bringing in the world in its place. Who was this writer? It was a Cistercian monk: Bernard of Clairvaux.

The abbey of Cîteaux, the mother-house of the Cistercian Order, had been founded in 1098 by Robert of Molesme, but in 1099 Robert was ordered by the pope to return to Molesme, and for some years it was questionable whether the new Order would survive. Its future was assured some fourteen years later when Bernard entered the monastery as a novice. Bernard was born in 1090 at Fontaines near Dijon and from an early age had shown a predilection for the monastic life. He entered Cîteaux in 1113 (having persuaded thirty young burgundian nobles to join him: Bernard was nothing if not persuasive), and two years later, in 1115, was sent by his abbot to establish a new foundation at Clairvaux[9]. Under Bernard's direction, Clairvaux became the real centre of cistercian monasticism, and in a remarkably short time the Cistercians had taken over from the Cluniacs as the preeminent monastic Order in Europe. Bernard, like Hugh, had the ear of princes, kings, and popes, and for a supposedly stable monk, his peregrinations and influence were astonishing.

But to what extent was his attack on the Cluniacs justified? Much depends, obviously, on whether one is Cluniac or

9. Clairvaux is now the most heavily guarded maximum-security prison in France.

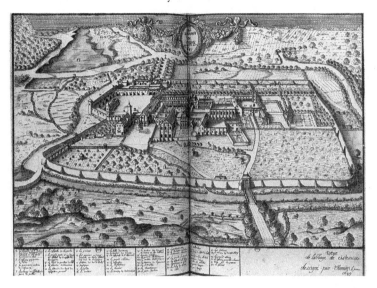

III-3 Cistercian monasteries were located in the countryside, nearly always in valleys. The mother-house of the order, Cîteaux, was founded in 1098 and by the time this drawing was made in 1689, had become an immense and prosperous abbey. Each abbey was conceived as an autonomous community and had a church, chapter room, dormitory, refectories, scriptorium, library, infirmary, storehouses and other conventual buildings; a bakery, guesthouse and industrial sectors; and a cemetery, orchards and gardens, all surrounded by a high wall. The Vouge River runs just outside the wall, but was also channelled inside the abbey for sanitation and a source of power for the mill. Conduits brought pure water from springs into the abbey. Located fourteen miles south of Dijon, Cîteaux owned numerous vineyards as well as surrounding fields and forests.

Veue de labbaye de Cisteaux, 1689. Thomain.
Paris, Bibliothèque nationale, Estampes Ve 26p T.11.
Photo: Bibliothèque nationale, Paris.

Cistercian. For the former, his comments were libellous; for the latter they might be regarded as satirical. Cluny had never aimed at the ideal of desert simplicity, but the cistercian Order, established some two centuries later, had been founded with the avowed intention of resurrecting that ideal to a new and better life. For Bernard and the Cistercians, their rule was to be the Rule of Saint Benedict, but the Rule of Saint Benedict in its original form and not according to the interpretation of Benedict of Aniane. In other words, the Cistercians were determined to reintroduce the healthy balance of prayer and manual labour which the first Benedict had specified, and to return to the poverty and simplicity which they saw in the original Rule.

During the life of Bernard and in the decades following his death in 1153, the Cistercian Order spread with great rapidity. By the end of the twelfth century there were more than five hundred cistercian abbeys, and the next century would see the establishment of at least another hundred and fifty. And although the fame and influence of the Order declined in the course of the thirteenth century, cistercian observances had a profound effect on other religious congregations, especially the Canons Regular.

The Canons Regular were a sort of hybrid of priest and monk. Their ultimate origins may be traced to the ideas of Eusebius of Vercelli whom we discussed earlier in this chapter, but it was not until the pontificate of Gregory VII that they achieved any real importance. For Gregory, it was all part of his programme of reform, and his argument was simple. He cited Acts 4:32[10] to prove that the apostles had been monks; he reminded the secular clergy that they were the heirs of the apostles; and he concluded that the secular clergy should therefore live in a monastic fashion. They should live the common life, renounce personal possessions, embrace celibacy, separate themselves from the world as far as was proper, and strive to display in their lives and conduct the teachings of Christ their Master. The rule the Canons adopted was the *Rule of Saint Augustine*, and in later centuries they came to be known as Augustinian Canons.[11]

Houses of Regular Canons began to appear in Italy and France in the middle of the eleventh century, but, for our purposes,

10. 'The whole group of those who believed were of one heart and soul, and no one claimed private ownership of any possessions, but everything they owned was held in common' (Acts 4:32 [NRSV]).

11. In England, 'Augustinian' was abbreviated to 'Austin', and the Austin Canons were a most important force in english monastic life.

the most important of these congregations were the Victorines, the Canons Regular of Saint-Victor in Paris. The house had been founded in 1113 by William of Champeaux, a famous scholar of his day, and when the time came for the Victorines to establish their own customs, they were strongly influenced by the ideals of the Cistercians, who, by that date, were the most influential Order in Europe. Nevertheless, the Victorines never lost the impetus for learning bestowed upon them by their famous founder, and although they never became very numerous, they produced some of the most brilliant theologians and contemplatives of the twelfth century.

Early in the next century yet another form of community life appeared in order to meet the changing conditions of european society. The representatives of this latest development were the two great mendicant[12] Orders: the Franciscans (the Friars Minor) and the Dominicans (the Friars Preachers). The one was founded by the best known saint of the whole medieval period, Francis of Assisi (1181/2–1226); the other by one not so well known, Dominic de Guzmán (1170–1221).

Francis was born to a wealthy family in Assisi in 1181/2, and after spending the first twenty years of his life as an irresponsible young-man-about-town, he underwent a series of psychological and spiritual crises which led, in 1209, to his total renunciation of money and possessions and the foundation of his Order. For Francis, a return to the Rule of Saint Benedict was not enough: behind Benedict lay the gospels, and it was in the words of Christ that Francis found his inspiration. The keyword of the Franciscan Order was poverty: poverty in goods and poverty of spirit. His friars (or brothers[13]) were to own nothing at all: they were to live by begging, and if that proved impossible, by the work of their hands. Their role in life was to preach, especially to the urban poor (the class most neglected by the regular clergy), and to show to all who needed it the charity and compassion

---

12. 'Mendicant' derives from the latin verb *mendicare* 'to beg'.
13. The term 'friar' comes from *frater*, the latin word for 'brother'.

of Christ. Francis laid no stress on learning—the gospels were enough for him—but his own charismatic personality attracted huge numbers, educated and uneducated, to the new Order, and the founder's ideals of absolute, corporate poverty, humility and simplicity inevitably began to crumble and fade away. Even before Francis's death in 1226 the Order had acquired property and wealth, and over the course of the next century would become very wealthy indeed. But not only did it become wealthy, it also became learned. In its preaching activities it often came in contact with adherents of heretical groups—we shall see in Chapter VI that the thirteenth century was riddled with heresy—and since the adherents of these groups could often provide intelligent and persuasive arguments in support of their own positions, it was incumbent on the Franciscans to counter these arguments with others equally persuasive. You cannot do it simply by telling bible stories. Even before Francis's death the Order could boast learned theologians, and in the decades that followed, more and more intellectual Olympians appeared within its ranks. Once the universities became established, franciscan professors were the rule rather than the exception. Francis himself would never have approved, but Francis was dead.

The second of the preaching Orders had emphasized education from the start. It was founded by Dominic de Guzmán, an austere, humble, and saintly Spaniard, and the sole reason for its existence was the eradication of false teaching. It was essential, therefore, that the Dominicans should be as well educated as their adversaries, and every one of their houses became a centre for teaching and study. Dominican friaries were to be found in virtually all university towns, and like the Franciscans (but perhaps more defensibly), Dominicans regularly occupied university chairs. They were superb organizers and devoted to the papacy which was then at the apogee of its temporal power. It was natural, therefore, that when the Inquisition was established in the first half of the thirteenth century, the Dominicans would be selected as papal inquisitors. This undoubtedly increased their power, but not their popularity. But for all that, some of the greatest medieval theologians were Dominicans—the most

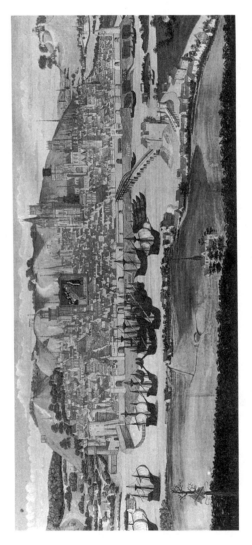

III-4 Skylines of medieval cities were punctuated by towers and steeples, many of them belonging to monasteries. Located on the Seine River between Paris and the sea, Rouen was a roman city which achieved civil, political, and ecclesiastical importance in the Middle Ages. In the course of the tenth century Rouen achieved its double role as a sea and river port; the density of housing, the many fortified gates and the ships in the harbour attest to its importance when this painting was made in 1525. The tallest building is the cathedral of Notre-Dame, rebuilt after a fire in 1200. Rouen also had a number of important abbeys and priories. This painting was made by a rich and prominent citizen of Rouen for his *Livre des Fontaines*, a book which describes in minute detail the conduits which carried water to the city.

City of Rouen, 1525. Jacques Le Lieur (c. 1480 - c. 1550).
Rouen, Bibliothèque municipale.
Photo: Bibliothèque municipale, Rouen.

famous example is Thomas Aquinas—and we shall meet some of them in succeeding chapters.

The brief survey we have presented here is not intended to be an exhaustive survey of western monasticism. There were numerous other Orders which we have not considered. Our principle for selection has been simple: we have mentioned only those of which representatives appear in the following pages. Those interested in the wider world of medieval monasticism will find abundant information elsewhere.

What, in sum, was the effect of the monastic movement? It can hardly be overestimated. Apart from the indeterminable effects of prayer (and we must not forget that prayer was the primary vocation for most monks and nuns), the movement had a profound effect in both east and west on almost all areas of life. In the world of politics, monks and abbots were advisors to princes, kings, emperors, patriarchs, and popes. Sometimes they were themselves patriarchs and popes. Economically, their dedication and hard work could result in astonishing achievements (the Cistercians dominated the wool trade in Europe), and the bequests and donations made to the various Orders (eastern and western) by those who hoped to ease their way into Paradise produced vast wealth, and vast wealth meant vast influence. Socially, it was the preaching Orders that had the greatest significance. They not only preached to the poor, but strove to educate them. They built hospitals, they operated homes for reformed prostitutes, and manifested a devotion to the dispossessed that was often lacking in the members of the other Orders.

For our present purposes, it was monastic contributions to learning that were most important. In the east this was less apparent, for eastern monasticism laid greater stress on the performance of the liturgy and on contemplation, and eastern monasteries never became centres of scholarship as did many of those in the west. This is not to say that all eastern monks were unlearned—some were, some were not—but there was a difference in emphasis. Eastern monasticism, both literally and metaphorically, remained closer to the desert than its western counterpart, and (as we shall see) eastern theology and spirituality has a flavour all of its own. Gregory Palamas was just as much a genius as Thomas Aquinas, but he was a genius in a quite different way.

In the west, it was the monasteries that kept alive the spirit of the Carolingian Renaissance, and even with the revival of the cathedral schools in the eleventh century, they still retained their importance. They remained one of the main sources for the copying of texts (something they shared with their eastern confrères) and produced a large number of impressive thinkers and theologians, some of whom we shall meet in the following pages. But with the development of the schools in the twelfth century, and especially with the development of the universities, the role of the monasteries as educational centres naturally declined. Indeed, as the rational and analytical techniques of the schools rapidly became more and more popular, the monasteries often appeared as reactionary bulwarks of an approach to the faith now outmoded. It is true that the contrast between the two is often too starkly drawn, but there was undoubtedly a difference of emphasis. The methods of the schools and of the monasteries were not always the same, and from Anselm of Canterbury onwards there had been an ever-growing struggle between the claims of reason and the authority of the faith. It is time now to examine that struggle in a little more detail.

IV-1 All seven liberal arts were sculpted on the Royal Portal of Chartres Cathedral, site of a famous school in the twelfth century. While the quadrivium represented the quadruple voice of worldly knowledge (bells and a stringed instrument pertaining to the discipline of Music are just to the left), the trivium was the triple voice of intelligence and persuasion. Here Grammar is the stern mistress with a switch, holding a book open before two unruly pupils. The sculpture of Chartres is admirable for its fine detail: the different ways in which hair is shown, the pleated bottom of the boy's cloak, and the beaded edges of garments. All the sculpture was once brightly painted.

Grammar, c. 1150.
Chartres, West façade, voussoir of south portal.
Photo: James Austin.

IV

Faith and Reason

ANSELM OF CANTERBURY, whom we met briefly in Chapter I, was one of the most important figures in the development of the scholastic approach to Christianity, but he was far from being the first to suggest that reason could and should be used in the service of the faith. The whole church, both eastern and western, taught that human beings had been created in the image of God (their authority was Genesis 1:26) and the whole church agreed that this 'imageness' was manifested primarily in human rationality. The argument is simple.

If we are images of God, and if God is eternal, it follows that we cannot be images of God in our physical and corruptible flesh since flesh is not eternal. But if our flesh is not eternal, what is?

The answer is obvious: our soul. The soul, however, was believed to have more than one part. The lower part served to animate the body and enabled it to move around. That is something we share with the animals. But the higher part enabled us to think rationally and comprehend abstractions, and that is something we share only with the angels and God. The church therefore maintained that human beings are images of God in the higher, rational part of the soul, and that reason is the greatest natural gift we have. But such a gift is given for a purpose. It is not to be squandered or neglected, but used appropriately in the service of the Giver, and the question of how much is appropriate was to challenge christian thinkers from the second century to the present day. Let us begin our investigation of the problem by examining the views of the western church.

Long ago, in the years when latin Christendom was slowly developing its own theological tradition and before the distinction between east and west had hardened into separation, Augustine of Hippo (354–430) had stated that belief involved thinking rationally about something and giving it your assent. It was he who introduced the phrase: 'Understand so that you might believe; believe so that you might understand.'[1] What did he mean by this? He meant that belief was not merely a matter of unthinking acceptance of authority, but that believing the tenets of the faith required a full understanding of their content. Once belief had taken hold, a line of communication was established with God and his grace, and then, by means of this grace, one was able to understand yet more of what the faith entailed. So the more you understand, the more you believe, and the more you believe, the more you understand; and we therefore ascend in a sort of spiral, becoming ever more knowledgeable in our understanding of the faith and ever more confident of its truth.

About a century after Augustine, the roman philosopher and statesman Boethius (c.480-c.524) translated certain logical

---

1. Augustine, *Sermo* 43.vii.9; *PL* 38: 258.

works of Aristotle and Porphyry, added commentaries of his own, and thereby provided the latin west with more precise and effective tools for the elucidation of the faith. He himself wrote a number of brief theological treatises and in them demonstrated clearly how logic and philosophy could be used in the service of Christianity. His logical works were of great importance, for until the rediscovery of other treatises of Aristotle in the first half of the twelfth century, they were the only guides the west possessed for the application of dialectic analysis.

Between Augustine and Boethius comes an obscure carthaginian writer named Martianus Capella. Around the time of Augustine's death in 430 he produced a curious and difficult volume with the title *The Marriage of Philology and Mercury*. It is a wildly allegorical piece of work which celebrates the uniting of Mercury and Philology before an assembly of pagan gods and philosophers. Mercury is attended by seven handmaids, all sisters, and these he presents to his learned bride. Each of the handmaids represents one of the seven liberal arts, and each in turn addresses the assembled wedding-party, setting forth what she does and why she is important. These seven liberal arts were to form the foundation of education in the schools, and, in due course, were established as the basis of western university education. What are they?

They were divided into two groups: the *trivium* and the *quadrivium*. We discussed the *trivium* in Chapter I and saw there that it comprised grammar, logic (or dialectic), and rhetoric. These three subjects were intended to enable a person to speak and write the latin language correctly, logically, and persuasively; and since the study of grammar involved the study of classical latin authors, the *trivium* also provided some exposure to literature. Once one had a basic command of the language, one could proceed to the *quadrivium*, which consisted of music, arithmetic, geometry, and astronomy. Music was music theory, not performance, and involved a study of the various scales and the numerical relationship between the notes; arithmetic was primarily 'ecclesiastical' arithmetic, and was especially important for calculating the date of Easter; geometry was essential for measuring land; and at this time, astronomy could hardly be distinguished from astrology.

This grouping of the seven liberal arts was adopted by Alcuin of York, the scholar appointed by Charlemagne to oversee the Carolingian Renaissance, and formed the basis of education in the carolingian schools. But because Alcuin was teaching unlettered Franks and Germans rather than urbane Romans, he had to start from scratch. He therefore stressed the *trivium* rather than the *quadrivium*, and for the four centuries between 600 and 1000 the *quadrivium* was hardly ever taught.

In the confusion of the Viking incursions and the breakdown of imperial institutions following the reigns of Charlemagne and Louis the Pious, the light of learning in the west flickered, dimmed, and almost died. Yet where they existed, learning was kept alive in the monasteries until the revival of the cathedral schools in the eleventh century, and then (as we saw in Chapter I) it was the cathedral schools that took over as the most important centres of western education.

The Viking raids effectively came to an end in 911 when the king of the West Franks gave the Viking leader, Rollo, all the land around the mouth of the Seine. Fire had been fought with fire, for since Rollo had no intention of allowing his own territory to be plundered, he also protected France from Viking raids along the coast of the English Channel. Once settled, the barbarian Northmen were rapidly transformed into civilized Normans, and within a century, those who had once been mainly concerned with ravaging monasteries were now more interested in founding them.

One of the greatest of these new norman abbeys, the abbey of Bec, located between Rouen and Lisieux, was founded in 1041. Anselm entered it in 1059 and was appointed prior four years later. In 1078 he was elected abbot and in 1093 he left the abbey to be consecrated archbishop of Canterbury. Anselm, as we have seen, anticipated the renaissance of the twelfth century and established the basic principles of the scholastic approach. He was at one with Augustine in stressing the interplay of belief and understanding, and it was he who coined the famous phrase *fides quaerens intellectum*, 'faith in search of understanding'.[2] But as with Augustine and all the fathers of the church, he began with faith, not reason; and although we have a God-given duty to use our reason to understand more fully the revealed truths of the faith, that is as far as we can go. It is like a game of chess. The truths of the faith, established by the authority of Christ, recorded in Scripture, and taught by his church, represent the edges of the board. Within that area, and in accordance with certain logical rules, we may do whatever we will. But if we once question these boundaries or attempt to overstep them, the entire game is forfeit.

While he was teaching at Bec, one of Anselm's pupils had been another Anselm, Anselm of Laon. Towards the end of the century he left the monastery, and together with his brother Ralph founded at Laon one of the earliest of the newly revived cathedral schools. The attitude of the new school was still very conservative—the authority of the Bible, the fathers, and the church remained the bedrock of Anselm's teaching—but we do find the hesitant beginnings of the use of formal logic in analyzing the faith. We also see the first attempts at a systematic arrangement of theological topics in the *Sentences* (which we shall consider a little later in this chapter), and the appearance of the technique of the *quaestio*. What happens here is that in any specific area (e.g. the sacraments) and sub-area (e.g. the eucharist), we ask a specific *quaestio* or question (e.g. does the bread become the true body of Christ?), determine what the fathers of the church and other recognized authorities had said on the matter, marshal the arguments for and against, consider both carefully and logically, and arrive at a solution. We then proceed to the next related *quaestio* and do the same thing. In the school of Laon, as we have said, this system was still in its infancy, but in due course it was to become the standard technique of scholasticism.

2. Anselm of Canterbury, *Proslogion, prooemium*; ed. F. S. Schmitt (Edinburgh, 1946) 2: 94.

The School of Laon was a famous place in its day and attracted some of the best minds of the time. One of these was Peter Abelard, a precocious and arrogant young man, whose contribution to the development of the scholastic approach was of major importance. Of equal importance is the way in which, during his tumultuous and difficult life, he focused attention on the question which affects virtually all areas of medieval theology: how far can reason go? What are the proper limits of human investigation? What do grammar, logic, and rhetoric have to do with faith? Where are the boundaries of the theological chess-board?

Abelard was born in 1079 at Pallet, near Nantes, and seems to have been an eager student from his childhood. About 1095 he moved to Loches to study under Roscelin (whom we shall meet again in Chapter VII), and some five years later went to Paris to benefit from the teaching of William of Champeaux. He then set himself up as a teacher of philosophy in his own right, first at Melun, then at Corbeil, then at Paris. At this stage of his career he determined to turn his attention more seriously to theology, and went off to the most reputable school of theology at the time, the School of Laon. Abelard, now about thirty-five, was not impressed. Anselm of Laon, he said, was wonderful with words but empty of reason; he could fill a house with smoke, but gave forth no light. He therefore left Anselm and set up his own school in the same city, but failed to obtain the necessary licence to teach from the local bishop. Two of Anselm's best students then put so much pressure on him that he decided to leave Laon and return to Paris. This he did in 1113–14 (accompanied by several students from Laon), and once in Paris he was offered a position at the cathedral school of Notre-Dame. He was happy to accept this, but it was here that he entered the most difficult period of his life.

In 1118 he accepted a collateral appointment as tutor to an intelligent and attractive young woman called Héloise. She was about seventeen at the time and was the niece of Fulbert, a canon of the cathedral. She and Abelard fell deeply in love and began a passionate affair—an affair that resulted, not surprisingly, in

Héloise becoming pregnant. In due course she gave birth to a son to whom Abelard gave the extraordinary name of Astrolabe. Abelard then offered to marry her, but wanted to keep the marriage secret, for at that time a teacher of theology was, as a cleric, supposed to live a life of irreproachable chastity. Héloise reluctantly agreed to this, but news of the marriage soon leaked out. Héloise, with great courage (or obstinacy), publicly denied that she and Abelard had ever married, but the situation was becoming extremely unpleasant, and to save Héloise from further abuse, Abelard sent her to a convent.

Fulbert was incensed by the whole business—not only his honour, but that of his entire family had been impugned—and he and certain of his relatives decided to take matters into their own hands. One night, when Abelard was in bed, they bribed one of his servants, broke in upon him, held him down, and castrated him.

It is difficult to imagine his physical and mental sufferings, and it may come as no surprise to learn that he decided to enter a monastery. There he remained for some time, but his reputation as a teacher was unimpaired and students persisted in coming to see him. His abbot therefore permitted him to open a school, but no sooner had he done so than he published a study of the Trinity which was immediately condemned as heretical by a Council at Soissons in 1121. Even within the monastery he succeeded in infuriating the monks by proving to them that their founder could not have been the venerable man they claimed he was, and it was not long before he found himself compelled to leave. During a short and unhappy spell as a hermit, he established a small oratory near Troyes called the Paraclete, but soon afterwards, in 1125, he accepted the abbacy of the Breton monastery of Saint-Gildas. The time he spent there was equally unhappy and after some six years he left the abbey. What happened to him over the next three or four years is unclear, but by 1135–36 he was back teaching in Paris. This was the time of his greatest literary activity, but he was again accused of heresy, and we shall examine the matter in some detail in Chapter VII. For the moment we need only note that he was summoned before a

Council at Sens in 1140 and there condemned. He immediately appealed to the pope and set off for Rome. But he had got only as far as the abbey of Cluny when he received word that the pope had agreed with his condemnation, and he went no further. He entered Cluny as a monk and there spent the last years of his life. Shortly before his death he moved to a cluniac priory near Châlon-sur-Saône and there he died, in peace, in April 1142.

Abelard is a strange and inconsistent character, impossible, I think, to assess. He was devout, arrogant, chaste, passionate, intolerant, kind, a superb logician, and wonderful with words. He loved to criticize, but hated criticism. His students adored him, but students tend to love flashy and iconoclastic lecturers. Much of his trouble he brought upon himself, and although he may have been guiltless of the heretical views of which he was accused, one cannot blame his opponents for accusing him. His language and terminology were sometimes dangerous, sometimes fool-hardy, and if he was misunderstood, he was misunderstood with good reason.

For all that, this dramatic and tragic figure played a crucial role in the development of the scholastic approach, for he took over the ideas of Anselm of Canterbury and the methods of Anselm of Laon, elaborated and refined them, and produced a study which would have a decisive effect on the logical analysis of the christian faith. We are talking about Abelard's *Sic et Non*, which means literally *Yes and No*, but which is normally translated as *For and Against*. It was probably written between the time he arrived back in Paris after his stay at Saint-Gildas and his condemnation at Sens in 1140.

In this work we find a long series of theological propositions such as 'Is God the author of evil?' or 'Does the Son have a beginning?' Most of these propositions are then followed by a series of statements drawn from the fathers. Their range and variety reflect Abelard's vast learning. But the statements from the fathers conflicted with one another—some were *sic* and some were *non*—and Abelard merely set them out side by side without presenting any solutions. This was to lead to serious problems.

What are we supposed to do with these lists of statements for and against? Abelard tells us in the introduction to his work.

The conflicts, he says, are more apparent than real, for the fathers, unlike us, were guided by the light of the Holy Spirit. We must never lose sight of our own inadequacy. He then proceeds to suggest a number of things which must be taken into account in seeking a satisfactory solution. The same word, for example, can be used in different ways; a number of treatises circulated pseudonymously and what appears as, say, Augustine is sometimes not Augustine; scribes who were copying manuscripts letter by letter often made errors; the fathers themselves occasionally changed their minds and revised or retracted statements that appear in their earlier works; sometimes, too, they are quoting other people and what they have written is not their own opinion. By thinking in such terms as these, we may come to realise that what *appears* to be contradictory is not, in fact, contradictory, and that the faith of the fathers remains sound and unshaken.

In other words, what Abelard wants us to do with his *Sic et Non* is to study his introduction, examine the materials, and then use our own natural reason to resolve the apparent conflicts and reconfirm our faith. Unfortunately, and despite his good intentions, the actual consequences were very different. Because Abelard himself had provided no solutions, it seemed to many orthodox churchmen that he was simply attempting to discredit the established authorities and set up fallible, human reason in their place. If the fathers cannot agree among themselves, he seemed to be saying, then throw out the fathers and do the thinking yourself! If their faith is based on such shaky foundations, let us invent our own! In his introduction to the *Sic et Non* Abelard makes it perfectly clear that he is not saying this, but even those who had read the introduction and were sympathetic to him might have been thrown into confusion by certain other comments that appeared elsewhere.

In a discussion of the nature of faith in a work that he wrote in his last years in Paris before his condemnation in 1140, Abelard defined faith as 'an *existimatio* concerning things not seen'.[3]

---

3. Abelard, *Theologia 'scholarium'* 1.2; CCCM 13: 318.

What is an *existimatio*? The latin word can mean opinion, judgment, consideration, supposition, evaluation, or estimation, but however we translate it, it is something which is the result of human reasoning. It therefore appeared that Abelard was stating categorically that faith is a matter of fallible human opinion, and when one juxtaposes this definition with the apparently destructive techniques of the *Sic et Non*, it is no wonder that more conservative churchmen began to get nervous.

Two of Abelard's most important opponents were William of Saint-Thierry and Bernard of Clairvaux. Bernard we met in the last chapter and at this time he was at the height of his power and influence. William had begun his monastic life as a Benedictine in the monastery of Saint-Nicaise at Reims and in 1119 was elected abbot of Saint-Thierry, another benedictine monastery set on a hill a short distance to the north-west of the same city. But at some time—precisely when is not clear— William had travelled to Clairvaux and had there met Bernard. A deep friendship developed between them, and after some years at Saint-Thierry William asked Bernard if he might relinquish his abbatial position, leave the Benedictines, and become a simple cistercian monk. Bernard did not agree, but William became more and more convinced that his calling to the Cistercians was a true vocation, and in 1135, perhaps against Bernard's wishes, he left Saint-Thierry and entered the newly-founded cistercian abbey of Signy, about thirty-four miles north-west of Reims. It was here that he came across certain writings of Abelard that an unnamed novice had brought into the abbey. William read them and was horrified. Two things in particular caused him major concern: Abelard's definition of faith and what he had to say about the Trinity. He immediately made a list of those ideas he found most repellent and sent it to Bernard with a covering letter. Once convinced of the danger, Bernard reacted with his customary speed and vigour, and the eventual result was Abelard's arraignment before the Council of Sens in 1140 and his subsequent condemnation. His trinitarian teachings we must leave for consideration in their proper place (Chapter VII), but his definition of faith demands our immediate attention.

IV-2 This statue of Saint Bernard, probably made for his tomb at Clairvaux, shows the saint as founder of abbeys, holding a model of a church in his left hand. He is depicted as an introspective and sensitive young monk, rather than the stern ascetic of later centuries. Carved from limestone, the statue stands thirty inches tall and still retains traces of paint. It was saved from destruction at the Revolution and was preserved in a bridge-chapel over the Aube River. When the chapel was bombed in 1940, the crozier—the emblem of abbatial office, which the saint once held in his right hand—was destroyed.

Saint Bernard, end of the fourteenth century (?)
Bar-sur-Aube, Bibliothèque municipale.
Photo: Photo Richard, Bar-sur-Aube.

For William and Bernard, Abelard's use of *existimatio* could imply only two things, and both were intolerable. He was either saying that the faith of the church was a mere matter of human opinion, or claiming that it was up to any one of us to make a selection from the truths of the faith just as our fancy dictates. In either case he was subverting divine and ecclesiastical authority and it was imperative that he be silenced.

What Abelard himself actually meant by *existimatio* is another matter. He seems to have been concerned with analyzing the psychological act by which we give our assent to the faith, and if we may translate *existimatio* as 'the process of deliberation whereby we give a reasoned judgment', he was not far wrong. But if that was what he intended to imply, it was not what he appeared to say, and there is not the slightest doubt that his terminology was dangerous. It did look as if he were equating faith with opinion, and William and Bernard were quite right to take him to task.

The furor that erupted around Abelard in the middle of the twelfth century had a number of effects. On the one hand it drove some of his contemporaries to redefine the nature of faith, to reassert its divine authority and its quality as a divine gift, and to reaffirm and tighten the position of the church as its transmitter and custodian. On the other hand, it drew attention both to the value and the danger of the scholastic approach. The meticulous logical examination of the tenets of the faith could clearly be of immense benefit, but one's language needed to be as precise as one's logic. Human reason, the greatest of God's gifts to humankind, was given us to be used, and to refuse to use it is blasphemous. The problem, as we saw earlier, lay in determining the extent to which it might be used appropriately, and that was a matter which called for very delicate judgment.

Despite the abelardian crisis, therefore, the methods of scholasticism continued to be cultivated, and less than ten years after Abelard's death they were used by Peter Lombard in the composition of the most influential of all text-books of medieval theology, a volume which was to remain for some four centuries the standard guide to western christian doctrine: the *Sententiarum libri quatuor*, the *Four Books of Sentences*.

Peter Lombard (or Peter the Lombard) was, as his name indicates, an Italian. He was born c.1100 in Lumello, not far from Novara in Lombardy, and educated at Bologna, Reims, and the abbey of Saint-Victor in Paris. For a time he was probably a pupil of Abelard (he had certainly read his books), and he knew Bernard of Clairvaux who thought highly of him. From c.1140 he taught at the cathedral school of Notre-Dame in Paris where he gained a great reputation, and in 1159, the year before his death, he was consecrated bishop of the city. By the early 1140s Lombard had already composed long commentaries on the Psalms and the Pauline Epistles, and his masterpiece, the *Sentences*, was compiled about a decade later, sometime between 1150 and 1156. It was not intended to be an original work, and in his prologue the author tells us that he has gathered together the opinions of the fathers into a single volume so that students, searching for authoritative statements, may not have to trouble themselves with tracking down a multitude of books. Students have always loved that sort of thing.

The four books of the work dealt respectively with God, creation, the Incarnation, and the sacraments. Lombard begins the first book with the mystery of the Trinity and moves on to consider such questions as whether human beings can know God, the unique generation of the Son, the simplicity of the divine essence, the distinction and equality of the three persons, the procession and mission of the Holy Spirit, the terminology of trinitarian theology, and God's omnipotence, foreknowledge, will, and predestination.

The second book deals with creation: the creation of the angels, together with a discussion of angelic natures, the creation of the world, and the creation of men and women. The author then proceeds to examine the nature of human beings before the Fall, the consequences of the first sin, its effect on free-will, the necessity of grace, the nature and causes of sin, and the role played by the human will in sinful acts.

Book Three discusses the Incarnation and the nature of Christ's human form, the relationship of divinity and humanity in the incarnate Christ, the question of whether Christ grew in wisdom and goodness, the extent to which he was bound by human infirmities, how we humans were redeemed by his death, the nature of his passion, and whether Christ possessed faith, hope, and love. He then proceeds to a more general discussion of these and other virtues (righteousness, fortitude, prudence, and temperance), and includes an account of the seven gifts of the Holy Spirit and the ten commandments.

In the fourth and final book we find an examination of the sacraments (Lombard is the first to provide us with the formal list of seven) and the four last things: resurrection, judgment, heaven, and hell. This last book is particularly important, for Lombard's teaching on the sacraments marks an important advance over earlier considerations, and we shall consider it in more detail in Chapters XV and XVI.

Lombard's approach to all these topics follows a standard pattern, the pattern which had begun in the school of Anselm of Laon and which had been perfected by Abelard. The author proposes a *quaestio*, he cites his authorities, he adduces arguments for and against, and he derives a solution. His arguments are taken from scripture, the fathers, the councils of the church, and treatises on ecclesiastical law, and Lombard had already accumulated much of the material when he was preparing his earlier commentaries on the Psalms and the letters of Saint Paul. His major authority is Augustine, who accounts for about ninety percent of all the patristic citations, but he does not restrict himself either to the west (Origen, John Chrysostom, and John of Damascus all make an appearance) or to the past (among his contemporaries, he quotes Abelard and Hugh of Saint-Victor).

Despite his skilful use of the scholastic method—the method of the *Sic et Non*—Lombard is far more cautious than Abelard. Nowhere do we find such dangerous terminology as *existimatio* and Lombard is careful to anchor his thought firmly and unswervingly to tradition and authority: the tradition of the church and the authority of the fathers. When he does use logic, he uses it extremely well, but for him the boundaries of the theological chess-board are not in doubt and he has no intention of challenging them. This did not stop some later writers from questioning the orthodoxy of certain of his opinions[4], but their accusations came to nothing, and from 1215 onwards Lombard's *Sentences* were established as the standard of western orthodoxy. For some three centuries it was the accepted text-book of theology and only the Bible had more authority. It was the set-text for the university degree in divinity; it was the basis for innumerable commentaries; it was to found in virtually every library; it presented the facts of the faith lucidly and comprehensively; and it was not until the sixteenth century that it was relegated to an inferior position and forced to take second place to the *Summa theologiae* of Thomas Aquinas.

Lombard's *Sentences* represent the high-point of the scholastic approach to theology in the twelfth century. But when Lombard died in 1160 western Europe was just beginning to feel the impact of the new translations of aristotelian works from muslim Spain. Until the early part of the century the only aristotelian treatises available were Boethius's versions of some of his logical works, but from about 1130 onwards we see first a trickle and then a flood of other and more important translations. First of all came further logical texts, and then, from about 1170, treatises dealing with physics, meteorology, biology and the other sciences. Finally there appeared the important and influential philosophical texts such as the *Metaphysics* and *Ethics*. By this time, however, William, Bernard, Abelard, and Lombard were all dead, and the real impact of Aristotle was not to be felt until the succeeding century. The study of theology then takes on a new dress and we will examine what happened in the next chapter.

One last point before we move on. Our discussion so far has been limited to theological developments in the latin world and we have said nothing yet about the interplay of reason and faith in the greek east. This is not because there is nothing to be said, but because we will consider the matter fully in Chapter VIII. In general, greek theology tended to lay greater stress on

---

4. He was accused of Nihilianism, a christological heresy which will be discussed in Chapter XII below.

the heart than on the head. There were 'Christian Hellenists' in the east—we shall meet Michael Psellos in due course—but the main lines of theological development were more spiritual than intellectual. Most modern westerners who know his work tend to think of Symeon the New *Theologian* as Symeon the New *Mystic*, but when the eastern church thought of theologians, it tended to do so in terms of the definition provided by a fourth-century monk and hermit, Evagrius of Pontus (346–99): 'A theologian is someone who truly prays, and someone who truly prays is a theologian'.[5] This, however, is a matter we shall consider in its proper place, and for the moment we will remain in the west and move on to examine the interplay of faith and reason in the first half of the thirteenth century.

---

5. Evagrius Ponticus, *De oratione* 60; PG 79: 1180B; CS 4: 65.

V-1 Almost all monastic libraries possessed a copy of Peter Lombard's *Book of Sentences*. The work summarized the whole of christian theology to the twelfth century and provided a basis for most thirteenth–century theological speculation. This copy, from the cistercian abbey of Pontigny in northern Burgundy, was made in the twelfth century and contains numerous thirteenth century interlinear glosses on the text. The initial C of the first word, *Cupientes*, takes the form of a fanciful bird in a bright blue frame.

Peter Lombard, Sentences, twelfth century.
Auxerre, Bibliothèque municipale ms. 9, f° 1.

V

The Limits of Reason

HUMAN BEINGS can look in four directions: outwards, upwards, inwards, and downwards. To look outwards is to look at the world we can see and sense, with its rocks, flowers, animals, humans, ugliness, beauty, life and death. To look upwards is to look to the Creator who, though bodiless and without form, may yet be known and experienced. To look inwards is to look at our own soul as the image of God, an image which, as we have already seen, is to be found in the highest part of the soul, that part which is capable of abstract and discursive reasoning. Looking downwards we shall ignore.

When the Arabs discovered the works of Aristotle, they found a philosopher who had been obsessed by a desire to understand

and explain these various directions. What is the process by which we perceive the external world and come to understand its nature? What is the relationship between creation and the Something or Someone that brought it all into being? Just what is the human soul, that remarkable entity that has the power to see and comprehend the created world and pose questions about its Creator?

That the christian scholastic philosophers of the thirteenth century were fascinated by these same questions will not come as a surprise. We saw in Chapter I that their main source of inspiration had been the muslim translations of Aristotle that had bedazzled the west during the renaissance of the twelfth century. They too wished to explain the relationship of Creator and creation, to analyze the affinity of God and the soul, and to explain the nature and importance of the processes of perception, cognition, and intellection. But philosophy, which leads to an intellectual and systematic understanding of the universe by the use of natural reason alone, is not our prime concern. We are more interested in theology, which stresses revelation more than reason. Reason should certainly be used to elucidate revelation—we demonstrated that in the last chapter—but philosophy and theology have different emphases. They may not be separate, but they are distinct.

Aristotle, however, was not always regarded in a particularly favorable light. The main philosophical foundations of the early church had been platonic[1], not aristotelian, and in general the early christian fathers regarded Plato and Aristotle as diametrically opposed. Plato was seen as the idealist, seeking the source and meaning of all things in God; Aristotle was seen as the materialist, the proto-scientist, looking for meaning in things themselves. Plato, they thought, always looked upwards; Aristotle always looked outwards. For Aristotle sense-experience was everything, and all could be explained in rational and materialistic terms. Furthermore, as we noted in Chapter I, Aristotle's

1. See *Cloud* 23–6, 43–53.

investigations in the various sciences had, in a sense, diminished the role of the Creator, for things which hitherto had been believed to be of divine origin were now thought to occur in accordance with natural laws. All in all, then, Aristotle was a temptation and a danger. He offered more to human reason than it had ever been offered before, but in so doing he tempted reason beyond its proper limits.

How, then, did the theologians of the latin west deal with this mass of new and potentially dangerous material? How did they accommodate their faith to the ideas of Aristotle? They could choose one of two ways. The easier way was simply to reiterate the facts of the faith and use Aristotle only to elaborate them. Any aristotelian ideas that contradicted or jeopardized those facts were simply ignored. This was an easy and convenient solution and offered few complications. The second way of dealing with the problem was much more difficult. Here one attempted a true reconciliation of Aristotle and the christian faith. It was not simply a case of missing out those bits of Aristotle that proved to be awkward, but of facing them fairly and squarely and establishing a rational aristotelian framework for the truth of christian revelation. The first of these two approaches is represented by Bonaventure, the second by Thomas Aquinas. Bonaventure is more a theologian than a philosopher; Aquinas is more a philosopher than a theologian. Both would have agreed that God is good and true, but Bonaventure was more interested in goodness and Aquinas more interested in truth. For Bonaventure, willing is more important than knowing; for Aquinas, knowing is more important than willing. Let us deal with Bonaventure first.

Giovanni di Fidanza was born near Viterbo in Tuscany in 1221. He became a Franciscan in about 1244 and at that time took the name Bonaventure. He then went to study at the University of Paris, and after fulfilling the necessary requirements, taught at the university for a number of years. In 1257, in company with Thomas Aquinas, he took his master's degree, but earlier that year he had been elected by acclamation as Minister General of his Order. Thereafter his life was fully occupied with administration and worldly affairs, for the burdens of his office were not light. By this time (as we saw in Chapter III) the Franciscans were numerous, wealthy, and powerful, but they were also rent by internal disagreements. Trying to govern a large and powerful body in a state of dissension and rapid change is no small task. In 1271 he played an important role in securing the election of Gregory X to the papacy and was rewarded two years later by being made Cardinal Bishop of Albano. He died in 1274.

Bonaventure's main work, composed when he was about thirty, is his commentary on the *Sentences* of Peter Lombard. And just as Lombard's *Sentences* cover the entirety of christian theology, so does Bonaventure's commentary, and we cannot hope to deal with all of it here. But his other main writing, the *Itinerarium mentis in Deum* (*The Journey of the Mind to God*), is very much shorter, and we shall have more to say about it in due course.

Bonaventure's master is not Aristotle but Augustine, and like Augustine and the whole patristic tradition, Bonaventure establishes his thought on the primacy of faith. Without faith, we have no link with God; without that link, we are deprived of a channel for his grace; without his grace we can know nothing of any real moment and cannot achieve salvation. Bonaventure is in full agreement with Augustine: 'Believe so that you may understand; understand so that you may believe'.[2] From faith we proceed to the use of reason, and from reason to contemplation: but faith comes first!

Once we have established this link with God (and since faith is God's gift, it is up to him whether it be established at all), we must then proceed to use our human reason to its fullest extent. How this should be done is set out by Bonaventure in the brief treatise we mentioned above: *The Journey of the Mind to God*. Here, in seven short chapters, the author delineates seven steps which lead us from a consideration of the traces of God we may discern in the world around us, through an examination of our own selves as images of God, to the contemplation of God

2. See Chapter IV, n. 1.

himself. The first six stages are within our control; the seventh, as we shall see, is not.

At the basis of Bonaventure's *Journey* lies Augustine's idea that when God created the universe, he left in it traces or vestiges of himself. Every created thing bears some likeness to its Creator, though some things resemble him more than others. So let us pose a riddle: how is a rock like God? The answer is simple: because both the rock and God *exist*, because both have being. Then, when we move up the scale to plants and animals, we find not one but two areas of similarity: plants and animals not only exist, they also live, as God exists and lives. And finally, when we come to human beings, we discover three levels of likeness, for human beings exist, live, and have the capacity for abstract reasoning. But because it is only human beings who possess all three of these powers, it is only human beings who can truly be called images of God.

The created universe, says Bonaventure, is a ladder that leads us to the Creator, and the chapters of the *Journey* represent the rungs of the ladder. In the first two chapters he looks outwards to the world around us; in the third and fourth chapters he looks inwards to his own soul; in the fifth and sixth chapters he looks upwards to God; and in the seventh and final chapter, it is God who looks at Bonaventure, not the other way round. But the author also makes it clear that this is far from being a purely intellectual exercise. Those who wish to undertake the journey must base their endeavours on faith. They must avoid sin and cultivate righteousness. They must live a holy life and put their trust in the grace of God, for without his grace, all our efforts are in vain.

In the first two stages of the ascent, we look outwards and see in created things not just the traces of a God who exists, lives, and thinks, but also of a God who is powerful, wise, and good. Here we can see the influence of Aristotle on Bonaventure. In saying that the created universe shows us something of the nature of its Creator, Bonaventure adds nothing to what Augustine had said eight centuries earlier. But Bonaventure is not content with saying this. He wants to know *how* we look at the world around us, how the act of perception is carried out, and how it is processed by the brain. Like the muslim transmitters of Aristotle, he is intrigued by the processes of perception, cognition, and intellection, and wants to know exactly what is going on when we look at the external world.

Exterior objects, he says, enter the mind through the five senses. How? First of all they produce a likeness of themselves on the medium that links them to us: the medium may be space (which carries light) or air (which carries sound). This likeness then passes through the medium to a sense organ (the eye, for example) and is transmitted through it to the faculty of apprehension. Once apprehended, the mind finds delight in the object and proceeds to judge it. It judges whether it is, say, black or white, helpful or harmful, and whether it is harmoniously proportioned. In this way, says Bonaventure, 'judgement is an action which, by purification and abstraction, causes those sensible species that have been sensibly received through the senses to enter the intellective power'.[3]

Whether one understands this is not too important. It is not presented here as an accurate and up-to-date account of the way in which we really do perceive the world around us, but as an example of the way in which the complexities of aristotelian thought could be used to elaborate an essentially simple augustinian thesis. One could make the matter even more complex by introducing such concepts as the active intellect, passive intellect, possible intellect, and agent intellect, the process of abstraction, being and existence, seminal reasons, and all the philosophical jargon of muslim-aristotelian speculation, but that is something we may leave to the scholastic philosophers. It would simply distract us from our main point. Our purpose here is to show that Bonaventure eagerly used Aristotle, but that for him, the ideas of Aristotle were useful only in so far as they served to elucidate the augustinian basis of his thought.

---

3. Bonaventure, *Itinerarium mentis in Deum*, ii.6; Quaracchi ed., accompanied by a French translation by H. Duméry (Paris, 1960) 50.

From a consideration of the external world, Bonaventure moves inwards to contemplate the nature and functions of his own soul. It is here that we find the closest created likeness to God, something that resembles him in being, living, and rationality, and which alone can be called his image. Unfortunately, it is an image which has been severely distorted by selfishness and sin, and an image that has been distorted can give us no more than a distorted glimpse of its prototype. To function properly, therefore, the image must be restored and repaired, and this restoration can only be carried out by clothing the image in the three theological virtues—faith, hope, and love—and thereby enabling it to be cleansed, enlightened, and perfected. Once again, Bonaventure draws us back to the need for faith and grace and reminds us that he is first and foremost a theologian.

From looking inwards and considering God in his image, Bonaventure now looks upwards and considers God in himself. He begins with a complex aristotelian analysis of pure Being, and shows how Being in its purity must be first in every respect, and how it must be eternal, perfect, immutable, utterly simple, utterly great, omnipresent, supremely one, the Unmoved Mover (an aristotelian description), and the efficient, exemplary, and final cause of all things. He then moves on to consider the trinitarian nature of the one God, and here too our human reason is stretched to its limits. He defines and discusses communicability, consubstantiality, coequality, coexistence, hypostatic plurality, essential unity, and the meaning of such terms as essence and person, and once again demonstrates how philosophy can act as a handmaid to theology and how natural reason, when used properly and to its fullest extent, can reveal a vast amount about the nature of its Creator. But let us note that all this difficult philosophical theorizing in no way imperils the faith: the boundaries of the theological chess-board are nowhere called into question.

This sixth stage of ascent represents the limits of our active investigation of the nature of the Creator. If we wish to go further, we must commit ourselves entirely into the hands of God and hope that he, by his grace, will draw us upwards into an extra-conceptual and ecstatic awareness of his inconceivable being. We must be carried out of ourselves and pass over into God. How can this be achieved? Not by any efforts of our own, not by the use of natural reason, not by the observation of the external universe, but by turning to Christ with faith, hope, and love, with devotion, admiration, and exultation. Christ is the way, Christ is the door, Christ is the ladder, Christ is the vehicle that will take us to the Father. All the operations of the intellect must here be relinquished and all our desire turned to God. None can speak of this save those who have experienced it; none can experience it save those who desire it; none can desire it save those who are inflamed by the fire of the Holy Spirit. Love now takes over from rational thought and joy supersedes language. And just as the journey of the mind to God began with his gift—the gift of faith—so it ends with his gift—the gift of an ecstatic, experiential, and incommunicable knowledge of his nature.

Bonaventure's theological thought is like a birthday-cake. Its main bulk is the augustinian tradition, deriving ultimately from Augustine himself and transmitted through Gregory the Great and the other orthodox fathers. The icing and decorations come from Aristotle and the muslim-aristotelian tradition, and the decorations are sometimes very elaborate. And the candles on the cake? These are Bonaventure's mysticism, his spirituality, the light of God's knowledge which crowns all our intellectual efforts and without which those efforts are no more than a sounding brass or a tinkling cymbal.

On the other hand, and despite his love for Augustine, Bonaventure is far more than a mere transmitter of augustinian ideas. In his commentary on the *Sentences* he covered the entire range of christian teaching, and in so doing, and in using Aristotle to elaborate this tradition, he transformed the diffuse and diverse ideas of Augustine into a comprehensive and coherent body of doctrine which is now generally referred to as 'Augustinianism'. But as we said earlier in this chapter, it is one thing to use Aristotle to elaborate and elucidate the faith; it is another to reconcile and harmonize the two and to produce, as did Thomas Aquinas, Christian Aristotelianism.

Thomas was born c.1225 at Roccasecca in Italy. His father was Count Landulf of Aquino (hence the name Aquinas) and at the age of five the young Thomas was sent to the monastery school at nearby Monte Cassino. His aristocratic family probably intended him to become abbot of the monastery when the time was right. In 1240, however, Thomas went to pursue his studies at the newly founded university of Naples and shortly afterwards, against his parents' wishes, decided to seek admission into the Order of Friars Preachers, the Dominicans, which had been founded by Dominic de Guzmán about twenty-five years earlier.[4] He entered the Order in 1244 and immediately left for Paris. For the next three years he studied at the university there and came under the influence of Albert the Great, who inspired him with his enthusiasm for Aristotle, and in 1248 he accompanied Albert to the new dominican house of studies at Cologne.

By 1252 he was back teaching and studying in Paris, and as we noted earlier, he took his master's degree in 1257 in company with Bonaventure. For the next dozen years he was teaching and writing in Italy until, in 1269, the Order recalled him to Paris. Here he met with considerable opposition from conservative theologians who had no love for Aristotle, and it may well have been a result of this antagonism that in 1272 he was sent by the Order to Naples to establish a dominican school. Two years later, on 7 March 1274, he was on his way to the Council of Lyons when he died at the cistercian abbey of Fossanova. He was not yet fifty.

Aquinas was a tireless writer and his output was immense. Like many other scholastics he wrote a commentary on the *Sentences* of Peter Lombard early in his career, and then went on to write a large number of commentaries on Aristotle, Boethius, certain books of the Old Testament, and the gospels. His two greatest achievements, however, are the two *Summae*: the *Summa contra Gentiles* (*Summa against the Gentiles*) and the unfinished *Summa theologiae*[5] (*Summa of Theology*). A *summa* or 'summary'

---

4. See Chapter III above.
5. Or *Summa theologica*, the *Theological Summa*. It is the same work.

was a general term used to refer to any compendium of theology or canon law in which the entries were logically arranged in accordance with the scholastic method of *quaestio*, authorities, arguments for and against, and final resolution. The *Summa contra Gentiles* was probably intended as a text-book for dominican missionaries in Spain (the 'gentiles' being the Muslims), and the *Summa theologiae* was a vast synthesis of the entirety of christian theology and a masterpiece of logical thought and precision. It is the greatest achievement of the scholastic method and remains one of the most important sources of modern Roman Catholic theology.

Aquinas's greatness comes not just from the phenomenal breadth of his reading and study, but from the way in which he was able to master all these materials, see them as a whole with all their inter-relationships, summarize their essential points, use them to build a new and harmonious structure, and explain that structure in logical, precise, and wonderfully lucid latin. Whereas Bonaventure used philosophy to elaborate faith, Aquinas used it to build vast interlocking scaffolding designed to support the weight of divine revelation.

For our present purposes, there are two areas in Aquinas's thought which demand our attention: what he has to say about the relative domains of faith and reason, and what he has to say about the importance of sense-perception. For a start, there is obviously a huge area in which natural reason is paramount. All that we would nowadays include among the sciences, for example. But when we come to such matters as the doctrine of the Trinity, the Incarnation, original sin, the efficacy of the sacraments, the resurrection of the body and so on, we are no longer in the realm of reason but the realm of revelation. Reason may certainly make contributions in this field—Aquinas demonstrates quite convincingly the existence of God as well as his eternity and simplicity—but when it comes down to it, you either believe these things or you do not. It is not the intellect that is at work here, but the will. You cannot *prove* that God became man in Christ, but if you use your will to believe it, that's what makes you a Christian.

So if the proper realm of human reason is not divine revelation, what is it? Aquinas's answer is the answer of Aristotle: the proper realm of human reason is the world of sense-perception. There is nothing we find in the understanding, he says, that was not first in the senses, and by this he means that the five natural senses are our *only* doors to knowledge. We must look outwards in order to look upwards.

This point of view is obviously very different from that of Bonaventure and his fellow Franciscans. Aquinas effectively limits himself to the first two stages of Bonaventure's journey, and refuses to accept any proof of God's existence by meditating on oneself as God's image or by establishing contact with the divine Ideas or by some sort of direct communication from God himself. Any proof of God's existence must be an objective, not a subjective proof: a proof which begins with the only things that natural reason can be sure about—the facts of the physical world.

Thus, at the beginning of the *Summa theologiae*, after some preliminary discussion of the nature and purpose of theology, Aquinas undertakes to demonstrate the existence of God and examine his attributes. Let us glance at the meticulous precision of his method.

Since we have shown, he says, that the principal purpose of holy teaching is to make God known, we will proceed by discussing (1) God, (2) how rational creatures can make the journey to God, and (3) Christ, who, as the God-man, is our path to God.

Our consideration of God will then fall into three parts: (1.a) the nature of God, (1.b) the distinction of the three persons, and (1.c) how God created the universe.

But in considering the nature of God, we must discuss (1.a.i) whether there is a God, (1.a.ii) what sort of a being he is, and (1.a.iii) the knowledge, will, and power involved in God's activity.

The first of these three questions—1.a.i—then gives rise to three further questions: (1.a.i.A) Is it self-evident that there is a God? (1.a.i.B) If not, can it be made self-evident? (1.a.i.C) Is there a God?

Our author then proceeds to prove (1.a.i.C.1) that it is self-evident that there is truth, but not a First Truth; (1.a.i.C.2) that it can, however, be made evident that there is a First Truth; and (1.a.i.C.3) that we can therefore show that there is a God, and that we can do this solely by using the evidence of our natural senses alone. How?

Aquinas provides five proofs of God's existence, every one of them based on our observation of the external world, and to illustrate the way he thinks and writes, here is a translation of his first proof:

> The first and most obvious proof is that which is based on change.[6] It is certain and evident to the senses that some things in this world are in a process of change. But anything in a process of change is being changed by something else. For although things which are changing possess the potential for [the actuality] towards which they move, they do not yet have it, whereas that which causes the change possesses it in actuality. To cause change is nothing more than to transform potentiality into actuality, but to transform potentiality into actuality can only be done by something in which the actuality already exists. For example, fire, which is hot in actuality, causes wood, which is hot in potentiality, to become hot in actuality, and thereby it brings about a change in the nature of the wood.
>
> Now it is impossible for something to be actually and potentially the same thing at the same time. It may, however, be actually one thing and potentially something else. For example, something which is actually hot cannot be potentially hot at the same time. It can, however, be potentially cold. So it follows from this that something which is changing cannot itself be the cause of the change and the result of the change at the same time: a thing cannot change itself. Anything that is changing, therefore, is being changed by something else. But if the thing that is causing the change is itself being changed, it is itself being changed by a second something, and this, in turn,

6. Or 'movement': *motus* in Latin.

by a third. But we cannot go on forever with this process, for if we do, there will be no First Changer to cause the first change and therefore no subsequent causes [to cause the subsequent changes]. A second cause will not produce change unless it is acted upon by a first cause. A stick, for example, will not move or change anything else unless it is itself first moved by the hand. It follows, therefore, that one is bound to arrive at some first cause of change which is not itself changed by anything, and this is what everybody understands by God.[7]

Once again, whether or not we are able to follow this argument of Aquinas does not really matter. It is simply intended to provide an illustration of his logical, aristotelian method. He is engaged in constructing a gigantic cathedral of philosophy and theology in which every part is firmly cemented to every other part. After establishing the foundations, he proceeds to build brick upon brick. Every brick leads logically to the next and eventually results in a wall. This wall then requires a second wall, and the procedure begins again. Once the four walls are raised, we proceed to the next level and lay the first brick of the next section of the building. And so we continue. Brick leads to brick and wall leads to wall; every division and sub-division has its appointed place, and everything plays its own logical role in the completed structure.

In this way, in Part One of the *Summa*, the author treats of the existence of God, the names and attributes of God, his trinitarian nature, the creation of the angels, the universe, and the human race, human intelligence, our likeness to God, and human government and order. In the second part he defines the highest goal of the human race as the return to God, and examines the ways in which this may be achieved. He therefore finds it necessary to analyze human acts, the principles of morality, love, desire, pleasure, anger, habits, virtues, sin and its effects, the nature of law, the need for grace and faith, the theological virtues, the

7. Thomas Aquinas, *Summa theologiae*, 1a.2.3; Blackfriars ed. (London/New York, 1964–81) 2: 12–14.

social virtues, justice and injustice, the active and contemplative lives, and the role of mysticism in the quest for God. Then, in the third and final part of the work, we find his account of Christ, who is the way to God. He considers his Incarnation, his divinity and humanity, his function as Mediator, the role of Mary his mother, his life, death, and resurrection, and then moves on to consider the importance of the sacraments, all of which were instituted by Christ, and analyzes their role in leading us back to our true home. The path he follows is similar to that of Lombard's *Sentences*, but it is far from being a slavish imitation.

The *Summa theologiae* is an immense and impressive work. One common latin edition contains about 2400 closely printed pages, and the standard bilingual edition—latin text with english translation—comprises sixty volumes. But despite the fact that it is a tour-de-force of logic and rationality, a gigantic paeon in praise of human reason, Thomas Aquinas is no materialist. While the whole of his work is grounded in sense-perception, it does not deny the need for faith and grace. We may not be able to apprehend the revealed truths directly, but they still remain essential for salvation. The very possession and use of reason are direct gifts from God, and Thomas, aristotelian though he may have been, never forgets that the human race is a fallen race and is in desperate need of restoration.

Our fallen nature has an immense potential to do good, but without grace this potential cannot be realized. We can love God to some extent now, but only with the aid of grace can we love him before all else. Without grace, we cannot attain eternal life, for the gift of grace exceeds the power of anything created and is actually a sharing of the very nature of God. Grace, therefore, does not destroy or abrogate the natural faculties: it perfects them! In faith, with love, and through grace our finite and rational minds may be lifted up by God to know and love him in a way which, at present, we cannot conceive. It is an ecstatic and experiential knowledge of the Divine Nature, a knowledge such as a lover has of a beloved, and it is knowledge which will be perfected only in heaven. With this Bonaventure would agree. But even when Thomas is discussing these high matters, his approach remains coolly logical and his language as precise as ever. Not for him are the vague and woolly babblings of so much so-called mysticism. He demonstrates clearly that ecstasy is the result of love; he defines the meaning of the term; he analyzes what happens in ecstasy in terms of knowledge (the apprehensive power) and will (the appetitive power); he distinguishes various forms of ecstasy, and so on and so on.

But to gain a glimpse of this logical and rational philosopher in perspective, let us not forget what the sacristan at Naples saw. When Thomas was in his last years, working on the final part of the *Summa*, the sacristan looked in his room and saw him before his crucifix, deep in prayer, but floating above the ground. A voice came from the crucifix: 'Thomas, you have written well of me. What reward can I give you for all your labours?' 'Nothing, Lord,' said Thomas, 'nothing but you'. And on 6 December 1273 when he was saying Mass, something happened to him. We do not know what it was, but after the experience he wrote nothing more. One of his friends thought he had suffered a breakdown and urged him to try to complete the last part of the *Summa*. 'I cannot', said Thomas, 'for compared with what I have seen and what has been revealed to me, everything I have written seems like straw'.

To Thomas Aquinas, then, we owe the creation of Christian Aristotelianism and the construction of a scholastic philosophical framework which would be common to the west until the Reformation and which, in due course, would become the bedrock of modern Roman Catholic theology. But Thomas's genius in christianizing Aristotle and in amalgamating his ideas with those of so many others in the production of this impressive system must not blind us to the fact that Aristotle was by no means everyone's favourite author. During the first half of the thirteenth century there was considerable opposition to his doctrines, and the study of Aristotle was more than once forbidden by the popes. Their concern was justified, for a number of aristotelian doctrines were diametrically opposed to those of Christianity, and unless they were treated with the utmost caution, they could all too easily lead the unwary astray. Aquinas, it is true, had given a new dignity to natural, human reason, but the unwise and incautious use of that reason combined with dubious philosophical ideas normally spelled heresy. And for the western church of the twelfth and thirteenth centuries, heresy—as we shall see in the next chapter—was a major problem.

VI-1 The façade of St-Gilles-du-Gard in Provence (southern France) has the largest exterior ensemble of sculpture of the romanesque period. The design of this façade was influenced by roman achitecture, especially triumphal arches. Another influence, this time in choice of subject, may well derive from the heresies raging in this period. The three portals narrate major events in the life of Christ, but the portrayal of the Crucifixion (a rare subject in romanesque sculpture), and the prominence given to the Last Supper probably reflect the strong stand taken by this monastery against an heretical group led by Peter of Bruys. Peter had denied the validity of the Mass and taught that crosses should be broken and burned because the cross, as an instrument of the Passion, was not worthy of veneration. To emphasize his point, he and his followers stole the wooden crosses from the monastery church of Saint Gilles and, on Good Friday, made a fire of them in front of the abbey, and over this fire they roasted meat, forbidden food in Lent. A few days later, Peter and his friends were burned as heretics on the same spot. These events may have taken place as early as 1126 and thus influenced the choice of subject matter on the portals, begun only a few years later.

Saint-Gilles-du-Gard

VI

Beyond Reason: Medieval Heresy

THERE ARE TWO types of heresy. Firstly, we have heresies which, in general, accept the fundamental principles of the christian faith, but interpret those principles in unorthodox ways; secondly, we have heresies in which these fundamental principles are rejected and an alternative Christianity or an alternative religion set up in their place.

Adherents of the first type of heresy acknowledge one God in three persons, recognize a clear distinction between the Creator and his creation, accept that God became man in Christ, and agree that the sacraments of the church are important for salvation. Their understanding of these four principles will not be that of the established church, but they are in general agreement as to their veracity. We discussed a number of cases of this sort of heresy in A *Cloud of Witnesses*—examples are Arianism, Nestorianism, Monophysitism, and Monotheletism—and we will deal with others in the course of this present volume.

We may include in this first type of heresy a number of groups who appeared in the west in the twelfth and thirteenth centuries and whose existence stemmed not from a dissatisfaction with the beliefs of the church, but from a disgust with its worldliness and corruption. We saw in Chapter I that by the time of Gregory VII the church was in dire need of reformation, but despite the various attempts at reform which we discussed in that chapter, the overall situation did not much improve. The wealth, laxity, dissipation, and immorality of all too many conspicuous ecclesiastics was an undoubted scandal, and it was only to be expected that some devout Christians would call to mind Christ's demands for poverty, humility, morality, and self-control.

Thus, in the early twelfth century, we see the appearance of wandering preachers, making their way through the towns and villages of the european countryside, and calling for repentance and a return to the poverty advocated in the gospels. They seem to have met with some success, and they may well have acted as focal points for wide-spread public dissatisfaction with the gross inequities in wealth and power which characterized the society of the time. Some of them quite deliberately combined their preaching with a call for political reform. A good example is Arnold of Brescia (a town in the north of Italy, at the foot of the Alps), an italian Regular Canon whose disgust with the worldliness of so many prelates led him to adopt a donatist position and maintain that unworthy priests could not distribute valid sacraments.[1] He also believed that truly spiritual people ought to have no secular power and should practice absolute poverty. The pope, he said, was a man both greedy and bellicose, and is owed neither reverence nor obedience. Arnold then led a

---

1. See *Cloud* 176–81.

popular revolt in Rome, but after some early successes, he was captured, condemned, and burned, and his ashes were thrown into the Tiber. The date was 1155.

A more serious outbreak of popular heresy occurred about twenty years later when, in 1173, a rich merchant from Lyon named Peter Waldo underwent a dramatic conversion. Like Saint Antony of Egypt, he too heard a reading of Matthew 19:21[2] and did as he was commanded. He sold all his goods and, just as Arnold had done, set out to preach evangelical poverty and to attack the prevailing corruption in the church. He met with great success and attracted many followers, both men and women, learned and unlearned. They called themselves the Poor of Lyon, but they are now generally referred to as the Waldenses after their founder, Waldo.

As the waldensian movement spread, the church naturally became alarmed and a series of pronouncements by a series of popes were designed to put a stop to their dangerous preaching. When this did not succeed, Pope Innocent III, in 1209, called for a crusade against them. Two years later eighty Waldenses were burned at Strasbourg, and over the succeeding decades the church continued its attempts to eradicate them. As it happens, they were not entirely successful and the movement survived to the Reformation, received support from the Protestant churches, and still exists today. There is a waldensian theological school in Rome, a waldensian community in the Piedmont in Italy, and a waldensian church in New York City. Their present numbers have been estimated to be about twenty thousand.

A different approach to the same problem may be seen in the apocalyptic ideas of Joachim of Fiore. Joachim, who was born c.1132, experienced a conversion to the religious life while on a pilgrimage to Palestine, and on his return to Italy he entered a cistercian monastery. Against his will, he was elected abbot of Corazzo in 1177 (Corazzo lies in the far south of Italy),

---

2. 'If you want to be perfect, go, sell your possessions and give to the poor, and you will have treasure in heaven.'

but resigned a few years later. He eventually founded his own monastery at Fiore not far from Corazzo and resided there until his death in 1202. With Joachim we see the same deep concern with ecclesiastical corruption, but Joachim thought not in terms of an immediate solution, but of one which was destined to occur in the future and which was part of God's divine plan.

The trinitarian nature of God, he said, is reflected in three great periods of world history. The first was the Age of the Father (the age of law) which came to an end with the Incarnation. The second is the Age of the Son (the age of grace), which Joachim thought would last for forty-two generations of about thirty years each. The third is the Age of the Spirit (the age of liberty) which would see the rise of new, pure, and unworldly religious orders, the conversion of the whole world to Christianity, and the establishment of a new Spiritual Church. Joachim himself never claimed that the Third Age had begun (though he expected it at any time between 1200 and 1260) and never challenged ecclesiastical authority. His followers did. Groups like the Spiritual Franciscans and the Fraticelli, reacting against the abandonment of the franciscan ideal of absolute poverty, became convinced that they were the 'Spirituals' of the new age and therefore combined with their calls for reform the conviction that they were cooperating with God in his plans for the world. The hierarchy of the church, needless to say, was not of the same opinion, and clamped down on the new movements. Excommunications were followed by burnings, and as a result of intense persecution, the numbers of Joachimite groups and followers gradually dwindled and faded away in the course of the fourteenth century.

Other groups similar to these also made their appearance in this period—the Humiliati, Poor Lombards, Poor Catholics, Reconciled Poor, and so on—but ecclesiastical opposition to these movements was directed not so much at the heretical nature of their teaching as at the disobedience of their members. At stake was the authority of the church rather than its beliefs, and the Waldenses, Spiritual Franciscans, and the rest might be regarded more as rebels than as heretics. This was not the case with those who may be classed as heretics of the second type.

In this case, as we noted at the beginning of the chapter, we are dealing not with unorthodox interpretations of fundamental christian principles, but with their straightforward rejection. We have here moved outside the traditional faith of the church and have established an alternative Christianity or an alternative religion. A heretic of this second type would be someone who claimed to be God, or who believed that Jesus was no more than a prophet, or who totally rejected the sacraments of the church, or who believed in two gods instead of one. It may come as a surprise to learn that such ideas were by no means uncommon in the Middle Ages, and one of them—the last mentioned—had an extraordinarily wide following both in the east and the west. The rest of this chapter will be concerned with this second type of heresy.

Let us begin our investigation where we left off in the last chapter: with the influence of Aristotle. Aristotle, as we know, had certain ideas that were very different from those of Christianity, and one of these involved the way in which the universe came into being. Christians believe that the universe was created by God out of nothing. The book of Genesis says so. But this was not the view of Aristotle, particularly Aristotle as he had been reinterpreted by the Muslims. The Arabs, in fact, had mixed up Aristotle with later platonic thought, and tended to think in terms not of creation but of emanation.

Emanation is not difficult to understand. Something like it happens every time you clean your teeth. When you squeeze the tube, a certain amount of toothpaste emanates out and manifests on the toothbrush, and the toothpaste on the brush and the toothpaste in the tube are identical in their composition. But if you apply this idea to creation, it can lead to serious problems. If God emanates the created order out of his own being, it is difficult to see any real difference between God and creation; and if there is no real difference between God and creation, what is to stop me from saying 'I am God'?

It seems that some people did say this, though because their writings were destroyed by the church it is not always clear just what they meant by it. A scholastic philosopher named Amalric

(Amaury in French), who came from Bène (near Chartres) and who had taught at Paris, was condemned by the church for pantheism (the doctrine that identifies God with the universe), and so too was another aristotelian philosopher named David of Dinant. But as so often happens, the followers of Amalric—Amalricians or Amaurians—took their founder's views to extremes and maintained that since God was perfect and immortal, they too were perfect and immortal. One of the leaders of the sect even asserted that he could neither be consumed by fire nor tormented by torture (he was wrong, by the way), and the Amaurians believed that they were the 'Spirituals' who had been predicted by Joachim of Fiore. Through them the Holy Spirit spoke to the world, and within five years, they said, everyone would be able to say 'I am the Holy Spirit' or, like Christ, 'Before Abraham was, I am.' But however startling these views might have been, they had only very limited circulation. They were confined to an obscure group of intellectuals and posed no real threat to the church.

More serious were a number of movements that emphasized not a philosophical or ontological identity with God or the Holy Spirit, but the possibility of mystical identity. The consequences, however, are much the same. If I can achieve such mystical union, or if I am utterly possessed by the Holy Spirit, then I am beyond the authority of the church, I am incapable of sin, I have no need of any sacraments or ecclesiastical organization, and I speak with divine authority. In 1022, a number of clerics and laymen were burned at Orléans, and although we do not know the details of their beliefs, they appear to have claimed some sort of direct interior illumination from God and to have rejected the sacraments, the Virgin Birth, and the Crucifixion. Their fate also provides us with the first reported case of burning as a punishment for heresy in the west.

Again, in the thirteenth and fourteenth centuries, churchmen became much concerned about something they referred to as 'the heresy of the Free Spirit'. Its adherents were also said to believe in some sort of direct mystical enlightenment, and although the designation may have been an umbrella-term that covered a diversity of groups, it does indicate the development of an individualistic and extra-ecclesial approach to religion and salvation. The claim to direct personal mystical experience often goes hand in hand with a rejection of the intermediary function of the church, for why should you bother with priests, bishops, popes, and sacraments when you can be in direct contact with the Holy Spirit?

It is understandable, too, that such a movement would have a particular attraction for women, for at this time women could play no part in the government of the church and they had only two choices in life: marriage or the convent. In other words, they would be required to obey either their husband or their abbess, and for many women, neither alternative was especially alluring. One of the most important texts to come out of the movement was written by a woman—the *Mirror of Simple Souls* by Marguerite Porete—but its author was burned as a heretic in 1310. It is only very recently, however, that the profound influence of such women on the development of medieval spirituality has been recognized. How many men and women accepted these mystical ideas is unknown, but the movement—or a group of movements sharing basically similar ideas—may have been very widespread. Medieval heresy was not a peripheral phenomenon.

By far the most dangerous of all these heresies of the second type were the dualist heresies: those which maintained that the deplorable condition of this world could only be explained by positing the existence of two principles or two deities, one good and one evil. The idea has its attractions. Some of these heretics believed in two gods, others in one god who had two sons, but all of them alike preached an alien version of Christianity and all of them proved remarkably popular. Dualism, especially in the west, was the greatest concern of the church in the late twelfth and thirteenth centuries and the greatest threat to latin Christianity. It still is, though most people don't realize it.

The story begins in the east, in Bulgaria, sometime between 927 and 940. A priest named Bogomil (Bogomil is the Old Slavic translation of Theophilus, 'God's friend') taught that the one God of the christian tradition had not one but two offspring.

The elder son, Satanael or Satan, revolted against God and was cast out of heaven. The events are narrated in Revelation 12:7–9. It was Satan, said Bogomil, who created the world, including human bodies. But since Satan was not capable of creating human souls, that had to be done by his father, God. Both God and Satan, therefore, have a claim on us—God for our souls and Satan for our bodies—and since the god of the Old Testament was the one who created the world, the Bogomils identified him with Satan.

Satan then seduced Eve, Eve tempted Adam, and humanity fell under satanic domination. Something had to be done. So God sent his second and younger son, Christ, down to earth to vanquish Satan and teach us how we might escape from matter and return to heaven. But because matter had been created by Satan and was therefore evil, the good Christ could not actually *become* human. Good cannot manifest as evil any more than a square can manifest as a circle. You cannot have both at the same time. Christ, therefore, only *appeared* to be human, or, in theological terms, the Bogomils were docetists.[3] After overcoming Satan, Christ returned to heaven, but left the Holy Spirit on earth to continue his work. That is the situation in which we find ourselves at present. What happens after that is not clear. Some Bogomils, perhaps the majority, thought that at the end of all things, Satan and sin would be entirely destroyed and both Christ and the Holy Spirit would be reabsorbed back into the Father. But this was not the only view in circulation and other bogomil teachers seem to have had different expectations.

Since created matter is evil, the Bogomils wanted nothing to do with it. They therefore rejected marriage and sexual activity, for sex leads only to the procreation of more evil bodies, and for the Bogomils, children were the production of Satan. They also banned as many material things as possible from their worship. They had no church buildings, they rejected icons, crucifixes, and all forms of religious art, they had no time for relics (unpleasant

3. See *Cloud* 92–3.

bits of evil bodies), and they did not use water for baptism or bread and wine for the eucharist. Their main form of worship was the recitation of the Lord's Prayer a certain number of times a day, and when they confessed their sins, they confessed them to each other. They were also strict vegetarians, refusing to eat meat, eggs, cheese, or any animal products, and they drank neither milk (another animal product) nor alcohol.

Their rejection of heterosexual sex led to them being accused of homosexuality, since in this way one could experience the pleasures of sex without the danger of procreation. And since the Bogomils were Bulgarians or Bulgars, the term Bulgar came to be synonymous with homosexual activity. The word then made its way into French and Dutch, lost its third letter *en route*, and ended up in English as bugger. But we should note that accusations of sexual immorality were commonly made against heretical groups, and there is no evidence that the Bogomils were any more interested in homosexuality than anybody else at the time. In fact, their ascetic and austere life-style was probably far superior to that of their orthodox rivals.

The Bogomils may never have been very numerous in Bulgaria and the movement became more important when bogomil beliefs spread to the Byzantine Empire. This seems to have begun in the mid-eleventh century and by the end of that century there were Bogomils in Constantinople. In c.1110 their leader was a monk named Basil who, we are told, had taught bogomil beliefs for more than forty years. He had numerous supporters among the upper classes and Constantinopolitan intelligentsia, but this did not prevent him from being arrested, together with his leading followers. Those who returned to Orthodoxy were pardoned; those who refused were sentenced to life imprisonment; Basil himself was burned.

In Constantinople, Bogomilism was provided with an impressive intellectual and philosophical framework, and in some quarters, it was transformed from dualism into ditheism. There were some, in other words, who believed not in one God who had two sons, but in two coequal and coeternal deities, one good, the other evil, who were engaged in perpetual and inconclusive struggle. But this extreme form of dualism was held only by a minority.

As a result of imperial and ecclesiastical control, Bogomilism was never a major threat to the eastern church. Bogomils or bogomil beliefs surface here and there until the fifteenth century, but since the term 'Bogomil' came to be used very loosely, it is often difficult to determine just what doctrines were being taught. Of far more consequence was the transmission of bogomil beliefs west along the shores of the Mediterranean to Italy and southern France in the late eleventh century, for once in the west, the system took root, flourished, and grew into the largest and most important heretical movement ever to trouble the medieval church until the Reformation.

In the west the dualists became known as Cathars or Albigenses. Cathar comes from the Greek work *katharos* 'pure' and the designation first appeared in writing in 1163. Albigenses is derived from Albi, a town in the south of France which was one of the centres of the sect. It lies on the left bank of the River Tarn, about forty miles north-east of Toulouse. We also find them called *Bulgari* or Bulgars, but that is not common.

Cathar beliefs, as we might expect, are similar to those of the Bogomils, and just as in Bogomilism we find both dualism and the more extreme ditheism, so too among the Cathars. Once again we have the idea of two antagonistic principles, the evil nature of created matter, the identification of Satan with the god of the Old Testament, docetism and a refusal to accept the reality of the Incarnation, the rejection of the sacraments, the renunciation of marriage and sex, and the avoidance of alcohol and any animal products. Fish were permitted because they were thought to be generated spontaneously from water.

The Cathars, however, introduced certain additional beliefs and practices. One of these was the introduction of severe fasting. Some major fasts were taken over from the established church of the time, but in addition to these, the Cathars demanded further fasting for three days each week.

A second additional idea was that since liberating oneself from matter might take some time, it was not a process that had

VI-2 This manuscript, written in Latin and Occitan (a medieval southern french dialect), consists of two parts: the New Testament and, beginning on this page, a collection of cathar ceremonies as they were practiced in the thirteenth century. The primitive drawing of a fish, in red and black, announces the opening of the second part, which includes invocations, prayers and various rites (such as the *consolamentum*), followed by the various phases of the liturgy: general confession of the Perfects, the consent of the assembled 'Christians' to administer the rite to the candidate, the washing of hands, the preparation of the table, the genuflexion of the candidate, and the prayers to be recited.

Cathar Ritual, thirteenth century.
Lyon, Bibliothèque municipale, MS. P.A. 36, f° 236.
Photo: Bibliothèque municipale, Lyon.

to be completed within the span of a single life. One's spirit could pass from body to body until the process of purification was complete, and then, transformed into ethereal substance, it would return to its true home. In other words, the Cathars introduced into their version of Christianity the doctrine of reincarnation. The importance of this idea, however, should not be overstated, for the reception of the *consolamentum* on one's deathbed was intended (as we shall see very shortly) to do away with the necessity for any return to the sinful flesh.

The most important of these additional beliefs was a recognition that not everyone was cut out for spiritual olympics, and that ordinary men and women might not be able to live the cathar life in all its purity and rigour. The movement therefore distinguished two classes of people: the Perfects and the Believers. The Perfects were expected to live ascetic, celibate, fast-filled, and vegetarian lives, and were assisted in so doing by the power of the Holy Spirit. This was communicated to them by the laying on of hands, just as in the orthodox rite of confirmation.[4] The Cathars called it the *consolamentum*, 'comfort' or 'consolation' (the Holy Spirit being the Comforter), and it is the nearest thing in Catharism to a sacrament. Once the *consolamentum* had been received, the one who had received it could then transmit it to others—but only so long as he or she (for both women and men could become Perfects) retained their sinless purity. On this point, the Cathars were similar to the Donatists, maintaining that the efficacy of the *consolamentum* depended on the sinlessness of its minister.

Ordinary believers would also receive the *consolamentum*, but only on their deathbeds. They could live normal, everyday lives, eating, drinking, and procreating like everyone else, but just before they died a worthy Perfect could bestow upon them the *consolamentum* and thereby guarantee them entry into heaven. In this case, the *consolamentum* was treated rather like the rite

4. See *Cloud* 186–7.

of baptism in the early imperial church: enjoy yourself here, but get your sins washed off at the last moment.[5] It is a splendid idea, but it calls for delicate judgment.

So what happened if such people recovered? In theory, they had two choices: they could either lead the life of a Perfect (they had, after all, received the *consolamentum*), or they could starve themselves to death. This last alternative was referred to as the *endura* or 'endurance', but it was not long before a certain laxity crept into the cathar system and other, less drastic, alternatives became possible. If such unwilling Perfects simply returned to their former lifestyle (and thereby began to sin again), they automatically ceased being Perfect; and since they were no longer bound by the rigorous demands of perfection, they could once again live a normal life and re-receive the *consolamentum* on their next death-bed.

The situation was further complicated by the idea that the efficacy of the *consolamentum* depended entirely on the sin-lessness of the Perfect. If, then, a Perfect had bestowed the *consolamentum* on a dying person (thereby ensuring entry into heaven), and had then sinned, the person who had entered heaven in this way immediately fell back to earth. This, too, required the readministration of the *consolamentum*, and led to a strict McCarthyish watch being kept on the morality and lifestyles of the Perfects.

Like the Bogomils, the cathar Perfects made confession of their sins to each other (this was done in public once a month), and again like the Bogomils, the main feature of their worship was the recitation of the Lord's Prayer. This was forbidden to the ordinary believers, for since they were still sinful, they could not address God as 'Father'. On meeting a Perfect, they were obliged to genuflect three times and say: 'Pray to God for me, a sinner, that he may make me a good Christian and bring me to a good

5. See *Cloud* 188.

end.' 'May God hear the prayer', the Perfect would reply, 'and make you a good Christian.'

Catharism spread rapidly. Part of its attraction was undoubtedly the contrast between the austerity of the Perfects and the dissolute worldliness of many of the catholic clergy. The Perfects, especially in the earlier days of the movement, tried to practise what they preached. It is, however, impossible to estimate the total number of Cathars at the height of their power and influence. One can make some attempt at guessing how many Perfects there were, but there is no way of calculating the number of ordinary believers. Estimates range from a hundred thousand to millions. But however many there were, their numbers were certainly sufficient to throw the church into panic. Bernard of Clairvaux had already preached against the heresy in 1145, and the prime purpose of Dominic de Guzmán in founding the Dominicans was to confront Catharism with learned and effective counter-arguments. Opposition came to a head in 1208 when a papal legate, a cistercian monk of Fontfroide, was murdered by a Cathar, and Pope Innocent III, eagerly supported by the Cistercians, immediately preached a crusade against them.

An army assembled in June 1209 and set off for the south of France under its leader, Arnold Amalric, abbot of Cîteaux. Béziers was the first town to fall, but when the crusaders had taken it, they found that not all the inhabitants were Cathars. Most were orthodox Catholics. The soldiers therefore came to Arnold and asked him what to do since they could not distinguish between them. 'Kill them all', said the abbot of Cîteaux, 'the Lord will know which are his.'[6]

Following the massacre at Béziers, other towns hastily submitted to the crusaders and paid ransom. Carcassonne held out for two weeks before lack of water forced it to submit. In the months that followed, the army gradually took control of the

6. This, at least, is the story as reported by the thirteenth-century Cistercian Caesarius of Heisterbach. It is only fair to note that not all accept his version of the events.

Béziers

VI-3 The early medieval town of Béziers was destroyed in 1209 by Simon de Montfort and its population massacred; at least 10,000 people were killed in the rampage, although only a small number of them were Cathars. The walls were rebuilt in 1289 but again destroyed during the wars of the sixteenth century. The great cathedral of Saint Nazaire dominates the old town from the extreme end of a plateau over the Orb River valley. It was rebuilt from 1215 onwards; the bell tower and upper parts of the nave and west façade date to the fourteenth century, and provide a fine example of the ecclesiastical fortifications common in southern France.

south of France (which had been its intention from the start), and although there was a certain amount of organized resistance from the Cathars, it was not particularly effective. The overtly religious part of the crusade came to an end in 1218 after nine years of brutality and bloodshed, and after that it was no more than a secular squabble for power and land. This was to have a profound effect on french politics, but it is not here our concern.

Catharism, however, had still not been exterminated. A cathar council was held in 1225 in order to reestablish the structure and organization of the sect, and despite the fact that the Albigensian Crusade had shown what could happen when the church took decisive action, cathar ideas once again began to spread through the south of France. In 1233, therefore, Pope Gregory IX charged the newly-formed Inquisition with rooting out the heresy and in 1252 Pope Innocent IV gave the inquisitors permission to use torture in extracting confessions and information. It was the beginning of the end. The dominican inquisitors were just as ascetic, devoted, and single-minded as their cathar enemies, and they were extremely effective. In a single year from 1245 to 1246 one inquisitor alone interrogated nearly five and a half thousand witnesses from thirty-nine towns and villages, and three years later, in 1249, eighty Cathars were burned in a single day at Agen. Persecution was now so intense that the cathar Perfects could move around only in the greatest secrecy, and even then their safety could not be guaranteed. Some were captured; some were burned; some fled to Italy. But the increasing pressure put upon them by an increasingly efficient Inquisition spelled doom to Catharism, and by the 1320s the heresy had virtually disappeared. The last known cathar bishop was captured in Italy in 1321.

Our discussion of Catharism is a convenient place to bring this chapter to a close. The next major problem to threaten the western church involved the proto-Reformation ideas of John Wycliffe and Jan Hus, but a consideration of their views is outside the scope of this present investigation. For the moment we must return within the portals of orthodoxy and continue our examination of the interplay of faith and reason. But whereas our discussion so far has been in fairly general terms, we will now turn our attention to more specific issues. Like Peter Lombard and Thomas Aquinas, we shall begin with a consideration of the nature of God, and we shall commence our investigation by examining what happens when reason and logic are applied to the doctrine of the Trinity.

VII-1 This miniature of the Trinity fills the entire first page of a manuscript containing the four gospels which came from the women's monastery of Notre-Dame-aux-Nonains in Troyes. The image of the Trinity belongs to a type known as the 'throne of Grace', which was very popular in the later Middle Ages. God the Father is shown seated, receiving in his hands the cross of his sacrificed son. Christ himself is supported—literally 'enthroned'—by his Father, while the Holy Spirit is portrayed as a dove. Surrounding the Trinity are the four living creatures which support the throne of God, described in Ezekiel 1:5–12.

Evangeliary, twelfth-thirteenth century.
Troyes, Bibliothèque municipale MS 2251, f° 2v.
Photo: CNRS (IRHT).

VII

Understanding the Trinity

IN THE COMPANION volume to this present study we traced
the development of the doctrine of the Trinity from its tentative
beginnings in the Apostolic Fathers to its final formulation in
east and west. We need not repeat that information here, but
it may be useful to summarise the conclusions of our earlier
investigation. We said there that by the end of the fourth century,
the eastern church had accepted a trinitarian doctrine that can be
described as 'Cappadocian Orthodoxy with Single Procession';
and that by the end of the fifth century the western church had
accepted 'Cappadocian Orthodoxy with Double Procession'.[1]
What does this mean?

1. *Cloud* 89.

It means first that both east and west had agreed that the view
of the Trinity developed by the Cappadocian Fathers—Basil the
Great (whom we met in Chapter III), Gregory of Nazianzus, and
Gregory of Nyssa[2]—was essentially correct, and that the Trinity
consists of three persons—Father, Son, and Holy Spirit—who are
coequal, coeternal, and consubstantial. No one person is better,
older, higher, more powerful, more divine, or more anything than
either of the other two; and since all three are one God, what can
be said of any one person can be said, equally, of each and all of
them. In other words, if we say that the Father is wise, we must
also say that the Son and Holy Spirit are wise; if we say that the
Holy Spirit is love, we must also say that the Father and Son are
love, and so on. Furthermore, since there is only one trinitarian
God, when the Trinity acts, it always acts as a unity. At no time
does the Father or Son or Holy Spirit act alone. If they did, we
would have three gods. All actions of the Trinity are effected *from*
the Father *through* the Son *in* the Holy Spirit.[3]

But for all that, there are still three persons. The Father
remains the Father, the Son remains the Son, and the Holy
Spirit remains the Holy Spirit. But if all three have identical
power, identical rank, identical eternity, identical substance, and
identical abilities, and if all three always act together as a unity,
how can we possibly distinguish between them? The answer of
the Cappadocians was simple: we can distinguish between the
persons of the Trinity not by what they do or what they can do,
but by the way in which they come into being. The Father, and
only the Father, is unbegotten; the Son, and only the Son, is
begotten; the Holy Spirit, and only the Holy Spirit, proceeds.
Beyond that there is nothing we can say.

As for Single and Double Procession, that is not something
with which we need trouble ourselves for the moment, and we
will defer detailed consideration of that complex question until
Chapter X.

2. See *Cloud* 71.
3. See *Cloud* 70–73.

For the greek east, the cappadocian definition was sufficient, and disputes over the Trinity within the eastern church were concerned not so much with how the Trinity should be *understood* as with how it could be *experienced*.[4] In this, the east remained true to form, for as we noted at the end of Chapter III, eastern monasticism tended to emphasize contemplation and the celebration of the liturgy rather than scholarship and learning, and the development of secular schools and universities was primarily a western phenomenon. It will come as no surprise, therefore, to learn that the major disputes and problems that arose from attempts to understand the Trinity intellectually were almost entirely confined to the west.

To understand the arguments in the following pages, we must first examine an important philosophical distinction which we find appearing in the west from the early Middle Ages onwards: the distinction between Nominalism and Realism. The history of the dispute between the rival supporters of these two positions is extraordinarily complicated, but the essential difference between the two views is not difficult to understand. Let us begin with three triangles:

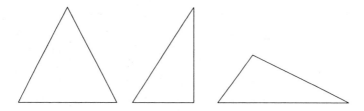

Each of these triangles is of a different size and different area, yet we recognize all three as triangles. How? Because all three share something in common, something we might call 'triangularity'. But just what is 'triangularity'? Is it an abstract concept that has no real existence outside our own minds? Is it simply a convenient word or term that we use to describe a certain shape? If you

4. This is a matter we shall consider in the next two chapters.

agree with this, you are a Nominalist, someone who believes that such concepts as 'triangularity' or 'dog-ness' or 'human-ness' or 'square-ness' are no more than names (*nomina*, in Latin) and that they do not have a real existence outside our own minds. I suspect that most people today are Nominalists.

There were others, however, especially Platonists, who disagreed with this. For them 'triangularity' or 'dog-ness' had a real existence apart from individual triangles and dogs, and we therefore refer to this group as the Realists. But what sort of real existence are we talking about? We obviously cannot pick up 'triangularity' and put it in our pocket. We cannot collect 'dog-ness' and 'human-ness' and 'square-ness' and stick them in a book like stamps. Of course not. But that is not to say that they do not exist. They exist, said the Realists, in the mind of God, the Divine Mind[5], and it is because our soul has a point of contact with this high level that we can recognize triangles when we see them and realize that a giant wolfhound and a tiny chihuahua are both dogs. For the Realists, we are not *creating* 'triangularity', we are *recognizing* it, and in this, the Realists were, in general, echoing the view of most of the early fathers.

Let us now introduce our first Nominalist and see what happens when nominalist ideas are applied to the doctrine of the Trinity. Roscelin[6] was born at Compiègne in the mid-eleventh century. He studied at the cathedral schools of Soissons and Reims and then went on to become a teacher in his own right. With the exception of a single letter, his own writings have perished, and we are dependent upon his enemies for an account of his views. This, obviously, necessitates caution, but so far as we can tell, Roscelin had no hesitation in applying human reason to the doctrine of the Trinity, and he seems to have thought that universal concepts like 'triangularity' were no more than mere words, mere sounds, mere puffs of breath.

If this is so, if such abstract concepts are really no more than mere words, what does it imply about the Trinity? The

5. See *Cloud* 23–25.
6. His name often appears in a latinized form as Roscellinus.

answer is clear. Just as we have three distinct triangles united by 'triangularity', so we have three distinct persons of the Trinity united by 'god-ness' or 'divinity'. But just as 'triangularity' has no real existence outside our own minds, neither does 'god-ness'. In which case, just as we have three separate triangles related only by a human word, so we have three separate persons of the Trinity related only by a human word. But if each separate person of the Trinity is God and the only thing that unites them is a word, a noise, a puff of breath, what we end up with is tritheism, three separate deities!

In 1092 Roscelin was summoned before a synod at Soissons and accused of tritheism. He denied the accusation, but was nevertheless condemned, and shortly afterwards spent some time in England where his views were opposed by Anselm of Canterbury. On his return to France he continued his teaching until his death c.1125.

The most famous of Roscelin's pupils was Peter Abelard, whom we met in Chapter IV. Abelard was neither entirely Nominalist nor entirely Realist but something in between, and he disagreed profoundly with the views of his former teacher. Abelard, rightly, had no time for tritheism and based his own doctrine of the Trinity on the assertion of the absolute unity of the one God. But in so doing, he swung too far in the opposite direction to Roscelin and put so much emphasis on the unity that he tended to blur the distinction between the individual persons. For this he was condemned at the Council of Soissons in 1121 and at the Council of Sens in 1140. What, then, were his trinitarian teachings and why were they considered to be wrong?

Although Abelard had no time for Roscelin's Nominalism, he agreed with him that human reason can and should be brought to bear on the doctrine of the Trinity. Augustine himself had said that he had found the doctrine in the writings of the pagan Platonists,[7] and if the Platonists could discover and comprehend the Trinity by means of human logic and reason, so too could Abelard. But whereas Roscelin had begun his analysis with the

7. Augustine, *Confessions* 7.ix.13; *PL* 32: 740.

three individual persons of the Trinity and had failed to unify them, Abelard, as we have said, began with an emphatic declaration of God's oneness. There is only one God in Christianity, he says, one God who is the Creator of all, one God who is one substance and in whom there are no divisions and no separate parts.

Nevertheless, within this immutable oneness there are three persons, coeternal, coequal, and consubstantial, who remain forever distinct. The Father is always the Father; the Son is always the Son; the Holy Spirit is always the Holy Spirit. The Father is unbegotten; the Son is begotten; the Holy Spirit proceeds. So far all is in perfect accord with Cappadocian Orthodoxy. The persons of the Trinity have been distinguished not by what they do, but by the manner in which they come into being. But Abelard was not prepared to stop here, and it is what he says next that gets him into trouble.

Is there any other way, he asks, that we can distinguish between the persons of the Trinity? Yes, there is. To the Father may be attributed power, to the Son wisdom, and to the Holy Spirit goodness. But even so, we must remember that when the Trinity acts, it still acts as a unity. How? Because whatever is done in power is guided by wisdom and established in goodness. You cannot have true goodness unless it is wisely guided, and wisely guided goodness is useless unless one has the power to put it into effect. So when the one God acts, he always acts in unity. This last point is also sound Cappadocian Orthodoxy and there is no problem with it. The problem lay with what preceded it: the separate attributions of power to the Father, wisdom to the Son, and goodness to the Holy Spirit. Despite the fact that there was abundant patristic support for such attributions, it was a dangerous idea, and Abelard's elaboration of it was even more dangerous.

The Father, he says, is especially (*specialiter*) power. Power is, in a special sense, his characteristic. The Son is wisdom, but wisdom is only a *sort* of power, the power of discerning and knowing things. And goodness, the special characteristic of the Holy Spirit, is neither power nor wisdom, but the effect of love. This kind of thinking can be dangerous. It looks very much as if we are saying that the Son has only part of the power of the Father and that the Holy Spirit has none at all. And if this is so, we are contradicting one of the fundamental principles of Cappadocian Orthodoxy, *viz.*, that what can be said of any one person of the Trinity can also be said of the other two. If the Father is power, so too is the Son and the Holy Spirit, and so on. But Abelard appears to have denied this, and if he has denied it, he is guilty of heresy.

Is there any way, then, in which we can avoid the difficulty? There is, but the solution is worse than the problem. We might say that there is only one God who is fully powerful, fully wise, and fully good, and that when this God acts, he sometimes acts in power (as at creation), sometimes in wisdom (as at the Incarnation), and sometimes in goodness (as at Pentecost). Acting in power, he is the Father; acting in wisdom, he is the Son; acting in goodness, he is the Holy Spirit. But there is only one God, one undivided Trinity, and in maintaining that this single deity acts as three different persons we are not maintaining that any one person is greater than or less than either of the other two. God is one, and the one God is powerful, wise, and good.

Unfortunately, if we accept this, we plunge head-first into Sabellianism, the view that the Trinity is no more than one single Being acting in different ways at different times. The heresy is named after Sabellius, an obscure third-century roman theologian, and had been condemned by Tertullian as early as the third century.[8] To understand it, we need only consider the actions of any human being: a woman may act as a mother (when she is with her daughter), as a daughter (when she is with her mother), and as a doctor (when she is at work). But there are not three distinct persons here, nor are the modes of activity limited to three. The same woman may also act as a grand-daughter, as a teacher, as a customer in a shop, and so on. But if we apply this idea to the Trinity, we are obviously in trouble: just

8. See *Cloud* 81–2. The ideas of Sabellius and Praxeas seem to have been virtually identical.

as the one woman is not three distinct persons, neither is the one God. Abelard appeared to be leaning towards this concept and therefore seemed to be guilty of heresy on two counts: not only was he saying that the three persons of the Trinity were not equally powerful, equally wise, and equally good, but he was also transforming them into mere qualities or attributes of God.

Some of his contemporaries certainly thought this was the case, and they were not slow to call him to account. In 1138 or 1139 William of Saint-Thierry, then a monk at the cistercian abbey of Signy, read some of Abelard's writings and was so horrified at what he saw that he laid aside the work on which he was then engaged (a commentary on the Song of Songs), wrote a rebuttal of Abelard's views, made a list of thirteen propositions he considered particularly dangerous, and sent copies to Bernard, abbot of Clairvaux, and Geoffrey, bishop of Chartres. Bernard then took up the matter and met with Abelard.

Abelard, according to all accounts, first agreed to amend his statements, but soon afterwards changed his mind and refused. He, the recognized scholar, seems to have resented being challenged by someone he considered, perhaps rightly, his inferior in scholarship. But because of his refusal, he immediately found himself accused of heresy, summoned to the Council of Sens in 1140, and precipitately condemned before he had even arrived at the Council to defend himself. He at once appealed to the pope and set out for Rome. But by this time he was old and ill and, as we saw in Chapter IV, he had travelled only as far as Cluny when he heard that the pope had ratified the condemnation and forbidden him to teach. He accepted the pope's decision and entered Cluny. A little while later the abbot of Cluny, Peter the Venerable, had him moved to the priory of Saint-Marcel for the sake of his health, and it was there that he died in 1142.

Abelard was probably not guilty of what he had been accused. A thorough examination of his trinitarian writings enables us to make a case in his favour, but to make such a case requires careful and sympathetic reading. Abelard's treatises were produced in more than one version and he himself was not always consistent. Sometimes, too, the subtlety of his thought is obscured by the

VII-2 The descent of the Holy Spirit at Pentecost is a common scene in Books of Hours. In this version, from the great Anjou prayer book, the Rohan Hours, it introduces the Hours of the Holy Spirit. The Trinity is depicted in the cluster of figures at the top: God the Father is shown as an old man holding the triply-flowering branch of the Trinity, a baby Christ wields the sword of justice while embracing the dove of the Holy Spirit who seems to carry both Father and Son on outspread wings. Surrounding the Trinity are angels outlined in gold, holding open their books, while the Apostles wait impatiently below for the Holy Spirit to descend upon them.

Rohan Hours, Use of Paris, c. 1420.
Rohan Master.
Paris, Bibliothèque nationale, MS lat 9471, f° 143v.
Photo: Bibliothèque nationale, Paris.

solidity of language, and many of his ideas are by no means easy to comprehend. Indeed, one of his defences at the Council of Sens was that his accusers were not sufficiently learned to understand his arguments. This may have been true, but it is not the language of diplomacy. Whatever the truth of the matter, one fact remains: on the surface Abelard does appear to be saying what he was accused of saying, *viz.*, that the three persons of the Trinity have unequal powers and capacities, and that Father, Son, and Holy Spirit are no more than three qualities or activities of the one God. Once again, William and Bernard were quite justified in taking him to task.

Roscelin, as we have seen, was a Nominalist, and his application of nominalist views to the doctrine of the Trinity led to his being accused of tritheism, of splitting up the one God into three. Abelard, who was neither Nominalist nor Realist, was accused, among other things, of just the opposite of this: of blurring the distinction between the persons of the Trinity and merging the three into one. Let us now turn our attention to a thorough-going Realist and see what happens when realist views are applied to the same doctrine.

Gilbert of Poitiers (or Gilbert de la Porrée) was born at Poitiers c.1075 and educated first at the cathedral school of Chartres and then at the school of Laon. His time at Laon was brief and he soon returned to Chartres, where he was appointed chancellor of the cathedral, and spent the next twenty years in the city. He then moved for a short time to Paris, where he taught theology and dialectics, but was soon afterwards elevated to the episcopate and consecrated bishop of Poitiers in 1142. He held this position until his death in 1154. He bears the distinction of being the only person attacked by Bernard of Clairvaux whom Bernard failed to have condemned.

Gilbert, as we have said, was a Realist. For him 'triangularity', 'dog-ness', 'tree-ness' and so on were real things that had real existence. But it was their very reality that got Gilbert into trouble. Let us consider the case of three people: you, me, and someone else. We are all three standing in a line, and we might be of different sizes, different shapes, different sexes, and different colours. What, then, unites us? Gilbert's answer would be 'human-ness' or humanity. Despite our differences we are all three human beings. But does this mean that you or I can be equated with 'humanity'? No, it does not. Nor can a spaniel be equated with 'dog-ness' or a pine-tree with 'tree-ness'. 'Humanity' or 'dog-ness' or 'tree-ness' is something greater than any one individual, and although all human beings share in humanity, none of us can claim it wholly for ourself.

So what happens if we apply this line of thinking to the Trinity? Just as I, you, and someone else are united by 'human-ness' or humanity, so the Father, Son, and Holy Spirit are united by 'god-ness' or divinity. But just as neither you nor I nor our friend can claim to be the whole of humanity, neither can Father, Son, or Holy Spirit claim to be the whole of divinity. By virtue of humanity I am a human being, but humanity is not me. By virtue of divinity the three persons of the Trinity are each God, but divinity is not God. The Father is God, but not divinity; the Son is God, but not divinity; the Holy Spirit is God, but not divinity. So what we end up with are two first principles: divinity (by which God is God) and God himself!

But if God is one and three, and if the oneness of God is divinity, and if the divinity is not God, then who *is* God? There can be only one answer: the Father is God, the Son is God, and the Holy Spirit is God. It is just the same with you, me, and our mutual friend. If the humanity that unites us is not a single human being, then who is a single human being? I am, you are, and so is our friend; and just as we are three separate and distinct human beings, so the Father, Son, and Holy Spirit are three separate and distinct gods. Gilbert of Poitiers seems to have reached exactly the same conclusion as Roscelin while starting out from exactly the opposite premise! Once again, we have tritheism, and once again, Bernard of Clairvaux summoned his forces and launched the attack.

Gilbert was arraigned before two councils, one at Paris in 1147, the other at Reims in 1148. He came very well prepared and his arguments were very lucid, but whether Bernard fully appreciated them is doubtful. Gilbert's latin terminology was the new, developing terminology of the schools, philosophical and precise, and for him the distinction between the Divinity who is God and the divinity by which God is God was perfectly clear. It was not so for Bernard. That, however, was of little consequence, for by this time Bernard was at the height of his power and wielded immense influence. Theological subtleties were overshadowed by clashes of personality, and the end result of the Reims council is unclear. Gilbert does seem to have made certain compromises and Bernard achieved the condemnation of the proposition that God and God's divinity are two separate realities; but according to one contemporary observer, Gilbert was still able to return to his diocese with his honour undiminished. Each side, in fact, could claim victory, and both seemed happy to do so.

We see, then, that purely logical approaches to the Trinity often lead to disaster. Nominalism and Realism can both produce tritheism, and Abelard's middle way seems to lead to a sort of unitarianism. All three approaches, in fact, are beset by the same problem and it was a problem of which Gilbert of Poitiers was acutely aware. There are certain principles, he says, which should be applied only to 'natural things', the things that belong to this world and the created order. If we apply these same principles to 'theological things', we are inevitably led into heresy. So what are we to do? We either say nothing whatever about God and make no attempt to understand him (a denial of our God-given gift of reason), or we take the bull by the horns, apply the principles that normally should be applied only to 'natural things', and hope for the best.

Neither William nor Bernard would have disagreed with the idea at the heart of Gilbert's thesis. There are things to be said about God, and human reason can and should be used to elucidate and elaborate the faith. As we saw in Chapter IV, the real question is not the *use* of reason, but its limits. How far should it go? To what extent can the principles applied to 'natural things' be applied to those that are 'theological'? According to William and Bernard, the scholars—Roscelin, Abelard, and Gilbert—had all gone too far and had ended up not by elucidating the faith, but by challenging or undermining it. How, then, would William or

Bernard have approached the doctrine of the Trinity? How would they have used human reason to probe the very nature of God while at the same time remaining irreproachably orthodox?

The best way to answer this question is by examining a short treatise called the *Enigma fidei* (*The Enigma of Faith*), a work composed by Abelard's adversary, William of Saint-Thierry, sometime between the condemnation of Abelard in 1140 and William's death in 1147 or 1148. It is a work in which William tries to present a doctrine of the Trinity which uses all the resources of human reason, but which uses those resources within their proper limits. It is simply a matter of knowing how far you can go.

William's first few pages, however, do not imbue us with much confidence as to the utility of human knowledge. The Trinity is utterly transcendent; God cannot be seen in this world; our human minds have the utmost difficulty in progressing beyond conceptual images; and questions pertaining to the consubstantial and coeternal nature of God are none of our business. Such a view is rather like that of Theravāda Buddhism: if there is a God, he is clearly infinite. The mortal mind is finite. Since the finite cannot comprehend the infinite, there is no point in trying.

So where do we go from here? Do we simply lapse into silence and say nothing at all? No, says William, that is not the case. Let us look first at God's own word, God's own revelation, and see what is stated there. The scriptures tell us that there is a Father, a Son, and a Holy Spirit; the scriptures maintain that all three are distinct; the scriptures make it clear that the three are one. And when it really comes down to it, says William, that—if we may quote Keats—is all ye know on earth and all ye need to know.

But William was well aware of the tenor of his times. He shared the enthusiasm of his contemporaries for reason and rational investigation, and he knew that although a simple belief in the Scriptures might be sufficient for salvation, it would not satisfy the intellectual curiosity of many of his readers. The spirit of Anselm and Abelard was alive and well, and few would have cared to maintain that the gift of human reason had been bestowed upon us to no purpose. Heresy itself, says William, had long ago demanded of the church greater precision in language and the definition of its doctrines. To combat Sabellius it had been forced to speak of 'persons'; to rebut the views of Arius it had found it necessary to coin the word *homoousios*.[9] William therefore proceeds to discuss and define such terms as number, substance, essence, person, *hypostasis*, attribute, quality, begetter, generation, and procession, and makes it quite clear (in opposition to Abelard) that we cannot and must not attribute power only to the Father, wisdom only to the Son, and goodness only to the Holy Spirit. All three persons are equally powerful, equally wise, and equally good.

Like Abelard, William asserts the unique unity of God, but he stresses again and again that in trinitarian mathematics, one equals three and three equals one. One person of the Trinity ranks no lower than the whole Trinity, and our failure to understand this intellectually only reflects our inability to comprehend what is by definition beyond our comprehension. I can call the Father Father, the Son Son, and the Holy Spirit the Holy Spirit, but beyond that there is little I can say. Apart from these names, all other names or qualities are common to all three persons. If the Father is X or Y, so too are the Son and Holy Spirit. I can never name one person without naming the other two at the same time. As God is one, the Trinity is one. We pray to the Father, who is unbegotten, through the Son, who is begotten, in the Holy Spirit, who proceeds from both, and if we cannot grasp the true meaning of these terms, that is simply a reflection of our inability to encompass in human thoughts or human words the unutterable mystery of the divine nature.

It may seem here that all that William has done is to take the augustinian doctrine of the Trinity—Cappadocian Orthodoxy with Double Procession—redefine the terms using twelfth-century vocabulary, and simply restate Augustine's ideas in a new and up-to-date fashion. He clarifies the concepts and shows us where the mystery lies, but he does nothing to explain it.

9. See *Cloud* 61–2.

Why, then, should we bother to read him? Roscelin, Abelard and Gilbert might have been condemned, but at least they were interesting. What does William have to offer?

From one point of view this is a fair criticism, but William is not arguing from one point of view. There is a companion volume to *Enigma Fidei* called the *Speculum fidei* (*The Mirror of Faith*), and in that work William deals not with the terminology of the Trinity, but with faith, hope, and love: faith in God, hope in God, and a love of God which, like true love between human beings, can lead to a knowledge of God which is not subject to logical analysis, but which is nonetheless real. It is like studying French. One can learn the grammar from a book, but to master the pronunciation and actually speak the language, one needs the help of a French-speaking teacher. For William, *The Enigma of Faith* provides one with the grammar; *The Mirror of Faith* shows the way to contact the teacher, in this case God. Where do we begin? With faith, obviously, the essential first step on which William believed Abelard had stumbled.

Faith is itself a gift of God and it puts us in contact with God. Faith establishes a channel of communication between us and the Trinity. Through this channel we experience the grace of God, and this experience has a twofold effect: it confirms and strengthens our belief in God's revelation of himself as one and three, and it fosters in us a love of God which leads us to an ever greater knowledge of him—a knowledge which is not defined by concepts and scholastic distinctions, but a knowledge which is based on experience. It is one thing to know that water comprises hydrogen and oxygen in a certain combination; it is another to drink it when one is dying of thirst in the desert and the vultures are waiting for the dinner-bell.

William's approach to the Trinity demands both understanding and experience, the head as well as the heart. Just as we need two eyes to see clearly the things on earth, so we need two eyes to see God, and those two eyes are reason and love. Reason provides instruction to love and love illumines reason; and while neither sees very far on its own, together they can accomplish great things. Reason and love cooperate and interact in raising our consciousness higher and higher until, ultimately, faith and reason fall away and we experience the Trinity by being in the midst of the Trinity—but that is not a matter for discussion in this present volume. Without reason, love sees its object dimly and indistinctly; without love, reason is sterile and fruitless. *The Enigma of Faith* and *The Mirror of Faith* represent the theory and the practice of our human approach to God. William, therefore, is not rejecting reason in favour of unthinking belief, but is asserting that reason alone cannot, by definition, comprehend what is beyond reason. If it tries to do so, it is doomed to failure, and if it persists in the attempt, it will be led into heresy. That, in his view, was exactly what had happened with Roscelin, Abelard, and Gilbert.

To what extent this is true is another question. It has become fashionable in recent years to draw a stark contrast between 'monastic' theology and 'scholastic' theology, the former reflecting the ideas and ideals of the contemplative life, the latter those of the active life. Monastic theology, we are told, bases itself on the Bible and the fathers, and its keywords are faith and experience. Scholastic theology bases itself on Plato, Aristotle, and the liberal arts, and its keywords are reason and logic. The contrast is convenient, but misleading. There *is* a difference between the two, but before the time of Thomas Aquinas it was a difference in degree, not in kind. Both monks and schoolmen recognized the authority of the Scriptures and the fathers, and although it is true that they approached the same texts in different ways, the difference lay only in emphasis. The schoolmen no more rejected faith than the monks rejected logic, and neither Abelard nor Gilbert had the slightest desire to substitute human reason for the church's authority. Both, in fact, had the best of intentions. Abelard tells us himself that he had no wish for his philosophy to resist Paul, and no desire to be so aristotelian as to separate himself from Christ. But as everyone knows, in matters of politics it is not what a person says that is important, but what he appears to have said, and what Abelard and the others appeared to have said was undoubtedly wrong. William and Bernard were perfectly justified in drawing attention to the problem.

We cannot, therefore, interpret the conflict of Bernard, Abelard, and the others simply as a conflict between the cloister and the schools. As we saw in Chapter IV, the essential problem was something much more subtle and much more difficult: what is the purpose of human reason and what are its proper limits? Where do we draw the line between natural truth (e.g. the moon goes round the earth and not vice-versa) and revealed truth (e.g. God is three and God is one)? To what extent can the principles we apply to natural things also be applied to theological things? We have seen that there was a large grey area between the two domains and that some western theologians were not at all sure of its extent. What, then, was the attitude of their colleagues in the greek east? That is the question for discussion in the next chapter.

VIII-1 In this sixth-century depiction of the Transfiguration, Saint Apollinaris (in whose church this mosaic is located) presents the event. The high mountain where Christ took Peter, James, and John is indicated by layers of rocks and trees, and the three disciples are shown symbolically as sheep. Sheep often represent the christian faithful; when there are twelve, as in the foreground, they represent the twelve Apostles. Moses and Elijah are witnessing the events from the clouds of heaven, while the hand of God appears out of the sky, bestowing approval: 'This is my beloved Son, in whom I am well pleased'. Christ is shown not as a man, but as a tiny face in the middle of the cross of the resurrection, placed at the curve of the half-dome. Candles on the altar reflect on the mosaic causing the cross to shimmer and sparkle against a blue star-filled sky. Few representations capture so well the mystery of the divine glory shining through the incarnate humanity.

Transfiguration. Interior, S. Apollinare in Classe, dedicated in 549, Ravenna, Italy.
Photo: Alinari/Art Resource, NY.

VIII

Experiencing
the Trinity

TO APPRECIATE the eastern approach to the Trinity we must

go back to the first century and listen to Saint Paul preaching in

Athens.[1] He calls the attention of the Athenians to their altar to

the Unknown God, moves on to discuss human beings as God's

children, and concludes by speaking of the resurrection of the

dead. Some people accepted these ideas and became believers.

Two are mentioned by name: a woman called Damaris and a

man called Dionysius. Since the latter was a member of the

Areopagus, or high court of Athens, he is commonly referred to

as Dionysius the Areopagite.

1. Acts 17:34.

About four centuries later there appeared in the east a group of writings which claimed to have been written by this same Dionysius. It is now known that they were not written by him, but despite the fact that doubts about their authenticity had been raised as early as the sixth century, it would be another thousand years before the attribution to Dionysius ceased to be generally accepted. It is now thought that the author was a late fifth/early sixth-century Syrian monk, and he was certainly deeply influenced by the ideas of later Platonism, especially the ideas of a fifth-century Neo-Platonist called Proclus. Since the real name of the author is unknown, he is universally referred to as Pseudo-Dionysius.

The God of Pseudo-Dionysius is a God who is known and unknown at the same time. He is known because when he brought the universe into being, he left in it certain traces or symbols of himself which are quite obvious to those who wish to see them. Being itself is a reflection of his being; life is a reflection of his life; rationality is a reflection of his rationality. We have already seen exactly the same idea in Augustine and Bonaventure.[2] But Pseudo-Dionysius does not limit himself to the natural world: he also draws attention to the importance of the church and its sacraments. Here, too, we may see symbols of God, and once the material substances used in the sacraments— water, oil, bread, and wine—have been blessed and transformed by the ministers of the church, they can reveal to us yet more of the nature of the Creator.

But God's revelation of himself is not limited to being, life, rationality, and the sacraments. There are many other names by which he is known, and each of them reveals something more of his true nature. It's just like a jigsaw puzzle: each piece you put in place reveals a little bit more of the final picture. Pseudo-Dionysius discusses the matter in a short treatise he calls *The Divine Names*, and there we find an examination of God as goodness, light, beauty, love, ecstasy, zeal, being,

2. See Chapter V above.

life, wisdom, mind, word, truth, faith, power, righteousness, salvation, redemption, omnipotence, peace, Holy of Holies, King of kings, Lord of lords, God of gods, and, finally, perfection and oneness.

This approach to God, an approach that gradually builds up an ever more complete picture of his nature, is often described as the *via affirmativa* or the 'affirmative way'. In theological jargon it is usually referred to as cataphatic theology. 'Cataphatic' is a greek word meaning 'according to words or ideas': the words or ideas which give us these glimpses into the nature of the Creator. The more glimpses we get, the better our understanding.

There is, however, a problem here. It is all very well to call God 'good', but what do we mean by it? Our acquaintance with 'good' is very limited, and we know it only by its contrast with evil, and in God evil has no place. So the goodness of God, a goodness which is perfect, infinite, and changeless, is not something we can understand. Similarly, if we say with Saint John that God is light[3], what sort of light are we talking about? Sunlight? Candle-light? Electric light? Obviously not. We are referring to some sort of eternal and uncreated light, and since we can only know light by its contrast with darkness, and since in God there is no darkness at all, our paltry understanding cannot hope to comprehend the nature of the incomprehensible Light which is God.

It follows, then, that God is good, but not good as we can understand it; he is light, but not light as we can comprehend it; he is being, life, and beauty, but not being, life, and beauty as we can conceive them. And the same is true of all the other divine names. Cataphatic theology cannot take us all the way in our quest for God, for although it certainly reveals some of the Truth, it does not and cannot reveal the whole Truth.

Pseudo-Dionysius was well aware of this, and he tried to clarify the matter by describing God's goodness as super-goodness, his being as super-being, his life as super-life, and so on. God transcends all being, all knowledge, and all goodness—but this

3. 1 Jn 1:5: 'God is light and in him there is no darkness at all.'

is not to say that he does not exist, does not know, and is not good!
His being, knowledge, and goodness are infinite and perfect;
and within the incommunicable oneness of the Divine Nature,
being, knowledge, and goodness are all the same thing. Here is
the domain of square circles and white blackness, of not-good
goodness and super-living life. God is beyond the concepts of
mind and soul. In him there is no imagination, no opinion, nor
even understanding as we can understand it. He cannot be described, cannot be comprehended, cannot be conceived. In him
there is neither number nor order nor greatness nor smallness
nor equality nor inequality nor similarity nor dissimilarity. He
does not move, does not stand still. He is not life nor light nor
darkness nor truth nor falsehood nor substance nor eternity nor
time. We cannot name him or know him.

> We may never affirm or negate anything of him, for although
> we may affirm or negate things apart from him, him we neither
> affirm nor negate. For the perfect and single cause of all things
> is beyond all affirmation, and the simple pre-eminence of his
> Absoluteness is above every negation and beyond all things.[4]

And so, says Pseudo-Dionysius, since none of our concepts
can ever encompass a God who is unknowable and beyond
concepts, we must know him through unknowing. Our human
understanding must withdraw back into itself, cast off all that
it thinks it knows—even its knowledge of the Divine Names—
and aim to achieve a mystical union with God which, in ecstatic
rapture, will provide it with an extra-conceptual knowledge of
him in what Pseudo-Dionysius calls 'the dazzling darkness of
the silence of hidden mystery'.[5]

This is the *via negativa*, the 'negative way', referred to theologically as apophatic theology. 'Apophatic' means 'beyond words and
ideas'. Pseudo-Dionysius also provides us with practical information as to how this knowledgeable unknowing can be attained,

4. Pseudo-Dionysius, *De mystica theologia* v; PG 3: 1048B.
5. *Ibid.* i; PG 3: 997B.

and his three stages of purgation, purification, and illumination were to become standard in both eastern and western spirituality. That, however, is not our concern in this present study. What is important for us is his conviction that such an experience was possible. It may be true that the Deity is ultimately unknowable in conceptual terms, but this does not mean we cannot know him. We simply have to change our idea of the nature of knowledge.

The influence of Pseudo-Dionysius was immense, and not only in the east. His works were first translated into Latin in the ninth century and had a profound influence on western theology and philosophy from the twelfth century onwards. Both Bonaventure and Aquinas were deeply influenced by him (Bonaventure called him the prince of mystics), and in later centuries we see his impact not only on the scholastics, but on the Rhineland mystics, the Carmelites, and the Jesuits. That, however, is another story. For the moment we must return to the east, make a leap of five centuries, and investigate a different approach to the Trinity: not that of mystical theology but of hellenic philosophy. This analytical approach is more akin to that taken by the western theologians we discussed in the last chapter, but in the east it was applied far more cautiously and never offered any real threat to the dominant influence of Pseudo-Dionysius. Nevertheless, despite the enduring preeminence of dionysian thought, no survey of byzantine trinitarian theology would be complete without a brief glance at the ideas of Michael Psellos and John Italos.

Michael Psellos, philosopher, theologian, historian, and statesman, was born in Constantinople in 1018. His family was not rich, but was able to provide its precocious child with an excellent education, and he went on to combine a life of scholarship with a somewhat chequered career in civil administration. By the time he was twenty-seven, he had been secretary to one emperor, Secretary of State to another, and professor of philosophy at the newly-founded University of Constantinople, a position to which he had been appointed in 1045. His involvement in court affairs, however, was not always happy, and in 1054 he incurred the displeasure of the emperor Constantine IX and was forced to take the monastic habit on Mount Olympus. He did not remain there long. A few years later, when Constantine died, he was able to return to court, but fared no better. Once again he became involved in various intrigues, and after a second fall from favour in 1072, he spent the rest of his life in obscurity. He died c.1080.

Psellos was fascinated by philosophy, especially the philosophy of Plato ('my Plato', he used to call him), and although he was eager to apply this philosophy to the faith, he did so with the greatest caution. The first thing you should learn, he said, is to worship Father, Son, and Holy Spirit, one God. This is what has been handed down by the fathers, and their authority was Christ himself. The tradition of the church is what we must believe, and if something different is suggested even by Plato, it must be ignored.

On the other hand, since there was only one God and one source of ultimate truth, it followed that the God who had revealed himself to the world in Christ was the same God who had inspired the poets and philosophers who had lived prior to the Incarnation. It would not be surprising, therefore, to find in their writings prefigurements of christian truth. A similar idea had been held by Justin Martyr as early as the second century.[6] Indeed, said Psellos, the doctrine of the Trinity was clearly anticipated by Plato, and in Homer we find not only the doctrine of the Trinity, but even the prefigurement of angels and saints. This is not to say that we accept the whole of Plato. Some of his ideas, said Psellos, were simply stupid, and Psellos always maintained that the church and its teachings took precedence over a thousand Platos and Aristotles. His view, in other words, was similar to that of Bonaventure whom we discussed in Chapter V: we may use philosophy and logic to elaborate the faith, but in any case of conflict, the faith comes first.

Furthermore, despite his philosophical devotion, Psellos (again like Bonaventure) was dionysian in his belief that the

6. See *Cloud* 36–7.

nature of God ultimately transcends all human concepts. However much we may analyze the Trinity and whatever terms we may use to describe it, God remains ultimately unknowable in intellectual terms. Philosophy, like cataphatic theology, can only go so far. An experiential, mystical experience of God is another matter altogether, but so far as we know, Psellos had no interest in mysticism.

Yet if God himself remains ultimately unknowable, that is not true of his creation. The way in which the universe was brought into being, the principles of causation, the order of nature, the complexities of cosmology, the problems of divine providence, chance, and determinism, the nature and divisions of the human soul, the processes of perception and cognition: all these were grist to a philosopher's mill, and Psellos was only too happy to apply his mind to their analysis. But for all that, he always retains his orthodoxy. He never proposes heretical ideas, and he demonstrates with great clarity which areas are safe to approach and which methods are safe to use when reason is applied to the faith.

His pupil and successor at the University of Constantinople may not have been so cautious. John Italos, as his name indicates, was born c.1025 in one of the greek communities in southern Italy and moved to Constantinople c.1049. He attended the lectures of Psellos and, as we have seen, went on to succeed him as professor of philosophy. What he taught is not entirely clear (some of the things of which he was accused do not appear in his published work), but he was condemned for heresy in 1076–77 and again in 1082. The reasons for the condemnations are simple: in general, he was accused of using too much philosophy in the analysis of the faith, and in particular, of believing Plato rather than the church on a number of important questions.

According to the council of 1076–77, the ancient philosophers were the first heretics and all subsequent heresies have sprung from that source. It follows, therefore, that whenever the church has condemned heretics, it has also condemned those philosophers who were ultimately responsible for the heresies. While a restricted use of philosophy is not necessarily bad—

Aristotle's logic can be useful—it is almost always dangerous. Plato was generally to be avoided, and the council accused Italos of maintaining platonic beliefs on the origin of the world, the pre-existence of souls, reincarnation, the eternity of matter, and of denying the resurrection of the body. It was the view of the council that if philosophy was to be studied at all, it should be confined to the classroom; and if it were to enter the church, it should do so only under conditions of the tightest security.

John Italos died shortly after the 1082 condemnation, but the councils' decisions were to have serious and long-lasting consequences for the greek east. They effectively put an end to the philosophical investigation of the faith (the east did not and could not produce a Thomas Aquinas) and established a deeply conservative theological attitude that was based firmly on the fathers and the tradition of the church. This is not to say that no heresies ever again appeared in Byzantium—they did, especially in matters of christology—but it remains true that one of the most characteristic features of byzantine theology is its patristic conservatism. The real impact of greek philosophical thought was to be seen not in the byzantine empire, but in the muslim world and the latin west. We therefore get the odd situation that in many ways the latin Aquinas was more greek than any Greek after John Italos!

In the west, after the eleventh century, the centres of theological study began to move from the monasteries to the schools and the universities; in the east, the monasteries remained the focal points of theological thought. And since contemplative monks are generally more interested in the practice of Christianity than in its academic study, it is not surprising to find that in the east experience was more important than intellectual understanding in the journey of the soul to God. This is not to imply that the western church did not also develop a rich and effective spiritual tradition. As we saw in the last chapter, William of Saint-Thierry demonstrates clearly that we need two eyes to see God, the eye of reason and the eye of love, and while the greeks would not, in principle, have disagreed with this, they did shift the emphasis and, in some ways, destroyed the balance. For the

VIII-2 When the new eastern end of the benedictine monastery church of Saint-Denis was dedicated in 1144, a new architectural era began, that of the gothic. This spacious ambulatory with its immense stained glass windows was unlike anything ever seen before: the ribbed vault of stone seemed to float miraculously above the colored light. The library of Saint-Denis possessed a copy of the works of Pseudo-Dionysius, and there can be little doubt that these influenced the design of the new church according to the taste and architectural wishes of the abbot, Suger. The impact of this structure was profound, for the amount of light and the technology which permitted it set a new standard for all subsequent building.

Ambulatory of the church of Saint-Denis (France), dedicated in 1144.
Photo: James Austin

greek theologians, the eye of experience was very much larger than the eye of intellectual analysis.

In turning to an examination of this eastern experiential tradition, there is no better place to start than with the ideas of Symeon the New Theologian. The 'old' Theologian could be either Saint John the Evangelist or Gregory of Nazianzus[7], and it is a sign of the esteem in which Symeon was held that the greek church was prepared to consider him their true successor.

Symeon was born in the small town of Galatai in 949 but was sent to Constantinople at an early age. He lived with a relative who held a position at the imperial court, and was himself originally destined for a career in the civil service. But when he was fourteen he met a monk from the monastery of the Studios who so impressed him that he determined to enter the religious life. This intention was strengthened when, in his early twenties, he underwent certain mystical experiences, and when he was about twenty-seven he took the habit at the Studios. This monastery, large and perhaps somewhat lax, did not suit him and after a short time he left it for the smaller and stricter community of Saint Mamas, also in Constantinople. Here he was soon elected abbot and held the position for about a quarter of a century. He was eventually forced to resign because of disagreements with his monks, who considered his spiritual demands too difficult, and he moved to a small ruined oratory at Palonkiton on the opposite side of the Bosphorus. Even here his withdrawal from the world was not complete. Although he produced some remarkable spiritual works, he was also involved in a series of violent disputes with his ecclesiastical superiors. He died at his oratory-hermitage in 1022 and, despite his disagreements with authority, was eventually canonized.

Symeon's theology is dominated by two principles, both of which derive from Pseudo-Dionysius. The first is the unknowable nature of a God who is beyond all concepts and beyond all logic.

7. See *Cloud* 71.

By the time of Symeon the apophatic approach to the Deity had become standard in the greek east, and Symeon accepts it without question. God is beyond all being, he says, beyond all natures, beyond time and eternity, beyond light, beyond our understanding, beyond our grasp, beyond all things. It follows from this that since we cannot hope to understand God intellectually, we must cast aside all our intellectual presuppositions and begin to 'unknow'. We must open ourselves up to him and rely on his grace to permit us entry into the 'dazzling darkness of the silence of hidden mystery', there to know by experience what we cannot know in any other way.

The second principle adopted by Symeon from the dionysian tradition was that this experience is an experience of God as light. Pseudo-Dionysius lists light as one of the divine names and sees the visible sun as a symbol of God. Just as the sun gives light to all things, so too does God. He gives his light to all who are capable of receiving it, and it is his light that creates us, gives us life, preserves us, and perfects us. By illuminating our minds, he drives out ignorance, and the more we yearn for his light, the more light he provides. In the beginning he bestows upon us only brief glimmerings, but as our love and longing grow, so he pours out his light upon us and within us in greater and greater abundance. It is clear, therefore, that for Pseudo-Dionysius light is not just visible light. It is a creative and illuminating power which is, in essence, God himself. 'God is light and in him there is no darkness at all' (1 Jn 1:5).

Symeon echoes and intensifies this dionysian concept. God's light, he says,

> shines around us without any diminution, without change, without alteration, without form. It speaks, works, lives and gives life, and transforms into light those whom it enlightens. It is we who bear witness that *God is light* (1 Jn 1:5), and those deemed worthy to see him have all seen him as light. Those who have received him have received him as light, for the light of his glory goes before him and it is impossible for him to appear without light. Those who have not seen his light

VIII-3 This portrayal of the Transfiguration combines traditional biblical imagery with the symbolic use of light. Peter, James and John lie dumbstruck at the top of the mountain (along the bottom of the wall); Christ inhabits a mandorla in the center, with Moses and Elijah on either side. Over Christ's head is a circular window flanked by angels. Though its original glass is now missing, it probably resembled the bright cloud out of which came the voice of God. This very passage (Matthew 17:5) is inscribed on the scroll held by God the Father in the topmost circle. In this way true light was incorporated into a wall-painting, while the architectural frame is a stage for the event.

Transfiguration, c. 1260.
Window-wall of the west gallery, Gurk Cathedral, Carinthia (Austria).
Photo: Bundesdenkmalamt, Vienna.

have not seen him, for he is the light, and those who have not received the light have not yet received grace.[8]

'Those deemed worthy to see him', says Symeon, and he himself was such a one. One evening, he tells us, when he was

---

8. Symeon the New Theologian, ed. B. Krivochéine, *Catéchèses* 28, 106–115; *SCh* 113: 136.

praying and saying silently 'God, have mercy on me, a sinner' (Lk 18:13), a divine light suddenly filled the room. He lost all consciousness of where he was and saw nothing but light. Indeed, it seemed to him that he had become one with the light, that he had been transformed into light, and that he had left this world altogether. He was overcome with tears and filled with unspeakable joy. Nor was this the only occasion when Symeon was so graced, and for him such mystical experience was neither particularly unusual nor particularly rare. Symeon, in fact, sees mystical experience as a normal occurrence for anyone living a truly christian life, and if we do not experience it, the fault is entirely our own. Don't blame God, he says, don't say it's impossible: we deprive ourselves of the experience through our transgressions and our neglect of the commandments, and the reason why we transgress and neglect the commandments is because we do not love God enough.

In the life of every Christian, therefore, there must be an element of asceticism, for the purpose of asceticism is to reduce our love of self and increase our love of God. The more we love him, the more we do his will; the more we do his will, the less we transgress; the less we transgress, the more likely he is to pour his grace upon us and overwhelm us with his light. But without God's grace, none of this is possible, and because God's grace is essential, so too was the Incarnation. To undergo baptism and chrismation (the eastern equivalent of confirmation) is to be initiated into the mystical body of Christ. It is to receive the gift of his grace and become part of a church which is the vessel of his grace. To receive the eucharist regularly is to receive his body, and to receive his body is to receive yet more of his grace, and this plenitude of grace enables us to relinquish our will for his will. Then, suddenly (a favourite word for Symeon), God may pour upon us a superabundance of grace and permit us to experience himself as light. The church and the sacraments, therefore, find their perfection and actualization in mystical experience, and this mystical experience is for *every* christian, not just the spiritual athletes.

Don't say that it's impossible to receive the Divine Spirit.
Don't say that it's possible to be saved without him.
Don't say, then, that we can possess him without knowing it.
Don't say that God does not appear to human beings.
Don't say that human beings don't see the Divine Light, or
    that it's impossible in these present times.
My friends, it is never impossible:
On the contrary, for those who wish it, it's obviously
    possible—
Though only insofar as their lives have purified their passions,
And made pure the eye of the mind![9]

We might point out that not everyone agreed with this, and if this was what Symeon was expecting of his monks at Saint Mamas, it is hardly surprising that they rebelled. Most Christians prefer an easier path to salvation: the simple security of church attendance and obligatory worship. But Symeon considered such laggards heretics and anti-Christs, and he had no time for them.

There is, however, a danger lurking in this way of thinking. It can very easily lead to a claim that one's own personal illumination is more important than any rite of ecclesiastical ordination, and although Symeon never says this explicitly, he certainly implies it. Only those, he says, who have led christian lives and have had such an experience are fitted to be priests and administer the sacraments, and if a person is consecrated bishop without having undergone such a revelation, he is nothing but an intruder. When it came to confessing his sins, Symeon preferred the spiritual direction of a lay-monk who was a genuine mystic to the absolution of an ordained priest who was not. This certainly casts doubt upon the validity of the institutional church, and Symeon's views on this matter may well have been at the bottom of his clashes with his superiors in his last years at Palonkiton.

When we consider Symeon's ideas on the unknowability of God and the necessity of experience, when we consider his

9. Symeon the New Theologian, ed. J. Koder, *Hymnes* 27, 125–34; SCh 174: 288.

authority as the successor to Saint John and Gregory Nazianzus, and when we combine this with the consequences of the condemnation of John Italos, it is obvious that we are not going to find anything in the greek world to compare with the rise of scholasticism in the west. Michael Psellos might possibly be called a greek Bonaventure, but there was no greek Aquinas. Nor was there any greek Roscelin or greek Gilbert of Poitiers. Philosophical analysis of the Trinity was forbidden ground to the eastern theologians, and in any case, once the apophatic ideas of Pseudo-Dionysius had become the norm, there was not very much to be said. There were, however, two areas which were to cause major theological problems: not the question of whether and how God was both one and three, but whether he could truly be experienced, and if so, how that experience might be realized.

Symeon does not provide us with much practical information on the means of experiencing the Divine Light. He seems to think that it is sufficient to live a good christian life and leave the rest to God. Others were more specific, but it is not until the late thirteenth century that we find the first clear and complete description of what came to be known as the hesychast method of prayer. The author of the text in question was a monk of Mount Athos and he is usually referred to as Nicephorus the Hesychast. He probably came from one of the greek communities in southern Italy, spent some years on Mount Athos, and eventually made his way to Constantinople. But not a great deal is known about his life.

The term hesychasm comes from the greek word *hēsychia* which means 'quietness' or 'stillness', and the techniques developed by the hesychasts were designed to quieten down both body and mind so that God could enter in. Most of us at any moment are like radios turned up full blast and tuned slightly off station. A continual noise pours forth from our minds as they boil and seethe with a million ideas and desires. The static—the result of our being tuned off-station—comes from our overbearing egocentricity with its insistent call of 'me, me, me'! With all this racket going on we cannot hope to hear either ourselves

or anybody else, much less God. Hesychasm is designed first
to turn down, then to turn off the radio; and then in the silence, to re-tune it to the One who made it. How is this to
be done?

According to Nicephorus, three factors are essential. First of
all, there is a certain bodily posture. If you sit on a low stool
(about nine inches high), draw up your knees, bend your back,
and rest your head and your hands on your knees, you should
be in approximately the right position. It is a curious posture for
meditation, and one reputable writer of the fourteenth century
tells us that it is extremely uncomfortable and causes pain in the
shoulders, chest, and neck.

Secondly, you must slow down and regulate your breathing
and make it coincide with the recitation of the Jesus Prayer: 'Lord
Jesus Christ, Son of God, have mercy on me'. In the earliest days
of hesychasm, the breathing exercises preceded the recitation
of the prayer, but from the late fourteenth century it has been
the practice to coordinate the breathing with the words. Modern
Orthodox hesychasts usually say 'Lord Jesus Christ, Son of God'
while breathing in, and 'have mercy on me' while breathing out,
but this is not invariable.

Thirdly, you must imagine your breath, the life-force (the
yoga term is *prāna* and we are dealing with precisely the same
concept), passing down into your heart, thereby merging heart
and head—affection and intellect—and preparing you to receive
an illumination which will be both experiential and revelatory at
the same time. At all costs, we must avoid thinking in concepts
and images: the radio must be turned off. Whenever a thought
arises, expel it with the Jesus Prayer.

Finally, when the intellect is emptied of all forms, when it is
wholly at rest, and when its attention is directed one-pointedly
on its Lord, it is inundated by the Divine Light and becomes one
with it. But the light which pours down upon it is not any created
light: it is the very nature of the Unknown and Unknowable God.
It is a light beyond light, a super-light, a hyper-light, a light which
not only shines but which also *transforms*. It is the dazzling

darkness of Pseudo-Dionysius and the hesychasts identified it
with the light of the Transfiguration.[10]

Where these ideas originated is unknown. Traces of hesychast
technique can be discerned in eastern Christianity as early as
the seventh century, and it is quite possible that we may detect
in them the influence of hindu yoga and muslim sūfism. The
influence of sūfism is, I think, certain. Some of the ideas, but
not all, appear in Symeon. There we find the unknowability
of God, the experience of his light, and the use if not of the
Jesus Prayer, of something close to it: 'God, have mercy on me, a
sinner'. But we find no mention of bodily postures or breathing
techniques. On the other hand, it is well known in spirituality
that the actual practice of mystical techniques may long predate
their first description in writing, and the early history and spread
of hesychasm still await further research.

Be that as it may, by the fourteenth century hesychast techniques were sufficiently well known to come to the attention
of a learned Greek from the south of Italy, the region known in
Latin as Calabria, who is generally referred to as Barlaam the
Calabrian. It was he who launched a violent and effective attack
on hesychasm and who precipitated the controversy which we
must examine in our next chapter.

10. See Mt 17:1–13, Mk 9:2–13, and Lk 9:28–36. According to Matthew,
Jesus's face shone like the sun and his clothes became white as light.

IX-1 This icon of Saint Gregory Palamas dates from shortly after his canonisation in 1368, nine years after his death. Many who knew him would still have been alive, and the icon may therefore resemble Gregory's actual physical appearance. He is represented as bearded and tonsured, as were all byzantine monks of the period, and he carries in his left hand a copy of the Gospels while his right hand is raised in blessing.

Saint Gregory Palamas, c. 1368-75.
Moscow, Museum of Decorative Arts.
Photo: Memorial University Photographic Services.

IX

Goδ anδ His Light:
The Hesychast Controversy

BEFORE BEGINNING any discussion of the theology of this important controversy, let us introduce the two main protagonists: Barlaam the Calabrian and Gregory Palamas.

Barlaam, as we saw at the end of the last chapter, was born c.1290 in one of the greek communities in southern Italy. We do not know where he was educated, but he seems to have been acquainted with western theological thought, though to what extent this influenced him is unclear. He moved to Constantinople c.1329 where he soon gained a great reputation as a scholar and philosopher and was appointed to a chair at the University. There he lectured on Pseudo-Dionysius, and it was his interpretation of Pseudo-Dionysius which, some four years later, would lie at the heart of his attack on hesychasm. In the 1330s he was a spokesman for the Orthodox east in certain negotiations with the latin church, but at the same time he was becoming ever more deeply involved in the hesychast controversy. As things turned out, his views were condemned at two synods in 1341, and as a consequence Barlaam turned his back on the east and returned to Italy. There he converted from Orthodoxy to Catholicism and was eventually appointed bishop of Gerace in that branch of the Greek Orthodox Church that had reestablished communion with Rome. He died in 1348.

His opponent was one of the greatest minds that Orthodoxy ever produced: Gregory Palamas.[1] He was born to a noble family, probably in Constantinople, in about 1296. His earlier training was in secular subjects (he had a very sound knowledge of aristotelian logic), but c.1316 he decided to embrace the religious life. He moved to Mount Athos in 1318 and there pursued the methods of hesychast prayer. Some years later, as a consequence of continual harassment from turkish pirates, Palamas left the holy mountain and made his way to Thessalonica where he was ordained priest in 1326.

Seven years later his conflict with Barlaam began, and his involvement in the controversy—which inevitably became tangled with politics and power struggles—was to last for almost twenty years. In the course of this long struggle, Palamas would be supported, condemned, exonerated, silenced, interned, released, excommunicated, restored, and eventually acknowledged as the voice of Orthodoxy.

In May 1347 he was consecrated archbishop of Thessalonica and administered his new archdiocese with notable success. But seven years later, in 1354, his life took an unexpected turn. While he was sailing from Thessalonica to Constantinople, his ship was forced by contrary winds to put in at Gallipoli, and the archbishop and his suite were captured by the Turks. They spent

1. The accent is on the last syllable of Palamas, not the first.

a year in captivity (but were very well treated), and Palamas returned to Thessalonica in the summer of 1355. Three years later he suffered an attack of an internal disease which had long troubled him, but this time he failed to recover. He died in Thessalonica on 14 November 1359 and was canonized nine years later.

So much for the personalities in the dispute. What were the problems? Barlaam makes two main points: (1) when the hesychasts say they experience God as light, they are mistaken; and (2) the use of such physical techniques as bodily postures and breathing exercises is grossly superstitious and has no place in true christian worship. On what did Barlaam base these opinions?

At the root of his first objection are the apophatic ideas of Pseudo-Dionysius. Pseudo-Dionysius, as we know, had established the principle that God was wholly beyond all concepts and was ultimately unknowable in any intellectual sense. Barlaam took this literally. If God is unknowable, we cannot know him; and if the hesychasts maintain anything contrary to this, they must be wrong.

On the other hand, Barlaam did not forget that Pseudo-Dionysius also made provision for an affirmative approach to God—the *via affirmativa* or cataphatic theology—and with this he had no problem. We can certainly know God, he said, but only through signs and symbols, and by far the most important of these signs are the sacraments of the church and God's own revelation of himself in scripture. Our knowledge of God, in other words, is a mediated knowledge which comes to us in and through the church. It is not an immediate knowledge that comes to us direct from God himself.

It follows from this that the light seen by the hesychasts cannot be the uncreated light of God. If you cannot see God directly in this life, and if God and his light are identical, it follows that you cannot see him as light either. Barlaam did not deny that the hesychasts experienced an altered state of consciousness, nor did he deny that they had a vision. But the light they saw could only have been a created light—much like sunlight, only brighter—and it was certainly not God. Light, after all, is one of the divine names discussed by Pseudo-Dionysius, and the divine names are part of the *via affirmativa* not the *via negativa*. Light, therefore, may be a symbol for God, but it is not God.

So what about the techniques used by the hesychasts to prepare themselves for this experience? Here, too, Barlaam had problems. What does it say in the gospel of John? 'God is spirit, and those who worship him must worship in spirit and in truth' (Jn 4:24). They do not worship him by concentrating on their navels, getting pains in their shoulders, and holding their breath. Further support for his argument could be found in Plato, for in this case there was no conflict between Plato and the scriptures. According to Plato the body was no more than a prison for the soul[2], and intellectual investigation was a matter for the mind, not the body. It is not our arms and legs that recognize God or the Good, but our immortal and immaterial spirit.

Finally, said Barlaam, by the use of these postures and breathing exercises, the hesychasts are reducing religion to mechanics: if you sit in a certain way and breathe in a certain fashion you will know God. So what need is there for the church and the sacraments? Why, indeed, did Christ bother to come to earth at all when he could more easily have communicated a book of instructions, a simple Teach Yourself Salvation?

These objections of Barlaam to the hesychast tradition were formidable and persuasive, and we must now turn our attention to the ways in which they were countered by Gregory Palamas. The last argument mentioned was actually the easiest to deal with, for on this point Gregory and Barlaam had no real dispute. The fourteenth-century supporters of hesychasm were unanimous in insisting that the physical methods used by the monks did not, of their own power, lead to the experience of the Divine Light. They were simply a convenient and effective way of preparing the body to receive God's grace and they went hand-in-hand with the keeping of the commandments and the obligations of christian worship. There were, it is true, certain monks who did

2. See *Cloud* 25.

IX-2 This twelfth-century miniature is one of numerous illustrations in a copy of a very popular and influential spiritual treatise, *The Ladder of Divine Ascent* by Saint John Climacus (c. 570–649). It represents a hesychast in prayer. He is seated on a rock, his knees drawn up, arms along his thighs, his head resting on his knees. This curious and uncomfortable posture (which may have been influenced by certain techniques in muslim mysticism), was radically different from the standing position in which eastern Christians usually prayed.

Hesychast in prayer, twelfth century.
John Climacus, *The Ladder of Divine Ascent*, 11th–13th c.
Vatican City, Biblioteca Apostolica Vaticana, ms. gr. 1754.
Photo reproduced courtesy of the Biblioteca Apostolica Vaticana.

regard hesychasm in a mechanistic way, but Palamas would have agreed with Barlaam in condemning them. Barlaam's objection, therefore, was here no more than a misunderstanding. Far more serious was his argument, founded on the unshakeable rock of Pseudo-Dionysius, that since God was unknowable, he could not be known; and that if the hesychasts maintained that they could know him, they had to be wrong. How was Palamas to deal with this?

Gregory's counter-argument was subtle and effective. Barlaam, he said, was both correct and incorrect: he was correct in maintaining, with Pseudo-Dionysius, that God is *ultimately* unknowable, but he was incorrect in maintaining that the only way in which we can know him is through signs and symbols. Gregory therefore made the very important distinction between God in his essence and God in his energies. What did he mean?

It may help if we consider ourselves. Each of us plays a variety of roles in our lives, and each of us comes into contact with a variety of people. Some of them will be no more than passing acquaintances; some may become friends; some we may decide to live with. All of them get to know us in a different way, and the longer the time you spend with them, the better they know you and the better you know them. But when all is said and done, you can never know anyone *completely*, and no one can ever know you as you are in your essence. Deep down, hidden away, there is always a secret chamber known only to you, and in that secret chamber are secret things—hopes, desires, guilty knowledge, emotions, reactions—of which only you are aware. My students in my classes may know ten percent of me; my friends may know seventy percent of me; my cat may know ninety percent of me—but it is only I, I alone, who can know all of me.

How much more, then, is this true of the infinite and incomprehensible God? We can never know God as he knows himself, as he is in his essence. Uncreated infinity can be known only by uncreated infinity, and since we are created and finite, we are excluded from that knowledge. Nevertheless, just as we, who remain unknown in our essence, may reveal something of ourselves to our friends, so God, who remains unknowable in his essence, reveals something of himself to us in a number of different ways. These ways are what Palamas means when he speaks of God's 'energies'. They are God's manifestations, the ways in which he shows us something of what he is. They are God-in-action, God in his relationship to his creation. Some of these energies or manifestations appear in the list of divine names provided by Pseudo-Dionysius, but just as Barlaam and Gregory disagreed in their interpretation of apophatic theology, so now they disagree in how they understand the cataphatic variety.

Barlaam does not deny that the divine names reveal God, but he regards them as *created* energies: manifestations of God which God has brought into being. Life, for example, shows us something of the living God, but God created life; beauty shows us something of the beauty of God, but God created beauty, and so on. In other words, just as Barlaam makes a radical distinction between the unknowable God and those who want to know him, so he also makes a radical distinction between the unknowable Creator and his creation. If we cannot know God, we cannot know the Creator; if we cannot know the Creator, we can know only his creation; if we can know only his creation, we can know him only by means of his *created* energies or manifestations. But this is not the view of Palamas.

Once again, let us consider ourselves. Anyone who reads this book will gain a glimpse into the mind of its author. Anyone who looks at a painting may see something of the mind of the painter. But in both cases what they see is transmitted to them by means of a created medium: in the one case print, and in the other paint. Even if I talk to you face to face and thereby reveal yet more of myself, it is still a created revelation, since the words I use are created by me and are no more than sounds produced by bursts of air passing over my vocal cords.

But what about two lovers or two old friends who, in loving and companionable silence, may gain from each other's company and learn more of each other in a very different but just as effective way? We are not dealing here with words or gestures, but with presence or *being*, and the sort of wordless communication we can have in these circumstances is perhaps the closest human

analogy to the experience of God's uncreated energies. But even
so, despite the fact that I may reveal myself without created
words, and despite the fact that it is really me who is being
revealed, it is not the whole of me. That secret chamber in my
heart still remains secret. In my essence, I still remain unknown.

According to Gregory, the most important of the uncreated
energies of God is his grace. Grace is not created, for grace is the
Holy Spirit, and the Holy Spirit is God. So when God shares his
Holy Spirit with us and communicates his grace, what we receive
is not only the gift of God, but God himself. Since grace *is* God, to
receive grace is to experience the very nature of God. Similarly,
when the hesychasts speak of light, the light they are talking
about is not a created light (as Barlaam would have us believe)
but the uncreated light which, like grace, is a true manifestation
of God's uncreated nature. God *is* light, says Saint John,[3] and
although the God who is Light also created light,[4] this created
light is not what we are talking about here.

The Uncreated Light is not a physical light, but a spiritual
light. Gregory is here echoing Symeon the New Theologian.
But although it is not a physical light, it can be perceived by
the physical senses provided they have been transformed and
properly prepared by the grace of the Holy Spirit. That is why the
Transfiguration of Christ took place before only three disciples.
They alone were ready to perceive it; and because they had undergone the requisite preparation, the light of the Transfiguration
was visible to them. Had the same event taken place before the
entire populace of Judaea, most of them would have seen nothing
at all.

The experience of the Divine Light, therefore, is a true experience of God, but an experience of God in his energies, not in
his essence. It follows that Barlaam was correct in maintaining
that God remains *ultimately* unknown, but he was incorrect in
suggesting that he could be known only through created things.
The divine light and divine grace are uncreated energies and true

3. 1 Jn 1:5.
4. Gen 1:3: 'Then God said: "Let there be light"'.

manifestations of the uncreated God who is himself both light and grace.

Barlaam's second major disagreement with the hesychasts centred upon the techniques they used to achieve their experience, but what appears at first glance to be no more than a squabble about mystical mechanics is actually something far more significant. Implicit in Barlaam's objection is a view of the human body wholly at odds with the christian tradition. Let us examine the arguments.

Barlaam had said that the worship of God was a matter for the mind rather than the body—the God who is spirit must be worshipped in spirit—and that physical contortions and weird breathing techniques had no place in christian adoration. In saying this, says Palamas, Barlaam has forgotten what happened at creation and (what is even more serious) what happened at the Incarnation.

At creation, God made human bodies to go with human souls, and when he had done his work and had taken stock of it, he saw that it was very good.[5] God did not exclude bodies from this general commendation, and if Barlaam thinks he did, then Barlaam is being a dualist. We met some of them in Chapter VI, but by the fourteenth century, Bogomilism had long been condemned.

Secondly, we are told by Saint John that at the Incarnation the Word was made *flesh* (Jn 1:14). It was not made mind. Ever since the Cappadocian Fathers the church had accepted that in Christ there was an unconfused union of Divine Logos, rational soul, and human flesh,[6] and to deny or ignore the human flesh is to lapse into docetism.[7]

Furthermore, when God became human in Christ, humanity—body and soul—was sanctified, and had bestowed upon it the possibility of deification. It is like dropping a spoonful of salt into a bucket of water: all the water becomes salty and, since it

5. See Gen 1:31.
6. See *Cloud* 91–9.
7. See *Cloud* 92–3.

is now a saline solution instead of ordinary water, it has different chemical properties from what it had before. Humanity before the Incarnation is like the water in the bucket; the Divine Word is like the salt. After the infusion of the Divine Word, human beings were not the same. Our nature had been changed—not chemically, of course, but spiritually—and as a consequence of the Incarnation, new and wonderful things could happen which could not have happened before.

To use our whole body in the worship of God, therefore, is to commemorate the Creator who brought it into being and the Christ who sanctified it. Remember too, says Gregory, that at the Transfiguration it was the whole of Christ that was transfigured, not just his spirit. And when he ascended into heaven, it was the whole of Christ that ascended. He did not leave his body on the ground like a discarded jacket. At the Last Judgment, it is our bodies that will be resurrected, not just our souls (we want no Origenism here[8]), and both soul and body—the new, glorious, spiritual body of the first letter to the Corinthians[9]—will enjoy the bliss of the Beatific Vision. When the hesychasts experience the Divine Light, they experience a foretaste of that vision here and now, though the full vision is possible only in the eternity and perfection of heaven.

It is the reality and importance of this final eschatological transformation that lies at the heart of Palamas's criticism of Barlaam. For Palamas, an acceptance of Barlaam's ideas involved a rejection of one of the fundamental concepts of Orthodox Christianity: the concept of deification or, in Greek, *theōsis*. Deification does not mean that we human beings become God— that can never happen—but that we become what God is. That is to say, we share or participate in his nature or qualities, just as we are promised in the second letter of Saint Peter.[10]

8. See *Cloud* 202–5.
9. See 1 Cor 15:35–54.
10. 2 P 1:4: '. . . he has granted to us his precious and very great promises, that through these you may escape from the corruption that is in the world because of passion, and become partakers of the divine nature' (RSV).

So what are the qualities of God? One of them is eternity, and we may share in his eternity. Another is perfection, and we may share in his perfection. A third is joy and bliss, and we may share in his joy and bliss, and so on. With some qualities, such as goodness, the process of participation begins on earth; with others, such as eternity, participation is reserved for the life to come. Deification, therefore, which, for Orthodoxy, is the goal of our human cooperation with the grace of God, begins here and is perfected in heaven, but as Palamas rightly points out, Barlaam's version of Christianity nullifies the principle of such participation and denies the possibility of deification. How?

Our hope, as we have said, is to participate in the qualities or attributes of God: his goodness, eternity, love, and so on. But these qualities are not created things. They are, on the contrary, the very nature of God himself. God did not create his own eternity: he *is* eternal. But Barlaam, it will be remembered, had established a gulf between us and the *uncreated* nature of God and had limited our contact with him to his *created* energies. But if we are unable to contact his uncreated nature, we cannot hope to share in his uncreated attributes, and deification becomes impossible. In separating us from the uncreated Creator, Barlaam also separates us from participation in the Divine Life.

Palamas, on the other hand, by distinguishing between God's essence and his energies, affirmed the possibility of our participation in his qualities, but showed at the same time that we can never be identified with him. To become God would be to know him in his essence, and that, as Pseudo-Dionysius had said, is impossible. To become what God is, however, is to participate in his energies, and this participation has now been made possible for us by Christ.

We may now perhaps see the reason for the intensity of the hesychast controversy. It was not merely a matter of defending the mystical techniques of a handful of monks on Mount Athos. In actual fact, Palamas was not particularly interested in the techniques themselves and considered them suitable mainly for beginners. His deepest concern was with the very survival of Orthodox Christianity. Barlaam had misunderstood the nature of creation, he had failed to realize the significance of the Incarnation, he had diminished the importance of grace, and he had denied the possibility of deification. According to Athanasius the Great, 'God became human that in him human beings might become God'.[11] It was in defence of this principle that Gregory Palamas spent twenty years of his life.

The hesychast victory was not achieved easily. Barlaam had strong support for his views, and initial palamite triumphs were rapidly followed by palamite defeats. A council held in 1341 at Constantinople supported Palamas and condemned Barlaam, but in the following year the situation was reversed and the writings of Palamas were condemned by two different synods. Two years later, in 1344, Palamas was excommunicated. These vicissitudes, however, were more the consequence of politics than of theology. From its earliest days the controversy had been enmeshed in political intrigue, and the question of whose teachings were approved and whose condemned depended to a large extent upon the sympathies of the reigning emperor. Thus, when a pro-palamite ruler usurped the throne in 1347, the excommunication of Palamas was lifted and he was appointed archbishop of Thessalonica. Four years later in 1351 the so-called Blacherna Synod excommunicated all the opponents of hesychasm and confirmed Gregory's teachings. Although this synod was not an Ecumenical Council, its decisions were eventually accepted by the entire Orthodox church, and from the second half of the fourteenth century, the views of Palamas and the views of Greek Orthodoxy were effectively one and the same.

Of those who followed in the footsteps of Palamas, by far the most important was a byzantine layman and civil servant named Nicholas Cabasilas. He is often relegated to very much of a secondary position in the history of hesychasm—a sort of appendage to Palamas, a mere fringe of his garment—but this is to do him an injustice and he deserves a fairer hearing.

11. Athanasius the Great, Ad Adelphium 4; PG 26: 1077A. See Cloud 58 and 159.

IX-3 This miniature was painted by order of the byzantine emperor John VI Cantacuzenus during his lifetime in a luxury manuscript of his own theological works (another portrait of John as emperor and monk appears in plate III-1). Here crowned, robed, and enthroned, he presides over the Blacherna Synod of 1351, flanked by four bishops (the second bishop on his right may be Gregory Palamas), and surrounded by monks (to his left) and civil functionaries (behind).

John VI Cantacuzenus presiding over the Blacherna Synod of 1351, 1370–1375.
John VI Cantacuzenus, Theological Works.
Paris, Bibliothèque nationale, ms gr 1242, f° 5v.
Photo: Bibliothèque nationale, Paris.

Little is known of his life. He was born in 1322 or 1323 in Thessalonica, but after receiving a sound education he moved to Constantinople where he joined the imperial civil service. For about ten years he was a friend and confidant of the emperor John VI Cantacuzenos, but when the emperor was deposed in 1354 and retired to a monastery, Cabasilas also retired from political life and devoted himself to theology. Sometime later he entered a monastery in Constantinople and, so far as we know, it was here that he spent the rest of his days. He survived until at least 1387, but the exact year of his death is unknown.[12]

His most important works are *The Life in Christ* and *A Commentary on the Divine Liturgy*, and it is the first of these which is of interest to us here. In a long and detailed examination of the nature and value of three sacraments—baptism, chrismation, and eucharist—the author takes the best of Symeon the New Theologian and Gregory Palamas and produces from them a new interpretation of the essential principles of palamite hesychasm. By the essential principles of hesychasm I do not mean the physical procedures, but the distinction between the essence and energies of God and the concept of our progressive participation in those energies.

One of the problems with the ideas of Symeon was his belief that mystical experience should be an everyday occurrence for Christians, and that it could be achieved simply by living a christian life. Most Christians, so far as I am aware, have never had such an experience and would be sceptical of Symeon's optimistic viewpoint. Gregory Palamas, however, maintains a very similar doctrine, except that in his case the effect is to be achieved by the use of certain psycho-physical techniques. Gregory himself does not restrict the use of these techniques to monks, but he obviously thought that the monastic environment would be the most conducive to their employment.

---

12. The person who suceeded Gregory Palamas as archbishop of Thessalonica was also called Cabasilas, but this was not Nicholas. It was his maternal uncle Nilus Cabasilas, although the two have often been confused.

For Nicholas Cabasilas, who was not a monk until his old age and who seems not to have had the temperament of a solitary, neither of these viewpoints was entirely correct. On the one hand, it was true that the experience of Christ was an experience to be enjoyed by every Christian, but such an experience might be neither quite so dramatic nor quite so direct as that envisaged by Symeon. On the other hand, although the monastery might be the best place to cultivate the christian life and although the use of certain postures and breathing techniques might facilitate such an experience, neither, thought Cabasilas, was essential for the ordinary believer. Let us examine his arguments in more detail.

First of all, he retains the emphasis on light so dear to Symeon and Palamas, but suggests that for most people the Divine Light will be experienced not directly, but through the sacraments. At the Incarnation, Christ, the sun of righteousness, entered this dark world like sunlight streaming into a house. He drove from it the shadows of evil and corruption and brought with him the possibilities of perfection and immortality. Even after his resurrection and ascension, he is still present with us: not in this case in his physical body, but through the Holy Spirit of his grace.

The light of Christ now enters each of us by way of the sacraments, especially the eucharist, and dwells within us. We are invaded by the brightness of the life to come and, by the uncreated energy of his grace, are transformed into his being. This, too, is the teaching of Symeon and Gregory, but Nicholas maintained that it occurs every time we participate in the Divine Liturgy. The wine which has become the blood of Christ, he says, transforms the human heart into a sanctuary for God, and it is a sanctuary more beautiful than the temple of Solomon. Christ's spirit is united with our spirit; his will becomes one with our will; his flesh becomes our flesh; and his blood flows in our veins. In the eucharist, we are united with God in the closest possible union and, as Saint Paul says, we become one spirit with him.[13]

13. 1 Cor 6:17.

188

IX-4 The Transfiguration was a meditative image of great importance to the hesychasts, for they too sought to be transformed by experiencing the light of the transfigured Christ. The greek icon painter who illuminated this manuscript has placed the event atop a craggy mountain. Christ's clothes are indeed 'as white as light', and one of the three disciples falls on his face, overcome with fear, while the other two seem to be fighting off sleep, a literal interpretation of the gospel account (Lk 9:32). The dominant colors are a range of blues and greys against a gold background which suggest otherworldly, non-temporal light.

Transfiguration, 1370–1375.
John VI Cantacuzenus, Theologial Works.
Paris, Bibliothèque nationale, MS gr 1242, f° 92v.
Photo: Bibliothèque nationale, Paris.

The energy that invades us does not leave us as we were. The iron that has become red-hot in the fire is no longer merely iron. When Christ infuses himself in us and mingles with us, he changes and transforms us into himself, and each of us is like a small drop of water which is plunged into an ocean of perfume and becomes one with it.

Furthermore, says our author, this is not something that is restricted to monks and hesychasts. You don't need to suffer hardship for it; you don't need to spend money; you don't need to retreat to the desert; you don't need to wear peculiar clothes or go on a weird diet. A general can remain in command of his army; an artisan can continue to work; no-one need leave his or her usual employment. It is quite possible for people who stay at home and keep all their possessions to devote themselves to 'the law of the Spirit' and experience the life in Christ. Symeon and Palamas are perfectly correct when they maintain that the experience of Christ can be achieved by every Christian, but with all due respect to Symeon, the experience may not be direct, and with all due respect to Palamas, monasticism and hesychasm are quite unnecessary. Nicholas, in fact, is in agreement with Barlaam when he says that the experience of God is mediated through the sacraments, but he is in agreement with Palamas when he says that what is mediated in this way are not the *created* energies of God, but his *uncreated* energies, especially his grace.

It is understandable, then, that Cabasilas recommends frequent communion, thus ensuring a continual transference of 'deifying energy'. But the life in Christ is not limited to those times of our lives when we are in church. Since God is present everywhere and since, in his love for us, he is eager to hear us and share himself with us (though his essence remains unknowable!), we can contact him any time we wish. You don't need to use special prayers, says Cabasilas, and you don't need to go to a special place. There is nowhere where God is not present and it is impossible for him not to be near us. To those who truly seek him, he is closer than their own heart.

For Cabasilas, the key to the whole process of deification is love: God's love for us and our love for God. In his love for

us, God became human that in him we humans might become
God. In our love for him, it is only natural that we should strive
to do his will, and the more we strive to do his will, the more
we experience his grace. But the more we experience his grace,
the more we love him; and the more we love him, the more our
will becomes his will, and so on. The light of all virtue is love,
says Cabasilas, and love is the life in Christ. Those who abide in
love abide in God and God abides in them[14]: it is that simple.
For Symeon the New Theologian, God is preeminently light; for
Palamas, he is preeminently light and life; for Cabasilas, he is
light and life and love.

We see, then, that although Cabasilas denies nothing of the
teaching of his masters, he nevertheless transforms it. The universality of the experience, the Divine Light, its transforming
quality, the uncreated energies, the importance of the Incarnation, our participation in the divine nature, and the goal of
deification: all these are present in Cabasilas, but all of them, in
a sense, have been brought down to earth. We are no longer in
the realm of mystical rapture or the restricted world of monastic
hesychasts: we are concerned with the sacramental life of ordinary Christians. In baptism, we are born to a new life and are
made an eye to see the divine light. In chrismation, the grace
of the Spirit is bestowed upon us and we begin to use that eye.
In the eucharist, which is the perfection and completion of all
sacraments, we see the light itself and are transformed by it
and into it. Christianity therefore becomes a living encounter
with Christ, and the vision of God something that is begun in
this world.

With the experiential theology of Nicholas Cabasilas we have
moved far from the academic rigour of scholasticism. There is
a world of difference between the nominalist approach to the
Trinity that we saw in Roscelin and the sacramental spirituality
of Cabasilas. The hesychast controversy had little effect upon the

14. 1 Jn 4:16.

west, and in any case, by this time the eastern and western understanding of the Trinity was dramatically different. Both east and
west would have agreed that the grace of God was essential for
living the christian life and for any correct understanding of the
christian tradition, and both would have agreed that this grace
was communicated by means of the Holy Spirit. Both, likewise,
would have agreed that the Spirit was truly God and the third
person of a consubstantial and coequal Trinity, and both would
have agreed that whereas the Father was unbegotten and the Son
begotten, the Holy Spirit proceeded. That, however, is as far as
their agreement would have gone. For the westerners, the Holy
Spirit proceeded from the Father *and* the Son; for the easterners,
it proceeded from the Father *through* the Son, and there is much
more to this than a trifling difference in words. To explain that
difference and to appreciate its significance will take us deep into
the realms of both theology and law, and that will be our task in
the next chapter.

X-1 The use of the dove to symbolize the Holy Spirit, third Person of the Trinity, was formally approved by the local council of Constantinople in 536 and is an image commonly used throughout the Middle Ages. After a fire destroyed Chartres cathedral in 1194, the dove shown here was added to a famous (and beloved) surviving stained glass window: Mary seated with the Christ Child on her lap. The dove signifies the presence of the Holy Spirit, its rays emanating down to the Virgin, and through her, to the Christ Child. A dove is sometimes present in scenes of the Annunciation to indicate the moment of Incarnation, and in other representations of the Virgin and Child (see XIII-4).

Notre-Dame de la Belle Verrière, twelfth century (Dove, thirteenth century).
Chartres cathedral.
Photo: James Austin.

X

The Procession of the Holy Spirit

BEFORE WE BEGIN the substance of this chapter it may be useful to review some of the material we considered earlier. In Chapter II we discussed the ninth-century schism of Photius the Great, patriarch of Constantinople, and Nicholas I, bishop of Rome, and we mentioned there that two factors played a major role in the controversy: the dispute over the papal claims and the question of the single or double procession of the Holy Spirit. The first of these is easy to understand: it was simply a matter of primacy of honour versus primacy of jurisdiction. The second is much more difficult and is our concern in this present chapter.

The essential features of the theology of the procession of the Holy Spirit were discussed in A *Cloud of Witnesses*, but it may be helpful to summarize the main points here. For the Greeks, the procession of the Holy Spirit can be likened to the distribution of electricity from power station to the outlet in the wall. The Father is the power station; the grid-system is the Son; and the outlet is the Holy Spirit. In other words, our immediate contact-point with God is the Holy Spirit, and the Holy Spirit proceeds *from* the Father *through* the Son. The Son is the channel by which the Holy Spirit is transmitted to us. Another analogy is the distribution of water from reservoir to tap: the reservoir is the Father; the pipes linking the reservoir to the tap represent the Son; the tap itself is the Holy Spirit. This view is referred to as single procession, since the Father is the one single source of the Spirit.[1]

The view of Augustine of Hippo was radically different from this, and it was Augustine's view that came to be accepted by the latin west. To understand his idea, we might imagine an electric battery—a car battery, for example—which has two terminals, one positive and one negative. If you join the terminals together, a current flows between them and the battery is in operation. In this analogy, we can regard Father and Son as the two terminals of the battery and the Holy Spirit as the current flowing between them. The Holy Spirit is here defined as the *interaction* of Father and Son, and just as both terminals are essential if the battery is to operate, so both Father and Son are essential in the production of the Holy Spirit. Interaction requires two persons: you cannot interact with yourself. For Augustine, therefore, the Holy Spirit does not proceed from the Father *through* the Son, but from the Father *and* the Son, and this is referred to as double procession.[2]

One final matter we need to consider before moving on to the substance of this chapter is the last section of the so-called Nicene-Constantinopolitan Creed. The origins and importance of this creed were briefly considered in A *Cloud of Witnesses*,[3]

1. See *Cloud* 86–7.
2. See *Cloud* 87–8.
3. See *Cloud* 123–6.

and all we need to note here are two points: firstly, that whatever its origins, the creed was given canonical approval by the fathers at the Council of Chalcedon in 451 and that the Council of Chalcedon was an ecumenical council; and secondly, that in its original version, the last section of the creed—the section dealing with the Holy Spirit—read as follows:

> . . . and in the Holy Spirit, the lord and life-giver, *who proceeds from the Father*, who with the Father and Son is together worshipped and together glorified, who spoke through the prophets.[4]

This is not the version used by the western church. Westerners maintain that the Holy Spirit 'proceeds from the Father *and the Son*', and we may justly ask where the additional words came from and why they were added. In Latin, the language of the west, the passage just quoted reads as follows: 'qui ex Patre, *Filioque* procedit'. *Filioque* means 'and the Son', and the dispute we are about to consider is usually referred to as the problem of the *filioque*.

It seems that the first time the additional phrase appeared in a western version of the creed was in 589 in Spain, at the Third Council of Toledo, and there is no doubt that it was a reflection of Augustine's theory of double procession. It may have been added to combat some form of Arianism, and whatever other problems might be associated with Augustine's idea, double procession leaves no room for a subordinate Son. If an electric battery is to produce twelve volts, you need the equal contributions of both terminals, and the idea that one terminal produces nine volts while the other produces only three is nonsense. Similarly, if we define the Holy Spirit as the interaction of Father and Son, both Father and Son must be equal partners in that interaction.

From Spain, the *filioque* made its way to England in the seventh century, and then, slowly, to France and Germany in the course of the eighth. Charlemagne eagerly espoused it, for

---

4. *Cloud* 124.

he knew that the Greeks did not agree with it and Charlemagne was quite happy to antagonize them. The popes were far more cautious and did not wish to provoke their eastern colleagues unnecessarily. Leo III, who owed his position entirely to Charlemagne and who had crowned the emperor on Christmas Day 800, refused to use it (though he agreed with the doctrine); and although the missionaries sent into Bulgaria by Nicholas I included it in their version of the creed, it was not adopted at Rome until after the year 1000. From that time on it was universally accepted in the west. In the east, however, it was universally condemned for three reasons: (i) because it was not in accord with divine authority; (ii) because its inclusion in the creed was a contravention of a fundamental principle of ecclesiastical tradition; and (iii) because it was theologically unsound. Let us examine the arguments.

The first (and simplest) reason for the eastern refusal to accept the *filioque* was, as we have said, simply a question of authority: not, in this case, the authority of the christian fathers, but the authority of Christ himself. In the gospel of John, when Christ is speaking to his disciples about the coming of the Holy Spirit, he says that he will send them the Counselor, 'the Spirit of truth, who proceeds *from the Father*', and that the Spirit will bear witness to him (Jn 15:26). Following this, a host of theologians, both eastern and western (the Greeks could gleefully include one of the greatest of the popes, Leo I[5]), had testified to single procession and, as we have seen, it had behind it the authority of the Council of Chalcedon.

The west, of course, did not deny the gospel of John, but laid stress on the context in which the phrase had been uttered. What was Christ talking about at the time? He was talking about the coming of the Counselor, the Holy Spirit, who would come into his own after Christ had left this world and had ascended into heaven. That had now been accomplished. The authority that had been present in Christ's physical body had now passed on

5. See *Cloud* 117–21, 175.

to his mystical body—the church—and under the inspiration of the Holy Spirit, much that was in the gospels had been expanded and elaborated by the fathers of the church. The west, therefore, had no trouble in finding plenty of respected theologians who, being guided by the Spirit, had recognized the *filioque* and who therefore supported the western case. Not the least of them were Ambrose and Augustine. But just as the Greeks had been able to include Latins in their polemic, the Latins had little difficulty in finding Greeks to include in theirs, and the argument from authority was, as usual, inconclusive.

The second reason for the eastern objection to the *filioque* was that it contravened a fundamental principle of ecclesiastical tradition. What tradition? The tradition that doctrines approved by the whole church acting in ecumenical council can be changed only by the whole church acting in ecumenical council. The Council of Chalcedon was an ecumenical council and the Council of Chalcedon had approved the creed. The Council had also stated that it was unlawful for anyone to propose, write, devise, intend, or teach any other creed, and that those who dared do so would be cursed and excommunicated. The fathers at the Council of Ephesus in 431, the Third Ecumenical Council, had said much the same thing. The Third Council of Toledo, however, was not ecumenical. It was no more than a local, provincial, spanish council; and since no ecumenical council had given its approval to the *filioque*, the west had no right to use it.

The western reply to this was that the phrase was not an addition but a clarification. It is true that the original version of the creed said that the Holy Spirit 'proceeds from the Father', but it did not specifically say that the Spirit 'proceeds from the Father and does *not* proceed from the Son'. The question was left open. At the proper time, therefore, and in order to combat erroneous ideas, the *filioque* had been added to the creed to safeguard belief in the full divinity of the Son. What was wrong with that? The reason it did not appear in the earlier version of the creed, said one western writer, was because the fathers at Constantinople and Chalcedon thought it so obvious as to be unnecessary. Times, unfortunately, had proved them wrong, and later theologians had been forced to add the phrase to ensure that the Trinity was understood correctly.

Furthermore, said the west, when the fathers at Chalcedon forbade any changes to be made in the creed, they did not mean changes in *wording*, but changes in the faith that was being expressed in that wording. If, then, the words were no longer adequate in expressing the faith, or if, because of their date, they were somewhat unclear, there was no reason why they should not be amended or clarified.

It need hardly be said that this argument held no water with the Greeks, and in any case, their objections to the *filioque* were not based on these grounds alone. Indeed, what might be called the legal case was merely the tip of the iceberg, and deep beneath the surface were major differences in the ways in which east and west approached the problem of the oneness and threeness of God. This leads us directly to the third, and by far the most complex, of the greek objections to the *filioque*—that it was theologically unsound—and we must now try to explain the reasons for this conviction.

It is important first to make a distinction between what happens *inside* the Trinity and what happens *outside* the Trinity. By 'outside' the Trinity, we mean what happens when the Trinity acts externally and affects us and the created order. Both eastern and western theologians were aware that Saint Paul had referred to the Holy Spirit as 'the Spirit of his Son' (Gal 4:6), and from the time of Augustine onwards, western writers had claimed this as clear evidence for the equal contribution of the Son in the production of the Spirit. Not so, said the Greeks: what we have in Saint Paul is a reference to the way in which the Holy Spirit acts *on us*. Even during his lifetime, Christ had promised us 'another Counselor' (Jn 14:16), and after he had ascended into heaven, the dramatic events of Pentecost bore clear and incontrovertible witness to the presence of the Spirit in the world. What we can say, therefore, is that with regard to operations or activities *outside* the Trinity, the Holy Spirit does indeed come from the Father (who brings it into being) *and* the Son (who sends it to us). But this has nothing to do with what is going on *inside* the

Trinity, and that is what we are dealing with here. As far as the Greeks were concerned, the words of Christ in John 15:26 left no doubt that within the Trinity the Holy Spirit proceeded from the Father alone.

Most of the reasons for the eastern insistence on this point appear at the time of the conflict between Photius and Nicholas. There are some in the west, wrote Photius, who are suggesting that the Divine and Holy Spirit proceeds not only from the Father but also from the Son, and such a doctrine (which he called 'the crown of evils') could, in his view, all too easily lead to very dangerous conclusions. Firstly, it could lead to ditheism; secondly, it could lead to Sabellianism; and thirdly, it undoubtedly lowered the status of the Holy Spirit. Later eastern theologians agreed with Photius, and we must now examine the ways in which they arrived at these conclusions. In the ensuing discussion I have not restricted myself to the arguments put forward in the ninth century and have presented the material more logically than it appears in the actual sources. Even so, the reasoning is not easy to follow. Let us begin with the first objection: that double procession leads to a form of ditheism, or belief in two First Principles.

First of all, said the east, whoever believes in a coeternal Trinity must obviously believe that all three persons are eternal. Secondly, if the Holy Spirit is indeed produced by the interaction of Father and Son—if the Holy Spirit is 'whatever is common' to Father and Son[6]—it follows that we need both a Father and a Son in order to bring the Holy Spirit into being. But if the Holy Spirit is eternal, and if the Holy Spirit is produced by the interaction of Father and Son, the Father and Son must also be eternal, and this is to imply *two* eternal First Principles. We have an eternal Father who had no beginning; we have an eternal Son who likewise had no beginning; and these two cooperate in producing the eternal Spirit. But to believe in two unoriginate First Principles is ditheism—belief in two gods—and that is directly contrary to christian teaching.

6. See *Cloud* 87.

The west had no real difficulty in countering this argument. The Son, they said, is certainly not a First Principle and we are not ditheists. At the beginning of all things, before all ages, the Father generated the Son and still generates him, for the generation of the Son is an eternal generation.[7] The Father puts forth the Son as the sun puts forth its light, and just as the sun was never without its light, so the Father was never without the Son. Contrary to the old ideas of Arius, there was never a time when he was not.[8] Then, to the Son whom he generated before all ages and who is coeternal with him, the Father gives the power to cooperate with him in the production of the Holy Spirit. We are not, therefore, talking about two unbegotten First Principles. The Father alone is unbegotten and the Son is begotten from the Father. But what is to stop the Father from giving a gift to his Son? The gift he gives is the capacity to join with the Father in bringing forth the third person of the Trinity.

Even if this were true, said the Greeks, there are still problems, for in defending yourselves against ditheism, you westerners have slipped into a second error. You have now blurred the distinction between the divine persons and are guilty of a form of Sabellianism! How does this follow? Let us agree that there are not two First Principles. But if there are not *two* First Principles, there can only be *one* First Principle, and that can only be the Father. The Father, as Gregory of Nazianzus said, is 'the fountain-head of Deity'. Augustine of Hippo had agreed with him. So if there is only one First Principle, and if that First Principle is the Father, it follows that both the Son and the Holy Spirit must have been brought into being by him *and by him alone*.

But you westerners, said the Greeks, are not saying this. What *you* are saying is that the Holy Spirit was brought into being by the Son as well as by the Father, and whether the Son does this by gift or by nature makes very little difference. The Son may certainly act as a channel for the Holy Spirit (i.e. the Holy

7. See *Cloud* 52.
8. See *Cloud* 55–8.

Spirit may proceed from the Father *through* the Son), but the Son is not the fountain-head of Deity and never has been. That is the characteristic of the Father alone. In other words, if the west were maintaining that Father *and* Son produced the Holy Spirit, and if the west were not suggesting the existence of two First Principles, what it was saying was that there is effectively no difference between the Father and the Son. Both Father and Son are fountain-heads of Deity. That smacks of Sabellianism and is certainly heretical. How was the west to respond?

The west responded by emphasizing the difference between something one has as a right and something one has as a gift: something one has by nature and something one has by grace. The President of the United States happens, at the moment, to be a male. That is not his fault and he had no choice in the matter. It is what he is by nature. He did, however, have a choice in whether he would run for office, and once he has been elected and installed, certain powers are bestowed upon him which he did not earlier possess. He can, for example, declare war on behalf of his country. The presidential powers, therefore, are certainly impressive, but they pertain to the office, not to the person. If the president is ousted or if he resigns, he no longer has those powers.

What happens in the Trinity, said the west, is that God the Father generates the Son eternally, and then, upon the Son whom he has generated eternally, he eternally bestows the power to cooperate with him in bringing forth the Holy Spirit. This is not a power that the Son possesses by right or by nature: it is a power he possesses by the grace of the Father. It is a free gift. Only the Father has *by nature* the power to bring forth the Holy Spirit, but he may share that power *by grace* with whomsoever he pleases. The west, therefore, was not saying that there is no difference between Father and Son. On the contrary. The Father remains the fountain-head of Deity, the sole First Principle, but what he decides to bestow on his Son is entirely up to him.

Even if we were to accept this, said the Greeks (and it need hardly be added that they did not), there are still difficulties. Westerners might be able to avoid the charges of ditheism and

Sabellianism, but they have still diminished the role of the Holy
Spirit and have failed to acknowledge its status as a full and
distinct person of the Trinity. How does this follow?

We know, said the Greeks, who and what the Father is: he
is the unbegotten creator and the fountain-head of Deity. We
know, too, that the Son is the second person of the Trinity and
is generated eternally by the Father. But who or what is the
Holy Spirit? According to the west, he (or she) is merely an
'interaction', something 'common to both'! The Holy Spirit is
no more than those bits of Father and Son which happen to
coincide, no more than the 'overlap' of Father and Son! This,
surely, is to denigrate the Spirit and to lower its status. To define
the Spirit not in its own terms but in the terms of Father and Son
may tell us something about Father and Son, but little about the
Spirit. Indeed, we might even say that the Holy Spirit is reduced
to a subordinate and derivative position in the Trinity, and that
would be to resurrect the long-condemned views of Arius and
his followers.

For the east, the Holy Spirit was every bit as real and distinct a
personality as Father and Son. Just as the Father had generated
the Son, so he had brought forth the Holy Spirit. The Spirit was
therefore just as real and just as individual as the Son, and it has
its own task to accomplish in the divine plan, its own work in the
world, its own involvement in the daily experiences of ordinary
Christians, and its own task in the church. In diminishing the
status of the Spirit and in reducing its importance, the west, once
again, was wrong.

To these objections the west could reply, with some justice,
that the east did not fully understand Augustine's view of double
procession. By the ninth century that was true. According to
Augustine, Father and Son are two infinite powers who have
everything in common. The only difference between them is that
one is unbegotten and the other is begotten. And since the Holy
Spirit shares *all* the powers of Father and Son, it follows that the
Holy Spirit is also an infinite power. The only difference in this
case is that the Holy Spirit proceeds, and is neither unbegotten
nor begotten. The Holy Spirit is the binding force that holds
the Trinity together, and just as the Trinity is one God, so the

Father and the Son and the Holy Spirit, three distinct persons, are coequal, coeternal, and consubstantial. To say that the western view of the Holy Spirit diminishes its stature is nonsense. The Holy Spirit is fully God just as the Father and Son are fully God, and no Christian would ever deny or ever wish to deny that the holy and divine Spirit has its own vital role to play in the life of the church. The west has never maintained anything different.

The series of arguments and counter-arguments outlined above reveal two things. They show how the doctrine of double procession could easily be misinterpreted, but they also show that it could be satisfactorily defended. At first glance, double procession does seem to produce a view of the Trinity much like a pawnbroker's sign—two golden spheres at the top (Father and Son) with one hanging down below them at a lower level (the Holy Spirit)—and it is easy to interpret this as implying two First Principles. On the other hand, the arguments in support of the doctrine that we have outlined here reflect the thought of Augustine himself rather than his later followers, and during the course of the subsequent centuries Augustine's ideas had sometimes been confused and had sometimes been stated in unfortunate terms. In other words, although it remains true that the east did indeed misunderstand the western doctrine of double procession, its misunderstanding was more justified than might appear from the discussion presented above. One example will suffice.

We have seen that according to Augustine, the Father generated the Son and then bestowed upon him the power to cooperate with him in the production of the Holy Spirit. This is what Augustine actually says:

> Anyone who can understand the timeless generation of the Son from the Father understands the timeless procession of the Holy Spirit from both . . . . For as the Father has in himself [the power] for the Holy Spirit to proceed from him, so he has granted to the Son [the power] that from him [too] the same Holy Spirit should proceed, and from both timelessly.[9]

9. Augustine, *De Trinitate* XV.xxvi.47; *PL* 42: 1094.

Or again:

> The Son speaks of the Spirit as 'proceeding from the Father'
> (Jn 15:26) because the Father, who is the source of his pro-
> cession, generated such a Son, and in generating him granted
> that the Holy Spirit should proceed from him as well.[10]

These statements of Augustine are clear and precise, and they
retain the important concept of the Father as the First Principle,
the single fountain-head of Deity. This, however, was not the
case when the same view was presented some centuries later.
The Spirit proceeds from Father and Son, said some western
theologians, *tanquam ex uno principio* 'as from one principle'.[11]
But if Father and Son are being regarded as 'one principle', the
distinction between them is certainly blurred, and the second
argument against double procession—that it leads to some form
of Sabellianism—appears to be justified. Once again, a careful
analysis of just what the west meant by this phrase reveals that
the problem is more with terminology than with doctrine, but
it cannot be doubted that such unfortunate expressions could
only exacerbate the differences between the two halves of the
christian world.

At the very basis of the dispute was a fundamental difference in the way east and west approached the doctrine of the
Trinity. The Greeks, from the Cappadocian Fathers onwards,
had tended to begin their discussion with the Father, move
on to the Son and the Holy Spirit, and then worry about how
these three distinct persons were one consubstantial God. The
Latins, from Augustine onwards, tended to view God as one
consubstantial Trinity, and then worry about how to distinguish
the three individual persons. It was inevitable, therefore, that as
far as the east was concerned, the west laid too little emphasis
on the person of the Holy Spirit, and that as far as the west was

10. Augustine, *Contra Maximinum* II.xiv.1; *PL* 42: 770.
11. The expression was used at the Council of Lyons and at the Council of
Florence. Both councils will be discussed later in this chapter.

concerned, the east teetered on the brink of tritheism. Neither side was actually guilty of the errors of which it was accused, but, as we have noted elsewhere, by the time of Charlemagne relations between west and east were very strained and neither east nor west was prepared to listen in a sympathetic and broad-minded way to the position of the other. It would not be long before the two churches separated, and ecclesiastical rivalries and political conflict ensured that the question of the *filioque* remained a point of contention.

How many people actually understood the theology behind the controversy is questionable. Photius certainly did, but Phot-ius was an exception. It is improbable that George down the street, who owned the constantinopolitan equivalent of the local pizza parlour, could follow its intricacies. A few centuries earlier the situation might have been different, for at the time of the Ar-ian controversy the question of the intra-trinitarian relationships was reputed to be a regular topic of conversation in the bars and taverns of Constantinople and Alexandria. But by the time of Photius and in the centuries that followed, the *filioque* was little more than a political slogan. To reject the *filioque* was equivalent to rejecting western christianity, western political ambitions, and especially the papal claims for a primacy of jurisdiction. It was a sign of being a good Greek. To accept it was to bow down to the west, submit yourself to an alien form of the christian religion, and grovel at the feet of the pope. The western view, of course, was just the reverse.

The *filioque* and the papal claims remained the two most important points of difference separating east and west until the end of the Middle Ages. They occupied centre stage at the only two attempts at reunification of the two churches between the sack of Constantinople in 1204 and the fall of the city to the Turks in 1453. What happened at those councils is not without interest and is yet another example of the way in which politics and theology went hand in hand.

The first of the two councils was held at Lyons in 1274. Both the byzantine emperor (Michael VIII Palaeologus) and Pope Gregory X desired it, but although both of them may have viewed reconciliation as a worthy ideal, their motives were primarily political. The beleaguered emperor needed the support of the pope to protect him from attacks from Sicily, and the pope wanted the support of the emperor in mounting a new crusade for the liberation of Jerusalem, a project very dear to his heart. The Council was attended by some extremely eminent western theologians. Both Albert the Great and Bonaventure were there (Bonaventure preached the sermon at the High Mass), and Thomas Aquinas was on his way to the council when he died.

Since the emperor's need was greater than the pope's, the easterners at the Council had no choice but to accept both primacy of jurisdiction and the *filioque*, and for about five minutes the eastern and western churches were once again united. What happened afterwards, however, will not surprise us. The terms of the union were rejected in all Orthodox countries by virtually all Orthodox Christians, clergy and laity alike, and the ephemeral union achieved by the Council was formally repudiated by the next emperor.

The second attempt at reconciliation was held at Florence in 1438–39. Once again, politics played a vital role. The east was under threat by the Turks (Constantinople would fall in 1453) and the only hope of the eastern emperor lay in getting western assistance and military support. The emperor himself attended the council as also did the patriarch of Constantinople, and despite the political pressures there was at least some attempt to reach an honest agreement. But once again, the promise of help in combatting the Turks obliged the Greeks to bow to western pressure, and although the actual wording of the article of union was deliberately ambiguous, the Greeks accepted both the papal claims and the *filioque*, despite the fact that this had been the major point of controversy. They also accepted the western doctrine of purgatory, a matter we shall discuss in Chapter XVIII. Only one of the Orthodox representatives at the Council refused to sign the agreement, Mark, archbishop of Ephesus, and in due course he would be canonized for his stand in defence of the Orthodox faith.

The west was delighted with the Union of Florence, but, as had happened with the earlier Union of Lyons, it had little effect on the east. Many of those who had signed the document revoked their signatures when they got home, and many Orthodox Christians agreed with the comment of a byzantine noble who said that he would rather see turkish turbans in the middle of Constantinople than latin mitres. And as we have seen, Mark of Ephesus, the sole Orthodox at Florence who refused to sign, was made a saint.

The *filioque*, both politically and theologically, played a dominant role in east-west relations in the Middle Ages, but the theological points at issue were not trivial. We are, after all, concerned with one of the fundamental doctrines of the christian tradition, and a correct understanding of it is obviously important. With the benefit of hindsight we can see that although east and west did indeed have different theories as to how the Spirit came into being, both were agreed that it was consubstantial, coeternal, and coequal with Father and Son. Heresy, in this case, was in the eye of the beholder.

Our primary concern in this chapter has been with events within the Trinity: the internal relations of Father, Son, and Holy Spirit. What happens outside the Trinity is a different matter. We then become involved with examining God's relationship with the created order (especially with human beings), and although the action of the Spirit is of major importance in this matter, it must take second place to the primary event of the Incarnation. The Counselor follows the Christ. We must therefore turn to a question we posed in the companion volume to this study, a question which is actually the title of one of the writings of Anselm of Canterbury: *Cur Deus homo?* Why did God become human? In A *Cloud of Witnesses* we considered what the early fathers had to say on this matter;[12] we must now examine some of the medieval answers to the same question.

12. See *Cloud*, Chapter XIII.

XI-1 Each of the cells in the carthusian monastery of La Chartreuse near Dijon contained a painting of the Crucifixion. Carthusians live as hermits, and this painted wooden panel would have served as a devotional focus. The suffering of Christ is strongly emphasized: his body sags, blood runs from his wounds. While depiction of this scene before the twelfth century showed four nails (two for the hands, two for the feet), only three nails are used in this painting. In the thirteenth century, artists were accused of heresy for reducing the number of nails from four to three, but artistic innovation triumphed over tradition and three nails became the norm in western art. Mary, who turns her tear-stained face away from her son, is as youthful in scenes of the Crucifixion as she is in scenes of the Annunciation and the Nativity, despite the fact that these events had occurred more than thirty years earlier. On the right is Saint John the Evangelist. who was charged by Christ with caring for Mary and who is always present in scenes of the Crucifixion. Only the white-robed carthusian monk, smaller than the three principal figures, is staid, neutral, and composed.

Crucifixion, c. 1440–1450.
Dijon, Musée des Beaux-Arts, inv. 1980-43P.
Photo: Musée des Beaux-Arts, Dijon.

XI

Why
Did God Become Human?

IN A CLOUD of Witnesses we glanced at some of the main

theories held by the early fathers as to why God became human,

and it may be useful to summarize those ideas here.[1] The earliest

view, that Christ came to earth primarily as a teacher in order

to tell us how to get to heaven, was always inadequate. A simple

teacher of spirituality does not need to be God incarnate and does

not need to die on a cross to illustrate his teaching. Both east-

ern and western theologians soon realized that this theory was

incomplete, and although neither ever denied the importance of

1. See Cloud XIII.

the pedagogic Christ, both went on to produce richer and more comprehensive explanations.

At the moment God became human, divinity was united with humanity, and the eastern church stressed that as a consequence of this, humanity had had bestowed upon it the capacity for deification. In the words of Athanasius, 'God became human that in him human beings might become God.'[2] The link with God that had been lost by the Fall had been reestablished by the Incarnation, and it was once again possible for us humans to become not God, but what God is: that is, to share in his qualities and participate in his perfection and immortality.[3]

The view adopted by the western church was less platonic and more legalistic, and, in general, western theologians laid greater emphasis than did those in the east on the importance of the crucifixion. To a large extent, this was due to the influence of Tertullian, a theologian of the late second/early third century who had been trained as a lawyer, and who saw the redemption as taking place in a divine lawcourt. We human beings are sinners and are guilty. Hell gapes before us. We stand in the dock condemned to death, for death is the wages of sin[4], and die we must unless someone is prepared to take our place and die in our stead. That, said Tertullian, is precisely what Christ has done, and Christ's willing acceptance of an undeserved death is central to Tertullian's thought. Christ has paid our debt; Christ has ransomed us; Christ has been crucified that we might be saved. For Tertullian, therefore, the death of Christ comprises 'the whole importance and benefit of the name Christian.'[5] The Greeks, of course, had never denied the necessity of the redeeming death of the Saviour, but to elevate it, as did Tertullian, to this supremely central position is a typically western point of view.[6]

---

2. See Chapter IX, n. 9.

3. See *Cloud* 158–60.

4. Rom 6:23.

5. Tertullian, *Adversus Marcionem* iii.8; ed. E. Evans (Oxford, 1972) 1: 192.

6. Further on Tertullian, see *Cloud* 79–83.

The last attempt at explaining the Incarnation that we discussed in A *Cloud of Witnesses*—the so-called 'theory of the devil's deception'[7]—is not one we need reiterate here. It continued to appear in medieval theology, but since it played no major role, we need not dwell upon it.

The obvious place to begin our discussion of medieval theories on the why and wherefore of the Incarnation is with the treatise whose title we borrowed for this chapter: the *Cur Deus Homo?* of Anselm of Canterbury. It was written in 1097–98 and was the first medieval work to attempt a systematic, rational, logical investigation of the mystery of the Atonement. Anselm's purpose was to show not just that the life and death of Christ were necessary, but that redemption could not have been achieved in any other way. How did he present his case?

Anselm, as we know, was a westerner, and it therefore comes as no surprise to see in his work the western, tertullianite emphasis on the importance of the crucifixion. Once again, we are in the law-courts. Once again, we stand condemned in the dock. Once again, there is need for the saving victim. Once again, it is Christ who takes upon himself the whole of humanity, stands in our place, and pays our debt. It is not we but he who dies upon the cross; it is not he but we who go free. The ransom has been paid; the judge has been satisfied; the case is over.

This idea of 'satisfaction' or *satisfactio* dominates western and anselmian thought on the Incarnation. *Satisfactio* is actually a latin law-term which means reparation or redress or amends for an injury committed, and although Tertullian himself did not use the word in quite this sense, he certainly anticipated its significance. Moreover, between Tertullian and Anselm stood the titan figure of Augustine, and one thing that Augustine stressed, especially as he became ever more deeply involved in the Pelagian Controversy, was human sinfulness. When we are born, he said, we are *una massa peccati*, 'one lump of sin', and we seem to spend most of our lives cultivating that sinfulness.

7. See *Cloud* 161–6.

It is an extraordinarily depressing viewpoint (Orthodoxy is far more optimistic), but it was the established view of the medieval church in the west. Anselm, therefore, stands in the wake of Tertullian's legalism and Augustine's stress on sinfulness, and both have had an obvious and major influence on the *Cur Deus Homo?*

Anselm begins his argument by demonstrating that the death of Christ must have been a free act of self-sacrifice on his part. Unlike us, Christ was sinless and did not deserve to die. That is not the case with us. We are not sinless—far from it—and if we are ever to attain our true goal, which is the eternal bliss of the Beatific Vision, then sin must be paid for and wiped out. Sin demands satisfaction. We have to pay for our pleasures.

Here, however, we might raise an objection. If God is truly all-powerful and all-loving, why can't he just forgive our sins? Why can't he just cancel them out as a loving parent might freely forgive an erring child? Anselm's answer is simple: God is indeed loving, but he is also just. Criminals in the dock may well repent of their crimes—most of them probably do—but they remain responsible for what they have done. If they are found guilty, the judge, whether he likes it or not, is bound by justice to render due and fitting punishment. God is no different. He is, in a sense, bound by his own laws, and justice or righteousness[8] is one of them.

What human beings have done, human beings must pay for. But what human beings have done is very serious indeed. When Adam and Eve sinned, they introduced sin into a sinless world. They were responsible for a difference not in degree, but in kind. The change was infinite, not finite. Imagine a sheet of spotless white paper. Take a pen and slowly bring it closer to the paper—closer, closer, closer. Suddenly—POW!—the point of the pen touches the paper and leaves a mark. The world has been changed. The spotless has become spotted. And although we may then spend the next hour putting dots all over the paper,

---

8. The latin word *justitia* can be translated as either justice or righteousness.

the difference between one dot and a thousand is no more than finite. The real difference is between a perfectly clean sheet of paper and a sheet of paper which is clean no longer, and that difference is infinite. So it was in the Garden of Eden.

It follows, then, that humankind is not only guilty, but infinitely guilty. So how can we finite creatures hope to render infinite satisfaction? The situation becomes even more depressing when we remember Augustine's doctrine of original sin: of our own power we can only fall.[9] If, then, we cannot do even finite good, how can we make reparation for infinite wickedness? Obviously we can't.

The only being who can pay an infinite debt is an infinite being, and the only infinite being is God. But since it is finite humans who have incurred the debt, humans are the only ones who can pay it. So what happened at the Incarnation? The infinite God, says Anselm, became finitely human, and, as the God-man, was the only one who could possibly deal with an impossible situation. Christ, God and man, offered himself as a free and willing sacrifice for the sins of the world. He offered to God what he did not owe to God—his death—and having thereby paid our debt and rendered infinite satisfaction, he claimed as a reward from God the salvation of the human race. To each sinner, doomed to eternal torment and with no way of escape, God the Father says: 'Take the Only-begotten, and offer him in your place'; and the Son says: 'Take me, and redeem yourself'.[10] In this exchange lies the whole of our salvation.

Such is the argument of the *Cur Deus Homo?*, and we may note that Anselm has tried to prove three points: (i) that Christ must have been fully and perfectly God, and therefore infinite; (ii) that he must also have been fully and perfectly human, and therefore finite; and (iii) that he had to die on the cross, for if he had not died, there would have been no legal satisfaction; and if

9. See *Cloud* 147–8.
10. Anselm, *Cur Deus homo?* 2.20; ed. F. S. Schmitt (Edinburgh, 1946) 2: 132.

the just God had not been legally satisfied, we would still be in our sins.

Anselm's argument is logical, but it was not without its critics. One of the main criticisms was levelled at its excessive legalism and its concentration on the juridical concept of satisfaction. Anselm's God is more interested in reparation and justice than with repentance and forgiveness; and Anselm's view of human beings leaves them little to do in the process of redemption. We are hardly more than spectators at the trial of Christ.

A quite different view of the atonement was presented by Peter Abelard, but as so often happened with that remarkable man, the merits of what he said were obscured by the antagonism he aroused. Once again we shall see a conflict between Bernard and Abelard; once again we shall see Abelard condemned; but once again, we shall see that there was real cause for Bernard's concern.

Abelard approaches the Incarnation from the point of view of God's mercy rather than God's justice. He also places much more emphasis than did Anselm on our role in bringing about our own salvation. For Abelard, the primary purpose of Christ's passion and death was to provide us with an unequalled display of God's love. 'No one has greater love than this, than to lay down one's life for one's friends' (Jn 15:13). This love, says Abelard, was clearly displayed in the crucifixion, and it should rekindle our cold hearts, give rise to a profound sense of gratitude, and inspire in us as much love for God as God has shown to us. 'It is clear', said one of Abelard's followers, 'that all this was done so that [God] might show how much love he had for human beings, so that human beings should be all the more inflamed with love for him'.[11]

To appreciate Abelard's argument, we must realize that for him the root of sin lies in one's intention. Without a deliberate, wilful, evil intention, there is no sin. In his view, no one can sin 'accidentally', and very young children and people who are

---

11. School of Abelard, *Epitome theologiae christianae* xxiii; *PL* 178: 1731D.

insane cannot sin. To sin is deliberately to turn one's back on one's Creator and treat him with contempt, and what this really signifies is a lack of love. The old principle enunciated by Augustine, 'Love God, and do what you will', is true: if you really love God, you will naturally wish to please him, just as lovers on this earth naturally strive to please each other. By the example of his obedience Christ teaches us the correct attitude we should have to God, and by exhibiting the highest degree of love, he inspires in us the love which, by producing a change in our attitude and intentions, will lead to a life lived in willing conformity to the will of God.

This is not to say, however, that Christ's death was no more than an encouragement or stimulus to a better life. Abelard never denies that it was also the payment of a debt. In Christ's blood, he says, we have been purchased, justified, and redeemed. The cross is the greatest gift of grace and by it we have been saved. On the cross Christ bore our sins and took upon himself the punishment for our iniquity. But the crucifixion is not where Abelard puts the emphasis. It is true that the events of Calvary were intended to free us from the servitude of sin, but they were also intended 'to gain for us true freedom as children of God, so that we may fulfil all things not through our fear of him, but through our love of him'.[12] Christ died for us to show us the magnitude of God's love, and we should always hold his passion in our mind's eye so that it may serve as our example and prevent us from falling away.

However much this abelardian doctrine might appeal to modern readers, there is no doubt that it poses problems. Bernard of Clairvaux saw it as a resurgence of Pelagianism[13], and it cannot be denied that he had a point. For Pelagius, the essential purpose of the Incarnation was to offer us instruction and encouragement and provide us with an example to follow. Abelard's ideas are suspiciously similar to this. Furthermore, in his suggestion that

12. Abelard, *Commentary on Romans* II; CCCM 11: 118.
13. For Pelagianism, see *Cloud* 144–7.

once human beings have had a change of heart they can take salvation into their own hands, Abelard again appears too close to Pelagius for comfort.

As we have seen earlier, a careful examination of Abelard's actual writings reveals that the accusations levelled against him were not entirely justified, but once again, what Abelard *meant* to say is not what he *appeared* to say. He does seem to diminish the importance of the death of Christ, and in his optimistic assessment of human nature he does appear to downplay the role of original sin and imply that the canonical views of Augustine on this matter were not quite correct.

So it was that at the Council of Sens in 1140, Abelard was condemned not only for his teachings on the Trinity and his definition of faith, but also for his christology. The view of the church was to be the view of Bernard of Clairvaux, and while Bernard neither denied nor wished to deny the inspirational and evocative quality of Christ's perfect life, he insisted on 'the sacrament of redemption' and the necessity of Christ's death. We *are* sinners, he says, and we are required to pay the price. In his life Christ is our model; in his death he is our Saviour. God is merciful, but he is also just. And Bernard tries to develop a doctrine that combines Anselm's emphasis on divine justice with Abelard's emphasis on love and grace.

There are three main factors, says Bernard, which must be considered in the work of salvation. The first is the form of humility by which God emptied himself and took upon himself the form of a servant; the second is the measure of love by which he loved us so much that he gave his life for us on the cross; the third is the mystery of redemption which was brought about by his death. Without the redemption, neither of the other two factors mean much. They provide wonderful models, to be sure, but without redemption they have neither foundation nor stability. You may as well try to paint on air. We are redeemed not merely through his teaching, but through his blood. We must eat the Paschal Lamb and drink his blood. It is one thing to follow him, one thing to hold him, but quite another to feed on him. We must be washed in his blood, washed in the blood that was shed by him for the forgiveness of sins. Only through the blood of Christ, said William of Saint-Thierry, will those who cling to him by faith escape the eternal death that is their due. In other words, whatever theory of the atonement we may have, the cross and the blood of Christ must be central to it.

Abelard's view of the Incarnation was never really representative of the western mind, and after his condemnation at Sens there was no further doubt about the centrality of the crucifixion for western theology. Bernard's own loving concern with the sufferings and death of Christ—those sufferings and death which were the greatest proof of his infinite love—were to have a major impact on the development of devotion to the human Jesus that found its fulfilment in the writings of the english Cistercian Aelred of Rievaulx (1109–67), sometimes called the 'Bernard of the North', of Bonaventure, and of the Franciscans. But although medieval western theology came to be dominated by the shadow of the cross, the old, hard-line, legalistic approach of Anselm had been softened by Bernard and his followers, and as we shall see shortly, the veneration of the Virgin also played an important role in this matter.

The sacrifice of Calvary, then, was essential for our redemption. From the time of Adam onwards, we have been steeped in sin and doomed to everlasting pain. From the very moment our first parents sank their teeth into the forbidden fruit, we have been condemned, and Augustine had made it eminently clear that when Adam fell, all his descendants—all of us—fell with him.[14] But what would have happened if Adam had *not* fallen? What would have happened if he and Eve had rejected the devil's overtures and overcome their temptations? Or, to put it in the words of the thirteenth-century scholastics: 'Would Christ have become incarnate if humankind had not sinned?'

This may seem to us a trivial question, much like asking what would have happened if the father of the Virgin had been impotent, or what would have occurred if the Holy Spirit had appeared

14. See *Cloud* 147.

as a vulture instead of a dove. It is not. It is actually of fundamental importance and is intimately related to the question we
are examining in this chapter: Why did God become human?
Are we to see the Incarnation as the epitome of love, the climax
of creation, the moment when God revealed himself in Christ
to human beings and united himself fully to their humanity?
Or are we to understand it primarily in terms of deliverance, of
God's involvement in human affairs simply because things had
got so bad that no other solution was possible. In the first case,
the Incarnation was not dependent on the sin of Adam; in the
second case, it was. Which view are we to accept?

In the west, the second alternative had the longer history. It
could claim the authority of Augustine; it gained great support
from the satisfaction-theology of Anselm; and a considerable
number of twelfth- and thirteenth-century theologians gave it
their approval. 'Oh happy Fall,' said one of them, 'that required
such a great Redeemer!' And there is no doubt that given the
western emphasis on the blood-stained centrality of the cross,
this approach is the one we might expect to prevail.

In the twelfth century, however, a different and richer view
of the Incarnation developed, a view in which Christ's humanity was seen not as something he assumed simply in order to
suffer death, but as an end in itself, as the consummation of
creation. One of the earliest writers to espouse this view was
Rupert, abbot of the benedictine abbey of Deutz (near Cologne
in Germany), who was born sometime between 1075 and 1080
and died in 1129. In Rupert's view, the delight of Christ was
'to be with the human race' (he is echoing Proverbs 8:31), and
it was part of God's original purpose that at the proper time,
he would reveal himself as his Image (Christ) to those he created in his image (human beings). The superabundance of sin
might have affected the conditions and the time at which the
Incarnation occurred, but it did not affect the event. Christ was
coming anyway. From its very beginning the expectant world
had awaited the revelation of its Maker; the ancient philosophers had hinted at it; the prophets had foretold it; and then
in Bethlehem of Judaea, a small hick town in a backwater of

the Roman Empire, the Infinite became finite and God became man!

How could it be otherwise, asked the thirteenth-century scholastic, Alexander of Hales?[15] God is without question the Highest Good, and the very nature of Good is that it seeks to share itself with others. Goodness always works outwards. In what better way, then, could God share himself with his creation than by becoming part of it? God did not become human only to endure the dreadful hours on Calvary: the Incarnation of the God-man involved his whole life, teachings, example, passion, death, resurrection, and ascension. The Incarnation was not contingent or dependent on our stupidity and wilfulness. God's revelation of himself to us in Christ was a supreme act of love (both Abelard and Bernard would have agreed), and it was an act of love which had been intended from the foundation of the world.

Most people nowadays would agree that this second view of the Incarnation is far more satisfactory, but it was not the view of either Thomas Aquinas or Bonaventure. Aquinas, as usual, began his examination of the question with a meticulous consideration of the evidence. He agreed with Alexander of Hales that the essence of the Highest Good is to share or communicate itself with others. He agreed that this sharing achieved its perfection when God actually became man. He agreed that the Incarnation exalted human nature and he agreed that it was the consummation of creation. But his final decision was based on the scriptures, and, according to Thomas, the scriptures everywhere proclaim that the Incarnation was first and foremost the remedy for human sin. 'I delivered to you (says Saint Paul) as being of first importance what I also received: that Christ died for our sins in accordance with the scriptures' (1 Cor 15:3). Nevertheless, adds Aquinas (leaving the door ajar), God *might* have become incarnate even if sin were non-existent, but we do not know that he would.

15. Alexander (c.1170–1245) was born at Hales in Gloucestershire, England, but was educated, and later taught, in Paris.

This debate remained unresolved at the end of the Middle Ages. The franciscan Bonaventure had accepted, somewhat hesitantly, the idea that the Incarnation was contingent upon the Fall, but later Franciscans generally preferred the opposite view. The Dominicans, as might be expected, usually followed the opinion of Thomas Aquinas.

In the eastern half of the christian world, the question had never really arisen. This was partly due to the fact that the Greeks had never developed an eastern equivalent of western scholasticism, but the main reason was that for the easterners the answer to the question *Cur Deus homo?* was obvious. It had long ago been answered by Athanasius the Great: 'God became human that in him humans might become God',[16] and since humans could not become God because of sin, that sin had to be taken away before deification could be achieved. If, therefore, human beings had not sinned, the Incarnation would not have been necessary. The only eastern writer to present the alternative view seems to have been Maximus the Confessor[17] who, like Rupert of Deutz, saw the Incarnation as the goal to which creation tended and as something foreordained by God independently of human sin. But the view of Maximus was, if not unique, certainly idiosyncratic.

Nevertheless, despite their recognition of the consequences of human sin and the way in which it necessitated the Incarnation, the Greeks never developed an anselmian theology of satisfaction. As we pointed out at the beginning of this chapter, they never denied the redeeming effect of the crucifixion, but that was not where they put the emphasis. For Orthodoxy, the goal of the christian life is deification, and the concept of deification has dominated eastern theology since at least the third century. The eastern answer to the question *Cur Deus homo?*, therefore, was not quite as complex as that of the west, and it may be found in convenient summary in the *Fountain of Wisdom*, a very

16. See n. 1 above.
17. See *Cloud* 137–8.

important compendium of christian doctrine compiled by John of Damascus in the eighth century.

Little is known of the life of the author, and what sketchy information we do possess is often contradictory. He seems to have been born c.675 in Damascus, the son of a wealthy christian family, and when he was about forty he retired to the monastery of Saint Sabas near Jerusalem where he was ordained. It was here that he spent the remaining twenty years of his life—he died c.750—and it was here that he composed his major works. Of these, the *Fountain of Wisdom* is certainly the most important, though his writings in defence of the Holy Icons played a major role in the Iconoclastic Controversy, and we shall examine them in detail in Chapter XIV.

The *Fountain of Wisdom* is divided into three parts—they deal respectively with philosophy, heresy, and orthodoxy—and the third part, 'On the Orthodox Faith', provides us with a clear, systematic, and comprehensive summary of the teachings of the greek fathers on the Trinity, creation (angelic, human, and physical), the sacraments, Mary the God-Bearer, icons, and, of course, the Incarnation, and it was used as the standard theological text-book throughout the Middle Ages in the greek east. It is a sort of earlier greek equivalent of the *Sentences* of Peter Lombard. We should also note that it was translated into Latin in the twelfth century and exercised considerable influence on both Peter Lombard and Thomas Aquinas. It is an extraordinarily useful summary of material, and it presents us with the accepted byzantine view of the reasons for the Incarnation.

In Eden, says John, Adam and Eve existed in a state of deification because they participated in divine illumination. This participation made them immortal, and it was this participation in God's immortality that would be lost when they sinned. Adam and Eve also possessed free-will and the capacity to do good, but as we know, they used that free-will to transgress the divine command and thereby submitted themselves to Satan and separated themselves from God. These conditions of submission and separation have been transmitted to us, their progeny, and we no longer have the ability to free ourselves by our own strength.

God, therefore, assumed human nature, body and soul, and became incarnate. In so doing he took upon himself the possibility of pain and death and bestowed upon us what we had lost: the possibility of deification, of regaining the incorruption and immortality that was ours in Paradise before the Fall. By sin, we had submitted to Satan; by conquering Satan, God in Christ restored us to his own dominion. By sin, we had separated ourselves from God; by uniting himself with humanity, God in Christ annulled that separation and brought us back into a right relationship with God.

The most obvious consequence of our submission to Satan lies in our mortality. Adam and Eve were immortal, but their immortality was bestowed upon them by grace. It was not something they possessed by nature. They were immortal because they participated in God's immortality, and their subsequent mortality was merely the clearest evidence of the loss of this participation. Our own mortality is no more than a consequence of their sin. The real significance of Calvary, therefore, was not just that Christ died, but that three days later he rose again. In his resurrection, he destroyed death, he conquered the devil, and he restored that participation in God that we had lost in Eden. Once again, we enjoy the possibility of deification, and once again we may look forward to everlasting life. Christ's triumph over death was his triumph over the author of death. Death is the last enemy[18], and our Saviour Jesus Christ has abolished death and brought us life and immortality.[19] Death has been swallowed up in victory.[20]

The east, therefore, did not deny the importance of the crucifixion, but saw it as a victory over death and the devil, not as a reparation or satisfaction for sin. For the Greeks, the resurrection was (and is) of greater significance than the crucifixion; and deification—its loss and restoration—remains the fundamental theme of byzantine christology.

18. 1 Cor 15:26.
19. 2 Tim 1:10.
20. 1 Cor 15:54.

Very occasionally, in later byzantine thought, we come across a theory somewhat akin to that of Anselm, but such views were wholly individual and played no significant role in eastern theology. There was a case in the twelfth century, for example, when Soterichos Panteugenos, a deacon of the church of Hagia Sophia in Constantinople and patriarch-elect of Antioch, began teaching that our redemption took place in two stages: the first stage occurred at the moment of the Incarnation, when divinity united with humanity and restored the possibility of deification; the second occurred at the crucifixion, when the Son offered himself to the Father in exchange for us. The views of Panteugenos, however, were condemned at two councils in Constantinople in 1156–57, and the spokesman for the councils, Nicholas, bishop of Methone, reiterated the view of John of Damascus and the whole eastern tradition. The birth, life, death, and resurrection of Christ—and also the coming of the Holy Spirit—were to be seen as a unity, and the work of Christ cannot and must not be reduced to some sort of legalistic exchange. We have been saved by the *whole* of the Incarnation, not only by three hours on Calvary, and the entirety of the work of Christ, from the moment of his conception to the events of Pentecost, are essential for our deification.

Our discussion in this chapter has been restricted to the 'why' of the Incarnation. We must now turn to the 'how'. We know that the possibility of redemption or deification is dependent on Christ being both fully God and fully human at one and the same time, but how is this to be explained? Did Christ take on his humanity like a garment? Did he merge with it? Was there any exchange between the godhead and the manhood? And if Christ were really God and man at the same time, what does this imply about his knowledge? Was he omniscient, as God, or limited in knowledge as we are? Did he progress in wisdom, or was he infinitely wise from his birth? Were his emotions exactly the same as ours, or was there some subtle difference? These questions, and others like them, we shall discuss in our next chapter.

XII-1 John of Damascus, slightly larger than life-size in this fresco in the monastery Church of the Saviour in Chora (Kariye Djami) in Istanbul, is shown with three other writers, each in a pendentive (the curved triangular portion of wall between the dome and the arches which support it). John occupies the most favoured of the four positions as befits his great fame as theologian, defender of orthodoxy during the first phases of iconoclasm, and writer of hymns. Dressed in monastic habit and turban, John is portrayed in the act of composition: he is sharpening a reed pen with a knife, surrounded by the furnishings of a scriptorium. The hymn he is composing can be identified from the lines on the parchment lying before him on the lectern. It is his *Idiomela for the Funeral Service*, which begins 'What joy of life remains without its share of sorrow. . . .'

John of Damascus, 1315–1320/21.
Monastery Church of the Saviour in Chora (Kariye Djami), Istanbul.
Photo: Byzantine Visual Resources, © 1994, Dumbarton Oaks, Washington, D.C.

XII

How
Did God Become Human?

THERE IS NO adequate answer to this question. In 451, the
fathers at Chalcedon had stated that

> we should confess that our Lord Jesus Christ is one and the
> same Son, perfect in his divinity and perfect in his humanity,
> truly God and truly man, possessing a rational soul and body,
> consubstantial with the Father in his divinity and consub-
> stantial with us in his humanity, like us in all things except for
> sin; made known in two natures without confusion, without
> change, without division, without separation; the difference
> of the natures being in no way removed because of the union,
> but rather the specific property of each of the two natures
> being preserved, and coming together in one person and one
> subsistence, not parted or divided into two persons, but one
> and the same Son and only-begotten God the Word, Lord
> Jesus Christ.[1]

1. The *Chalcedonian Definition of the Faith* as quoted in *Cloud* 121–2
(abbreviated).

This is a clear statement of unconfused union, and the principle, though not the terminology, was accepted by the whole
christian world, east and west. The problem of terminology was
another matter, but the development of Monophysitism and the
conflict between Monophysites and Chalcedonians is not here
our concern. A brief account of the matter was presented in
Chapter II.

The fathers at Chalcedon did not provide any explanation
as to how the divinity and the humanity were related in this
unconfused union and they were content to leave the matter to
faith. Their successors were neither so wise nor so cautious, and
from the fifth century onwards, in both east and west, we find a
variety of attempts at explaining how the one person of Jesus of
Nazareth could have been 100% God and 100% man at the same
time. None of these theories is entirely satisfactory, but the fact
that we are dealing with a unique phenomenon which cannot be
explained in conceptual terms did not stop people from trying.
Their attempts were sometimes very complex and very subtle
and a detailed investigation would lead us far into the realms of
scholastic philosophy. That is not our interest. What we shall try
to do here is to draw attention to the essential problems which
lay at the bottom of these philosophical schemes and discuss,
in more general terms, the differences and similarities between
Jesus of Nazareth and us.

At the heart of the matter lies a longing on the part of medieval
theologians to have the best of both worlds. They wanted Christ
to be fully God and fully man, but they did not want the manhood
to interfere in the business of the Godhead. Christ's manhood
had to be a true manhood, on that there was no disagreement,
but it needed to be a sort of *passive* manhood, a manhood which
in no way diminished the divinity of the Divine Logos and in no
way obstructed it in its divine mission.

Let us take an example. According to the fathers, the agony
in the Garden of Gethsemane was the classic case of a conflict
between the divine and human wills in Christ. His human will,
reasonably objecting to crucifixion, said: 'Father, let this cup pass
from me'; but his divine will said to the Father: 'your will be

done'.[2] That there was a conflict here is not in doubt: it caused
Christ to sweat blood. But neither was there any question as to its
resolution. The divine will was going to win and everybody knew
it. So what we need, said the theologians, is for Christ to be truly
human, possessing both a human soul and human flesh, but not
so human that his humanity would present a real challenge to
the divinity and put our redemption in question. How was this
to be resolved?

The medieval explanation was that Christ assumed human
nature, but not a human *personality*. What makes a personality?
It is essentially the product of the interaction between soul and
body. The soul provides us with free-will and the capacity to live
and sense; the body is the means by which the immaterial soul
can operate in the material world. As thinking, living, and sensing
human beings, we have certain likes, dislikes, attitudes, ideals,
aspirations, and points of view which make each one of us unique.
These take time to develop and sometimes, when one set of
characteristics meets another, we have what we call 'personality
clashes'. Some people (we think) have a 'good attitude', some
have a 'bad attitude', some we like, some we don't like: each of
us has a different personality.

If, then, the development of 'personality' is dependent on
the interaction of soul and body, the obvious way to prevent a
personality from developing is to make sure that soul and body
do not interact. How could this idea be applied to Christ? It
was not difficult. The theologians simply maintained that at the
very instant that Mary conceived Jesus, his soul and body were
assumed by the second person of the Trinity and united with
it. In other words, we do not give the human soul and body of
Jesus any time to begin that interaction which would lead to the
development of a distinct human personality. Thus, in Jesus, we
have true human nature, but not an independent human person.

If, then, Christ is truly human, but not a human person, how
was the humanity combined with the divinity? All that we have

2. See *Cloud* 96. For the the biblical account, see Mk 14:36 and parallels.

said so far pertains to both eastern and western theology, but we must now distinguish between them. For the easterners, there was only one main theory; for the westerners, deeply affected by the ideas and principles of scholasticism, there were three. Let us begin with the east.

Once again, the most convenient summary of the greek view is provided by John of Damascus in his *Fountain of Wisdom*, but to understand what he is saying, it may be helpful if we introduce an analogy. Put a poker in the fire and wait until the end glows red-hot. Take it out and look at it. What do we have? We have two things coexisting at the same time and in the same place: iron and heat. The iron, in this case, can exist apart from the heat, but the heat cannot exist apart from the iron. You cannot remove the 'redhotness' from the tip of the poker and examine it under a microscope. The 'redhotness' is certainly real (try holding the poker by the hot end), but it exists *in* the iron and cannot be separated from it.

This idea of one reality or nature existing *in* another lies at the basis of John's christology. He did not invent it. The credit for that goes to Leontius of Byzantium, a sixth-century anti-monophysite theologian of whom hardly anything is known. For John and Leontius, Christ's humanity is the 'redhotness' and the iron is his divinity. Christ's perfect humanity was included *within* the divinity, but it was not lost or swallowed up or consumed or annihilated. Just as the iron and the 'redhotness' are both real, united, yet distinct, so too the humanity and divinity of Christ are both real, united, yet distinct.

Furthermore, because Christ took upon himself human *nature* rather than a human *person*, he has restored to all of us the possibility of deification. He assumed the whole of humanity, not just one individual. Had it been just one individual, what Christ achieved would have been limited to himself, but that is not the case. Jesus was the Second Adam, and just as the First Adam was the root and foundation of our physical existence, so the Second Adam is the root and foundation of our spiritual existence. We, who were born in Adam, have been reborn in Christ. He is the beginning of the new creation, and we are created anew in him.

If, then, Christ's human nature is true human nature, does this mean that his humanity is identical to ours? It does not. As the fathers at Chalcedon had said, he is 'like us in all things *except for sin*'. So how are we to explain his sinlessness? John does so by pointing out that in every human being there are two wills. Men and women, he says, were not only created good, but were also created in the image and likeness of God, and this means that we have a natural tendency to turn back towards God and to do his will. This tendency is what John calls our *natural* will, for we possess this will as a consequence of our nature as innately good human beings. We can feel our natural will in action in the promptings of our conscience. Every time we say: 'I know I *shouldn't* do this, but . . .', it's the natural will that is acting.

In addition to our natural will, however, we also possess free-will. John calls this the determining or deciding will, since we use it to determine the direction we will take: whether to God or away from him. Our natural will says: 'I know I shouldn't'; our determining will says: 'but I'm going to anyway'. In the First Adam, the determining will desired what was contrary to the divine will (and contrary to his own natural will), and that is what led to his transgression and our problems. In the Second Adam, this was not the case. Why not?

Let us remember two things. Firstly, Christ was born of a pure Virgin by the power of the Holy Spirit[3], and it was the unanimous opinion of the fathers that the sin of Adam—original sin—was not transmitted to him. He, who was born in a unique way, was uniquely free from the stain of sin that contaminates all of us. Secondly, the Divine Logos assumed a human body and soul at the very instant of conception. There was no time for soul and body to interact, and no time for the soul to use its determining will—its free-will—to develop an independent personality. So when the divinity assumed the humanity, (i) it assumed a humanity which had not been corrupted by the sin of

3. The question of Mary's sinlessness and the development of the doctrine of her Immaculate Conception will be discussed in the next chapter.

Adam, and (ii) it assumed a humanity whose human free-will was immediately put into the service of the divine will. Christ's free-will, therefore, never rebelled against the divine will and never led him into sin. His human will, though real, was no more than an instrument of the divine will and wholly obedient to it.

We see, then, that in the view of John of Damascus, Christ had a human will, but that it was always passive in relation to the divine will. The divine will always won. So what about human emotions? Did Christ have passions? Did he feel things in the same way as we do? And if so, did his free-will ever tempt him to sin? John's answer is simple: it all depends on what you mean by emotions. There are two kinds of emotions: some are natural and blameless; some are unnatural and culpable. Examples of blameless emotions are hunger, thirst, tiredness, sorrow, fatigue, tears, fear, anger, dread, anguish, comfort, pleasure, and delight. The culpable emotions are those which are 'contrary to nature' and thereby contrary to the will of God. The most obvious of these are lust and greed. We must also note, however, that those emotions which are blameless can easily be transformed into those which are not. Hunger, for example, can become gluttony; pleasure can become hedonism; fear can become cowardice; anger can become sadism. It was by giving in to these culpable emotions that the First Adam fell.

When Christ became human, he assumed the natural and blameless emotions—he felt pain, thirst, sorrow, and so on—but not those which were culpable. In other words, the humanity Christ assumed was the humanity of Adam as it had been *before* the Fall, when Adam, too, lived and felt 'naturally', i.e. in accordance with God's will. Indeed, since Christ is the Second Adam, this was only fitting. Furthermore, said John, the idea that Christ's humanity, though perfectly real, was that of Adam before the Fall provides us with a clear explanation of Christ's attitude to sex.

It was the view of a number of respectable eastern theologians (e.g. Gregory of Nyssa, John Chrysostom, Maximus the Confessor, and Symeon the New Theologian) that procreation by sexual intercourse had not been God's original intention. John shares this view. Adam and Eve in Eden did not lust after each other, and if they had not fallen, the distinction between male and female might have been miraculously abolished. The human race would then have reproduced itself in the same manner as the angels, though John does not provide us with details of the process. Sexual desire, therefore, was a passion that was not felt until our first parents ate the forbidden fruit and it was not a natural part of unfallen human nature. But since the human nature assumed by Christ was that of Adam as it had been *before* the Fall, it follows that in Christ there was no sexual desire and he was never tempted to sexual sins. This is just as well, for if he had been tempted and had fallen, and if his consort had produced a boy, we would have been in the curious position of having a second Son and a fourth member of the Trinity. That, says John, is theologically impossible. If his consort had produced a girl, the situation would have been even more interesting, but that is a possibility John quietly ignores.

One final question remains to be answered in this eastern understanding of the Incarnation. If Jesus was both true God and true man, and if God is omniscient, how are we to understand the statement in Luke's gospel that Jesus 'advanced in wisdom' (Lk 2:52), or, in Mark's gospel, his admission of ignorance as to the time of the end of the world (Mk 13:32)? How could Christ have been omniscient and ignorant at the same instant? John's answer is logical, but although it was shared by the great majority of byzantine authors, it remains unsatisfactory.

Jesus, says John, was never ignorant. It is true that the human nature he assumed was possessed of human ignorance, but as a result of its union with the omniscient Word, it was enriched with divine knowledge and thereby transcended its human limitations. Jesus of Nazareth, therefore, was indeed omniscient. But if he were omniscient, how can Luke say that he 'advanced in wisdom'? He only advanced, John tells us, in the sense that as he grew up, there was a progressive manifestation of his omniscience that kept pace with his bodily growth. When this achieved its fulfilment John does not say, but it certainly occurred long before the commencement of his ministry. If Christ professed ignorance after that, it was only because he did not wish to manifest his omniscience. It was something done for the sake of the disciples, a mere pedagogical technique.

Not all byzantine authors agreed with this. Some did maintain that Jesus really was ignorant about certain matters, but they were quite unable to reconcile this with his divinity and the fact that there was, after all, only one acting person of the incarnate Christ. They recognized a problem, but they were unable to provide a solution. To say that Christ was ignorant in his humanity, but that his humanity was separate from his divinity, was Nestorianism. To maintain that there was no distinction between the humanity and divinity, and that Christ was simply omniscient, was to confuse the natures and resurrect the old heresy of Eutyches.[4]

The views of John of Damascus were not the only views entertained in the greek east, but they do represent the majority opinion. They also give rise to considerable difficulties. John provides us with an asymmetrical or unbalanced christology, a christology that is heavily weighted towards the Divine Word. Yes, there is a human nature, but not a human person. Yes, there is a human will, but it is no more than an instrument of the Divine Will. Yes, Christ took upon himself humanity, but humanity as it had been before the Fall. Yes, Jesus felt emotion, but not the emotions connected with sex—and that, after all, is where we find most of our problems. The analogy we used earlier still holds true: if I'm holding a red-hot poker and someone asks me what I have in my hand, I reply: 'A poker'. I don't say: 'A redhotness'. Similarly, in the byzantine doctrine of the Incarnation, it is the Divine Logos that predominates, and although we can never accuse John or his followers of denying the humanity of Christ, that humanity certainly plays a subordinate role. Whether the western theologians could do any better is a matter we must now consider.

Let us begin by going to Spain and investigating a heresy. It seems that in the eighth century there were certain heretical

4. See *Cloud* 117–8.

view in circulation in Spain that denied the true humanity of the incarnate Christ. These views may have been associated with some form of dualism and, as we saw in Chapter VI, christian dualists always tended to be docetic. Whatever it was that was being taught, it caused the archbishop of Toledo, Elipandus (c.718–802), together with his friend Felix, bishop of Urgel (a much more competent theologian who died in 818), to assert a strongly contrary view. The humanity was fully real, they said, and Jesus of Nazareth was not just the Divine Word appearing to be human. In him there was the fullness of divinity and the fullness of humanity, and between the divinity and humanity there was no confusion at all.

Felix explained the theory by carefully distinguishing between the Divine Word, who alone can be called the Son of God in the strict sense, and the fully human Jesus who was born of Mary. The human Jesus was not *by nature* the Son of God, but because of his association with the Divine Word, he was *adopted* as Son of God and thereby came to merit the title not by nature, but by grace. It follows from this that we must distinguish between two sorts of Sonship: natural Sonship, which is applicable only to the divinity in Christ, and adoptive Sonship, which applies to the humanity. This theory of the Incarnation, therefore, came to be known as adoptionism.

When did this adoption occur? According to Felix, it took place in two stages. The first stage was Jesus's baptism in the Jordan when a voice came from heaven saying: 'This is my beloved Son with whom I am well pleased' (Mt 3:17). The second stage occurred at the resurrection, and, according to Felix, it was this event to which the words in Psalm 2:7 referred: 'You are my Son, today I have begotten you'.

It is obvious that this view of the Incarnation would prove unacceptable to the church. It distinguishes too clearly between the humanity and divinity in Christ and comes close to separating the natures.[5] Elipandus and Felix were, in fact, accused

5. See *Cloud* 102–3.

of Nestorianism, and although they could defend themselves against the accusation, their views did tend in that direction. Furthermore, the humanity they were dealing with was not just human nature, but an independent human *person*. If the first stage of Jesus's adoption as Son of God did not occur until his baptism, he had plenty of time to develop his own personality, and if this were so, all sorts of problems arise. Could Christ have sinned before his adoption as Son of God? *Did* he sin before his adoption? What happened to his personality after his adoption? And so on. As we saw above, the general tendency among all theologians was to restrict the humanity of Christ to human *nature*, and thereby avoid the difficulties of dealing with the assumption of a human person.

Other theologians pointed out that although adoptionism may have prevented any confusion between the divinity and humanity in Christ, it did not prevent a confusion between Christ and us. If the incarnate Christ had merely been adopted as Son of God, how do we explain such passages as Galatians 4:5 which speaks of *our* adoption as children of God? If Jesus is adopted and if we are adopted, we are both adopted, and there is no real distinction between Jesus's relationship to God and ours. In this case, Christ has been too 'humanized', and in emphasizing his similarity to us, we have lost sight of his true divinity.

It is not surprising, therefore, that adoptionism was condemned at a number of synods held in the last decade of the eighth century. There were occasional resurgences in later times (there was one in Constantinople in the twelfth century when a monk named Nilus was condemned for adoptionist teachings), but in the extreme form in which it had been stated by Felix, adoptionism soon faded away. The essential principle behind it, however, lasted much longer, and there is no doubt that adoptionist ideas did have certain advantages. Adoptionism provided an easy way of understanding the Incarnation: Mary conceives an ordinary human baby who is then assumed by the Divine Logos. It recognized a human personality in Christ (though it did not know quite what to do with it), and thereby did away with some of the asymmetry which appears in the view of John of Damascus. It also put the divinity and humanity in Christ on more of an equal footing. In a modified form, therefore, adoptionism was to survive well into the twelfth century and, as the theory of the *homo assumptus*, was the first of the three prevailing theories of the Incarnation summarized by Peter Lombard in a famous section of his *Sentences*.

The term *homo assumptus* means 'man assumed', and according to this view, Mary conceived the child Jesus as a real human being, complete with body and soul, and this human child was immediately assumed by the Divine Logos before any human personality had time to develop. In this way we avoid the problems posed by pure adoptionism. But by this act of assumption, the humanity of Christ became possessed of all the divine knowledge, wisdom, and power of God himself. He *became* God, in fact, though by grace and not by nature. Similarly, because the divinity became one single person with the humanity, we can also say that God *became* a man. He did not just appear to be human, he did not just indwell humanity, but was actually transformed into a real, living, mortal human being.

Lombard then points out various objections to this theory. By far the most significant is that it tends to lead to a confusion of natures. By maintaining that God actually *becomes* a man, we imply that the unchangeable and eternal Deity has become changeable and subject to time. That is logically impossible: you cannot both have your cake and eat it. And if we believe that the human Jesus possessed all the wisdom and power of God, can we really be talking about humanity in any real sense? Lombard himself obviously has no time for the theory of *homo assumptus*, but it seems to have been widely accepted in the twelfth century.

Lombard then moves on to consider the second theory of the Incarnation: subsistence theory. This theory is virtually identical to that of John of Damascus, but this is not surprising. We mentioned earlier that by the twelfth century, John's impressive summary of the Orthodox faith was available in latin translation and that Lombard himself had been influenced by it. Here we see solid evidence for that influence. Before the Incarnation, says Lombard (quoting John), there was only the one nature of the Divine Logos, but at the moment of the Incarnation, there came into being a 'composite person' (again the term is John's) composed of two natures or three substances. The two natures were divinity and humanity; the three substances were divinity, the human soul, and human flesh; and the 'composite person' was Jesus of Nazareth, God incarnate. But if you cannot understand this rationally, says Lombard, don't let that worry you: it is actually inexplicable. Subsistence theory, therefore, is no more than a latinized version of the views of John of Damascus, but despite his admiration for John's work, Lombard was well aware that subsistence theory was not without its problems.

The major difficulty with the theory is that it implies that Christ was made up of various separate parts, rather like a jigsaw puzzle. The problem occurs with any theory that asserts that Christ was 'composite'. The overall picture may be clear, but you can still see the separate pieces, and in these circumstances it is unclear to what extent we can really refer to the incarnate Christ as 'one person'. In both English and Latin, the term 'composition' is not normally used for something that is a real unity, and if Christ is not a real unity of Godhead and manhood, are we not implying a *separation* of the natures? This is certainly possible, so let us see whether the third theory is any more satisfactory.

This is the theory of the *homo habitus*, which we might translate as 'the garment of manhood'. This view is intended to do away with any idea that God was actually transformed or changed into a human being (the first theory), and it removes any concept of Christ being made up of various independent bits (the second theory). According to this third theory, after Mary had conceived Jesus, the Divine Word took over the manhood like a garment, clothing itself in humanity so that Christ could appear on earth in an appropriate form. The human soul and human flesh acted as a sort of covering for the Divine Word, much as our clothes act as a covering for us, and just as the Divine Word remained unaffected by the garment it put on, so the garment was unaffected by the Divine Word.

This approach is certainly easy to understand, but there are obvious problems associated with it. To think of Christ's humanity as no more than a pair of trousers is clearly dangerous. Trousers come off and go on at a moment's notice, and there is really no unity between my trousers and me. It is true that I rarely appear in public without them, but trousers do not make the man. If the connection between Christ's humanity and his divinity is no more than the connection between me and my clothes, then it is a very loose sort of connection, and it is better described as conjunction rather than union.[6] In other words, the *homo habitus* theory undoubtedly leans in the direction of Nestorianism.

Furthermore, it is a perilously short step from saying that Christ's humanity is no more than a garment to saying that it has no proper reality, that it is really nothing. If I am summoned to appear in court for some misdemeanour and send my trousers in my place, it does me no good. The real me has not appeared. The real me is not there. So if the humanity of Christ is no more than a garment, is the garment really Christ? This is no trivial question, for it bears directly on our redemption. If a mere garment, not the true God-man, was nailed to the cross at Calvary, then what was accomplished? It will not come as a surprise, therefore, to learn that 'Nihilianism', the doctrine that Christ, in his human nature, was nothing (*nihil* in Latin), but that the whole of his essential being was contained in his divinity, was condemned by Pope Alexander III in 1170 and again in 1177.

In his *Sentences*, Lombard has presented us with three different theories of the Incarnation. He has pointed out their advantages and disadvantages, but he has left it to us to decide which we prefer. The Greeks had already decided—they had chosen subsistence theory—but Lombard's account makes it clear that in the west there was a wealth of dispute and disagreement over the relative merits of the various views.

As the twelfth century merged into the thirteenth, the first and third theories gradually gave way to the second. The idea

6. See *Cloud* 110.

of God actually being transformed into a man (the first theory) posed uncomfortable problems, and the concept of God simply wearing his humanity like a coat (the third theory) had become too closely associated with Nihilianism. In addition to this, the growing influence in the west of John of Damascus played an important role in popularizing subsistence theory, and after it had been taken up and elaborated by Thomas Aquinas, it became the predominant view of western theologians from the thirteenth century to the end of the Middle Ages. Let us see, then, what Aquinas says on this matter and how he deals with questions relating to the personality of Christ, his human will, his sinlessness, his emotions, knowledge, and ignorance. We shall find that his views are often similar to those of John of Damascus, and it is as pleasant as it is unusual to find an area in which west and east are so much in agreement.

At the very instant of Incarnation, says Thomas, the divinity and humanity became one 'composite person', subsisting in two natures and three substances; and at the precise moment of this union, the Divine Word hindered or impeded the manhood from arriving at any independent personality. Furthermore, just as the human soul in us is the link between our material bodies and the immaterial God, so in Christ the human soul acted as the link between the flesh and the Divine Word. Christ, therefore, was a single composite person, just as John of Damascus had said.

Aquinas also follows John in what he has to say about Christ's human will, though he changes John's terminology and expresses his ideas in the language of thirteenth-century scholasticism. Human will is twofold: one part of it naturally tends to do good and act in accordance with God's will; the other part, following the laws of fallen human nature, prefers to go its own way. But since Christ was conceived without original sin and is unfallen, the two wills in Christ coincide; and if ever a conflict should occur, the human will would be no more than an instrument of the divine will.

Again like John, Aquinas maintains that Christ was subject to the blameless or sinless emotions, but that these never changed into their culpable or sinful counterparts. Aquinas differs from

John, however, in laying much more stress on the role of human reason. The appetites and desires of the senses, he says (following Aristotle), are natural to all human beings, and since Christ was truly human, his flesh naturally desired food, drink, and sleep—everything, in fact, that could *reasonably* be desired. It is only when desires break free from the reins of reason that they become sinful, and in Christ this never occurred. His natural emotions were always subject to his human reason, and his reason was always subject to God. It follows from this that in him there was no lust and he was never guilty of sexual sins. Let us consider the argument.

To begin with, Aquinas does not agree with John that before the Fall Adam and Eve would have produced offspring without sexual intercourse. Why else would God have created two different sexes and why else would he have provided them with genitals?[7] No, he says, the manner of conceiving would still have been by copulation, and copulation would still have been enjoyable, but the enjoyment would have been tempered by reason. This is not to say that the pleasure would have been diminished (Aquinas is here disagreeing with Bonaventure and Alexander of Hales), but the natural desire for pleasure would not have gone beyond the bounds of reason. In other words, you don't have to be a glutton to enjoy good food. But since pleasure that transgresses the boundaries of reason is lust, it follows that in Eden there would have been fruitfulness without lust.

As a consequence of the Fall, however, human beings have inherited original sin and have been burdened with concupiscence of the flesh—an inordinate, possessive, self-centered, grasping for pleasure and gratification—and this inevitably leads them into sin. But since Christ was conceived without original sin, and since his emotions were always subject to reason (and his reason always subject to God), in him there was no concupiscence

---

7. John's answer is that our genitals were given us by God because he knew in advance that we would fall, and would therefore have need of them *after* our expulsion from Eden.

or 'spark of sin'. As John of Damascus had said, quite rightly in Aquinas's opinion, the human nature of Christ was that of Adam as it had been before the Fall, but in Christ, innocence was combined with the fullness of grace and the perfection of virtue and knowledge. Does this then mean that the human Jesus was not only sinless but also omniscient? Let us consider the question.

In typically scholastic fashion, Aquinas distinguishes three sorts of knowledge in Christ: beatific knowledge, infused knowledge, and acquired knowledge. In his *beatific* knowledge, which is the knowledge possessed by God the Son, Christ is wholly omniscient. As a consequence of the union of God and man, this beatific knowledge is infused into Christ's human nature, but because he is limited as a human being, he cannot contain all of it. How much can he contain? By his *infused* knowledge, Christ knows everything that human beings can possibly know, whether by reason or by revelation. He therefore knows all that has been, is, and will be, but not what *could* be or what *might* be. That is known only to God and is a matter of beatific knowledge. As for his *acquired* knowledge, this refers to everything that can be known by the use of the human intellect alone.

So the answer to the question: 'Was Christ ignorant?' is both Yes and No. In his acquired knowledge he would have been ignorant of the time of the end of the world, but not in his infused or beatific knowledge. In his infused knowledge he would have been ignorant of what *might* be, but not in his beatific knowledge. But since there was only one person of the incarnate Christ in whom all three forms of knowledge coexisted, and since we are not going to become Nestorians and separate the natures, it follows that Christ was not ignorant of anything. 'Just as the fullness of grace and virtue in Christ excludes the spark of sin, so the fullness of knowledge excludes ignorance, which is the opposite of knowledge. Therefore, just as in Christ there was no spark of sin, so there was in him no ignorance.'[8]

8. Thomas Aquinas, *Summa theologiae* 3a.15.3; Blackfriars ed. 49: 198.

How, then, did he 'advance in wisdom and stature'? He could not have advanced in beatific knowledge, for beatific knowledge is omniscience. Nor did he advance in infused knowledge, for he knew from the beginning all that any human being could possibly know. But acquired knowledge, says Aquinas, is the product of the active intellect, and the active intellect does not learn things all at once (*simul*), but step by step (*successive*).[9] Only in his acquired knowledge, therefore, did Christ 'advance' in accordance with his age, but in those forms of knowledge which were a direct result of his union with the Divine Word, no advance was either possible or conceivable.

In general, the views of Aquinas on the 'how' of the Incarnation are representative of the west in the thirteenth century and, in due course, would become the established views of Roman Catholicism. It must be remembered, however, that they represent the end of a long period of intense speculation and argument, and however meticulous may be the logic of Aquinas, the fact remains that 'unconfused union' is not an expression that is really susceptible to logical analysis. Nor are the ideas of Aquinas much of an improvement on those of John of Damascus. The essential problems still remain unsolved and the human mind remains incapable of providing a satisfactory solution.

Let us therefore leave this examination of the ultimately incomprehensible and concentrate on matters closer to home. Whatever view we may have as to the 'how' and 'why' of the Incarnation, one essential fact remains: had it not been for Mary, the Incarnation would not have taken place at all, and it seems appropriate therefore to turn our attention from the Son of God to the Mother of God and investigate the attitude of medieval theologians to Mary the God-bearer.

9. *Ibid.*, 3a.12.2; Blackfriars 49: 144.

XIII-1 The Annunciation was a common and beloved scene in the high Middle Ages. In this thirteenth-century manuscript, the initial D (*Deus*) is illuminated with the angel Gabriel, who holds in his left hand the scroll of scripture announcing the birth of the Saviour, while his right hand points to Mary, the chosen vessel for the Incarnation. Artists of this period usually portray Mary in a receptive position, graciously accepting the angel's news, although in later centuries she is sometimes shown recoiling from the idea. Here Mary acquiesces to the will of God, albeit a bit timidly. The book she holds is the New Testament, in which she, as the Virgin Mother of Christ, will play an essential role.

Annunciation, thirteenth century.
Sacramentary from Paris, adapted for Senlis.
Paris, Bibliothèque Sainte-Geneviève, MS. 102, f° 291v.
Photo: CNRS (IRHT).

XIII

The Veneration of the Virgin

THERE CAN BE NO more obvious place to begin an examination of the role of Mary in medieval Christianity than with her title. In Greek, the use of the word *theotokos* or 'God-bearer' dates back to the early years of the fourth century. In Latin, *Mater Dei* or 'Mother of God' is first recorded in the writings of Ambrose of Milan (c.339–97). Of the two terms, *theotokos* is not only the older but was also the focus of one of the most violent conflicts to trouble the early church: the christological controversy of the fifth century. We have already discussed this in A *Cloud of Witnesses*[1] and there is no need to repeat all that information

1. See *Cloud* Chapters IX-X.

243

here. Nestorius, it may be remembered, had been accused by Cyril of Alexandria of refusing to use the term *theotokos* and of thereby implying that Jesus was a mere man. The accusation, as we know, was unjustified, but it precipitated the third and fourth ecumenical councils—the Council of Ephesus in 431 and the Council of Chalcedon in 451—and at both of those councils the title was given the official approval of the universal church.

It is an important title, since it makes it clear that the veneration paid to Mary is not paid to her in isolation. It is, in fact, a christological rather than a mariological title. Mary is venerated as the Mother *of God*, and as such, veneration of the Virgin is an acknowledgement of the reality of the humanity of Christ. The title was always popular, and its popularity played a major role in Cyril's victory over Nestorius. It was just too widely used to be challenged.

Mary's motherhood, however, was always recognised to be unique, for she, alone among women, was both mother and virgin at one and the same time; and just as the medieval church inherited the concept of Mary as *theotokos* from the early fathers, so it also inherited the idea of her perpetual virginity. In Greek, the title *aeiparthenos* or 'ever-virgin' had a history that was just as long and just as respectable as *theotokos*. It had been used by Athanasius the Great and had been given conciliar approval at the fifth ecumenical council held at Constantinople in 553. It had not, however, gone unchallenged. The fathers, both eastern and western, were united in their belief that Mary had *conceived* as a virgin, but whether she had retained that virginity through the birth of Jesus was another matter.

A few, such as the latin Tertullian and the greek Origen, refused to accept the idea on the grounds that it implied docetism. If the flesh and body of Christ were truly human, how could a human body have been born from a woman without breaking the hymen? But their concerns, though justified, were those of a small minority, and most theologians were prepared to accept the doctrine of Mary's *in partu* and *post partum* virginity as a

XIII-2 These larger-than-lifesize limestone sculptures of the annunciate angel and Mary by the Joseph Master are located on the façade of Reims Cathedral, arguably the most important cathedral in France, because the kings of France were crowned there. On the left is the famous 'smiling angel' whose mirthful face with its crinkled eyes, kinked hair tied back with a sweatband, and jauntily turned head contrasts with Mary's serene pose, sculpted by a different artist in the 'Amiens style'. They were once painted, and are part of a series of statues which pay homage to both the Virgin Mary and Christ with scenes from the infancy depicted on the central portal of the west façade.

Annunciation, c. 1240.
Angel by the 'Joseph Master'; Mary in 'Amiens style'.
Cathedral of Reims (France), façade, central portal, right jamb.
Photo: James Austin.

matter of faith.[2] The earliest explicit witness to the idea in the west is probably Zeno of Verona who died c.375, but once the doctrine had received the unqualified support of Augustine and a number of popes, it rapidly became the official teaching of the western church. By the Middle Ages it was unquestioned, and the prophecy in Ezekiel 44:2 was universally accepted in the west as referring to this miraculous event: 'This gate shall be shut; it shall not be opened and no-one shall pass through it, for the Lord, the God of Israel, has entered by it; therefore it shall remain shut'.

How it was possible for Mary to give birth and retain her virginity at the same time was another matter. A twelfth-century poem incorrectly attributed to Bernard of Clairvaux likened Jesus's birth to the light shining from a star. As the star puts forth its light yet remains unsullied, so the Mother of God put forth the light of the world and likewise retained her purity. This idea was then elaborated by suggesting that just as a starbeam or sunbeam can shine through a window without breaking the glass, so the Son of Man could be born from his mother without destroying her virginity. And just as the light passes through the window without causing the window any pain, so Mary suffered no pain when she brought forth Jesus. By the thirteenth century, these ideas had proved very popular and were very widely accepted.

How, then, do we explain those passages in the gospels that refer to Jesus's brothers and sisters? How can multiple siblings be reconciled with Mary's *post partum* virginity? This was no problem. The so-called brothers and sisters of Jesus were either Joseph's children by an earlier marriage, or they were Jesus's cousins or adopted siblings. The first view was generally preferred by the Greeks (together with an occasional Latin, such as Ambrose or Hilary of Poitiers) and it explains why Joseph is often depicted iconographically as being much older than Mary. The

---

2. *In partu* = 'in the act of giving birth'; *post partum* = 'after the act of giving birth'.

second view was that of Jerome, who prized virginity so much that he thought it inappropriate to restrict it to Mary alone. Joseph, too, should be a virgin, and the idea of a previous marriage was unnecessary and irreligious. It was this idea that became standard in the west.

In the matter of virginity, Mary stood in marked contrast to Eve. What the former had retained forever, the latter had lost in sin. Eve, with Adam, had been tempted in Eden and had fallen, and after their expulsion from Paradise, stained and corrupted with iniquity, they had sexual intercourse for the first time and produced Cain.[3] As a consequence of Eve's transgression, she and her female descendants (Mary alone excepted) would have to suffer the pains of childbirth, and all of us would be subject to concupiscence and the lusts of the flesh.

Mary, however, not only conceived Jesus as a virgin, but retained her virginity even after his birth; and whereas Eve, while still a virgin, had been disobedient and had fallen, Mary, a virgin forever, had been totally obedient. 'Behold the handmaid of the Lord', she had said to Gabriel, 'be it done to me according to your word' (Lk 1:38). It was only natural, therefore, that just as the church saw in Christ a second and perfect Adam, it would also see in Mary a second and perfect Eve.

At the basis of this idea is a theory we discussed in A *Cloud of Witnesses*: the theory of recapitulation.[4] It is a simple idea that had its origins in Saint Paul, its development in Justin Martyr, and found its perfection in Irenaeus of Lyons, who died c.200. According to this theory, everything that the First Adam did wrong has been cancelled out by what the Second Adam did right. The First Adam was disobedient, sinful, and imperfect; the Second Adam was obedient, sinless, and perfect. The First Adam was tempted and succumbed to temptation; the Second Adam was tempted and overcame the Tempter. 'For since death came through a man, the resurrection of the dead has also come

3. See Gen 3:16 and 4:1.
4. See *Cloud* 96–8.

through a man. For as all die in Adam, so shall all be made alive in Christ' (1 Cor 15: 21–2).

Theologically, of course, there is no need for this theory to be applied to Eve. When Christ became human, he took upon himself humanity, not just masculinity, and when he cancelled out the sins of Adam he did not save only the male members of the race. But it is easy to see how the principle of recapitulation would have been applied to Eve, and we have evidence for it from a very early date. Justin Martyr, who was executed c.165, was one of the first to set out the doctrine. When Eve was still a virgin and incorrupt, he tells us, she conceived the word spoken by the serpent and brought forth disobedience and death. When Mary was still a virgin and incorrupt, she conceived the word spoken by the angel and obediently brought forth the Saviour of the World, the Saviour who destroyed both death and the devil.

Following Justin, both eastern and western writers regularly cited the parallel and devised a number of neat phrases to express it. Through a virgin we were expelled from Paradise, says John Chrysostom, and through a virgin we have found eternal life. Jerome is even more economical: through Eve, death; through Mary, life. The former drove us from Paradise; the latter leads us to heaven. Through Eve, we are told by Bernard of Clairvaux, folly was transmitted to all her descendants, but now the Virgin has brought us wisdom.

In the west, this saving work of Mary could be encapsulated very neatly in a pun. In Latin, Eve is *Eva*. What happens if we reverse the letters of *Eva*? We get *Ave*, the first word spoken by Gabriel in his salutation to the virgin: *Ave, gratia plena*, 'Hail, full of grace' (Lk 1:28). Mary, therefore, has reversed the work of Eve and, through her perfect obedience, has cooperated with her Son in the work of redemption. It is this cooperation which leads us to our next consideration: Mary as *mediatrix* or 'mediatress' and her role in bringing about the salvation of the world.

The origins of this idea lie far back in the second century. Irenaeus of Lyons speaks of Mary as becoming, by her obedience, a cause of salvation for herself and for us, but he does not use the word *mesitis*, the greek equivalent of the latin *mediatrix*. Its

XIII-3 The central event of Mary's life was the nativity of Christ, here combined with the adoration of the shepherds. This painting shows a combination of biblical narrative and apocryphal stories (the midwife holding out her hand, withered as punishment for doubting Mary's continued virginity after Christ's birth). The scene is set in a naturalistic world that shows a new interest in daily life—that of Flanders in the early fifteenth century, with a bounty of details: the shabby frame structure of the animal shelter, trees newly pruned in winter, wattle fences, brick houses, fishing boats. In contrast are the jeweled dresses of the midwives, the colorful angels, and the Holy Family in the center, with Mary in a copious white robe, and a tired and aged Joseph holding a candle that seems to shed no light at all compared to the golden rays emanating from the Christ Child.

Aдoration of the Shepherds, c. 1420.
Robert Campin (Master of Flémalle), (1378/79–1444).
Musée des Beaux-Arts, Dijon.
Photo: Musée des Beaux-Arts de Dijon.

first appearance seems to have been in the middle of the fifth
century, but it was not until the eighth century that the title
was used freely and the doctrine taught in a clear and explicit
manner. The person most responsible for this was Andrew of
Crete who, of all the early fathers, was the most prolix in his
veneration of the Virgin. He was born c.660 in Damascus, trained
as a monk in Jerusalem and Constantinople, and eventually
appointed archbishop of Gortyna in Crete. He died in 740.

Andrew loves to dwell on the concept of Mary as *theotokos*,
telling us how she bore him who bears all things, how she
nourished him who would nourish all creatures, how she carried
in her womb him whom the whole world could not contain, how
she, who was created, gave birth to her Creator. He teaches, as
we might expect, her perpetual virginity, and he calls her the
mediatrix of law and grace. She is blessed in heaven and glorified
on earth. She is the mother of life. Through her fragrance, all
things have been sanctified. Through her, sin has been abolished
and the woes brought upon us by our first parents have been
transformed into joy. She, who is the mother of the Maker, is the
mediation between his sublimity and the lowly nature of corrupt
and corruptible flesh.

After Andrew, Mary's mediation became a standard theme in
eastern theology and reached its culmination in the fourteenth
century in the startling ideas of a follower and defender of
Gregory Palamas: Theophanes, archbishop of Nicaea, who died
in 1381. Theophanes likens Mary to the earth, from which grew
the Second Adam, and to heaven, the very throne of God. In the
view of Theophanes, just as there would have been no Christ
without Mary, so it is impossible to approach Christ without
Mary. Mary is the way to Christ, and no human being nor any
angel who wishes to participate in the divine gifts which flow
from the Son of God—in other words, no one who wishes to be
deified—can come to these gifts save through Mary. If Christ
is the head of the church, Mary is the neck which leads to that
head. Through his ineffable goodness, Christ wished to be called
our brother and to bestow upon us the uncreated energies of
the Divine Spirit which make us his siblings (here we recognise

the voice of Gregory Palamas), but according to Theophanes, Christ bestows on Mary the power to distribute these gifts, and it therefore follows that while we are deified in and through Christ, that deification can be applied to us only through his mother.

Theophanes, in fact, goes even further than this and suggests that as a consequence of the intimacy of the union between Christ and Mary, certain of his attributes and titles have been passed on to her. Mary, it seems, has the same sort of relationship to the Divine Word as the Divine Word has to the humanity it assumed. Thus, we find him referring to her as omnipotent and omniscient, and even as God and Lord and King of kings. And if this were not enough, he goes on to raise Mary almost to the level of a fourth member of the Trinity. She is linked to the Father by their common Son (Theophanes actually calls her the Father's spouse); she is linked to the Son because she is his mother; she is linked to the Holy Spirit because she was conceived by the Spirit from barren parents (a common byzantine idea which we shall discuss shortly), and because the Spirit was actually more present in her than in heaven.

It is obvious that some of Theophanes' ideas are theologically suspect, but they well represent the esteem in which Mary was held in late Byzantium. This is clearly reflected both in the Orthodox liturgy and in Orthodox icons, and by the eighth century in the east and the eleventh in the west, it had become commonly accepted that Christ was to be approached through his mother. She is our intercessor in heaven and our representative with her Son. 'Do not weep', she says to Adam and Eve in a sixth-century greek hymn, 'I shall become your advocate with my Son. Do not be sad, for I have brought joy into the world.'

In the west, the first occurrence of the term *mediatrix* appears to be in a sixth-century text, but, as we mentioned above, the real development of the doctrine did not take place until the eleventh century, rather later than in the east. An eleventh-century liturgical passage for the Feast of the Assumption refers to Mary as 'Our *mediatrix*, who, after God, is our only hope', and asks her to present us to her Son so that we may sing Alleluias in the heavenly courts. And according to the benedictine Peter Damian

XIII-4 The privileged place accorded Christ's mother in this lavishly colored illustration indicates the devotion she inspired among Cistercians. She stands at the top of a tree of the sleeping Jesse (not shown here), in whose lineage were the ancestors of Christ. Mary wears a long emerald-green dress, red tunic with jewelled border, and blue mantle; a purple veil covers her head. The Christ Child clings tenderly to her, and angels proffer gifts. The flowering rod in her left hand is proof of fulfillment of the words of the prophet Isaiah (11:1, 10) 'and there shall come forth a rod out of the stem of Jesse.' The dove of the Holy Spirit perched on her nimbus confirms the reign of God on earth through the incarnation of Christ. While this standing figure owes much to byzantine painting, the rather humorous presence of the dove, the graceful poses of the angels, and a suggestion of movement with the slight bend of Marys's left foot breaks the rigid frontal pose seen in byzantine icons.

Virgin of Cîteaux, c. 1120–1133.
Saint Jerome's Commentary on Isaiah.
Dijon, Bibliothèque municipale MS 129, f° 4v.
Photo: CNRS (IRHT).

(1007–72), a famous monastic and ecclesiastical reformer, since it was through Mary that the Son of God condescended to come down to us, so we must come to him through her. The principle is not difficult to appreciate, and, in the east, it found its clearest expression in the sermons of Theophanes of Nicaea, and in the west, in the writings of Bernard of Clairvaux.

Mary, says Bernard, was the way in which the Saviour came to us. Only through her, therefore, can we ascend to him who, through her, descended to us. In this way, he who through her was given to us, might, through her through whom he was given, take us to himself. Bernard summarizes the matter thus: 'Let us venerate Mary with the whole of our hearts, with all our most intimate affections and desires, for this is the will [of God], who has willed that we have everything through Mary'.[5]

> The royal virgin (he says) needs no false honour, for she is abundantly endowed with true titles of honour and marks of dignity. Honour her indeed for the purity of her flesh and the holiness of her life. Marvel at the fruitfulness of a virgin. Venerate her divine offspring. Extol her who knew neither concupiscence in conception nor pain in giving birth. Proclaim her as revered by the angels, desired by the nations, foreknown by patriarchs and prophets, chosen from among all, placed before all. Glorify the one who found grace, the *mediatrix* of salvation, the restorer of the ages. Finally, exalt her who was exalted above the choirs of angels to the realms of heaven.[6]

Furthermore, says Bernard, it was only fitting that someone so pure and so holy, the very Queen of virgins, should, by a unique privilege of sanctity, lead a life that was free from all sin. She, alone of all women, was 'full of grace' (Lk 1:28), and where there is truly fullness of grace, what room can there be for iniquity? Most, though not all, theologians agreed with this, and the belief that Mary did not sin was not a matter of major dispute. A few of the earlier greek fathers had expressed doubts on the matter, and no less an authority than John Chrysostom thought that her intervention at the marriage at Cana indicated a love of vainglory. But this view was not shared by John's successors and it was emphatically denied in the west. By the Middle Ages, both east and west were in agreement that while Mary was alive, she had remained without sin. Far more troublesome was the question of whether she had been *born* sinless, or whether, like all other human beings, she had been tainted with the corruption of concupiscence that was the universal heritage of the Fall. In other words, we must now move on to

---

5. Bernard of Clairvaux, *Sermo in nativitate beatae Mariae (De aquaeductu)* 7; SBO*p* 5: 279.

6. *Idem, Ep.* 174, 2; SBO*p* 7: 388–9.

consider the development of the doctrine of Mary's immaculate conception.[7]

The content of the doctrine is simple: God, by a unique grace and privilege, preserved Mary from all stain of original sin from the first moment of her conception. The history of the doctrine, however, is unclear and is not helped by the fact that many passages are ambiguous and unclear. The eastern theologians certainly entertained doubts about it—John Chrysostom, as we have seen, did not believe that Mary had been perfectly sinless even in her life—and part of the problem lies in the different emphases placed by east and west on the importance of original sin. The west, as a consequence of the teaching of Augustine, laid great stress on inherited guilt, whereas the east laid far more emphasis on inherited mortality.[8] And since no one ever suggested that Mary was immortal, it was difficult for the easterners to see how she could have escaped the consequences of the Fall. It is true that from the seventh century onwards we find passages in some greek writers stating that Mary was cleansed from sin 'in advance', but the precise moment of the cleansing is not specified. It is possible, therefore, that some Greeks did accept the doctrine of her Immaculate Conception (Gregory Palamas and Theophanes of Nicaea seem to have done), but it was certainly not widely accepted. We might also note that Orthodoxy has never made any official pronouncement on the subject, but that most modern Orthodox do not accept the idea. Nevertheless, towards the end of the seventh century, the eastern church had introduced a feast intended to celebrate the conception of the Virgin (a feast celebrating her *birth* had been in existence for more than a hundred years), and we may justly inquire as to how and why this anomalous situation arose.

---

7. It is a common error nowadays to confuse the doctrine of the Immaculate Conception with the doctrine of the Virgin Birth. The Immaculate Conception refers to the conception of Mary; the Virgin Birth to the conception and birth of Jesus.

8. See Chapter XI above.

The major reason for the introduction of the feast was the influence of a very popular apocryphal text originally called *The Nativity of Mary* but nowadays usually referred to as the *Protevangelium of James*. It purports to have been written by James the apostle, but this is obviously not the case since the work dates from the middle of the second century.

We are told in this treatise that the parents of the Virgin were Joachim (a charitable man of great wealth) and Anna, but that Anna, unfortunately, was barren. On one occasion, when Joachim had gone to the temple in Jerusalem to make an offering, the High Priest rebuked him for his childlessness and told him that this was a sure sign of God's displeasure. The pious Joachim was horrified at this and fled into the desert to do penance for forty days. Meanwhile, back at their house, Anna is walking in the garden and bewailing her barrenness, and her sense of inadequacy is reinforced when she sees a nest full of baby sparrows. But in the midst of her tears and sorrow, an angel appears to her, tells her that her prayers have been heard, and promises her a child. Another angel then announces Anna's pregnancy to Joachim, and since Joachim has been away in the desert, and since Anna's virtue is not in question, he realises that a miracle has occurred. Straightaway he rushes back to Jerusalem where he meets Anna at the city gate. They warmly embrace each other (this scene has often been painted) and in gratitude to God, Anna promises to dedicate her child—Mary—to his service. It was this popular and widely believed miracle-story which lay at the basis of the feast of Mary's conception.

When the feast was introduced into the west is unclear. It may possibly have been brought to Ireland in the ninth century, but it was certainly known in England c.1060. After the Norman Conquest it faded away for a time, but was revived about 1127–28 and was then taken over to Europe. It reached France in the 1130s but was opposed by no less an authority than Bernard of Clairvaux, and it was Bernard's opposition that marks the beginning of western controversy over the doctrine. Why, then, did Bernard, who was so devoted to the Mother of God, object to celebrating her conception?

XIII-5 The abbey of Fontenay was dedicated to Mary, as were all cistercian abbeys; it is therefore not surprising to find an image recalling her perpetual presence as patron. This standing Virgin and Child from Fontenay's church is two meters in height and was originally painted. Mary's right leg is bent slightly to create a graceful pose and she carries the infant Jesus on her left hip. This fine late thirteenth-century work, showing a delicately intimate exchange between mother and child, anticipates a series of similar statues that proliferated throughout Europe in the course of the next century.

Virgin and Child, late thirteenth century.
Abbey of Fontenay (Burgundy).

For a start, Bernard stood firmly in the augustinian tradition, and although Augustine had made no specific pronouncement on the matter of Mary's immaculate conception, the impression he gave was generally negative. For Augustine, the transmission of original sin was intimately linked with the act of sexual intercourse, and Augustine did not accept the apocryphal stories of Anna's miraculous conception. Nor did Bernard. It was true that Mary conceived by the Holy Spirit, but she was not herself conceived by the Spirit. That was a unique privilege reserved for her Son. Mary was conceived by the normal processes of human reproduction, and she was therefore conceived in sin.

Bernard, however, goes on to point out that this is no denigration of the Mother of God. Far from it. She herself would not wish to be confused with her Son and Lord, and she has honour enough without adding something which is irrational and supported neither by scripture nor by tradition. To celebrate the feast of Mary's birth is admirable; to celebrate the feast of her conception is indefensible. In any case, if we were to celebrate *her* conception, should we not also celebrate the conception of her parents? And of her grand-parents and great-grand-parents? Ridiculous!

Nevertheless, says Bernard, if Mary were indeed to be a proper and sinless vessel for the Lord of the World, something had to have happened between the moment of her conception and her birth. Sometime during that period she was cleansed from original sin by a specific act of God's grace, and it was when she was *born*, not when she was conceived, that she was unstained and immaculate. She was, admittedly, not alone in this—Jeremiah and John the Baptist had likewise been cleansed of sin while in their mothers' wombs—but Mary received something greater than either of these. She received a blessing which not only sanctified her in the womb, but preserved her from sin throughout her whole life. And this, says Bernard, is something we believe has not been granted to any other human being. Let us therefore celebrate her holy birth, not her conception. How can a conception be holy if it were not by the Holy Spirit? And if Mary's conception were not by the Holy Spirit, how can we keep the feast of something not holy? No, says Bernard, there is no place in the church for a Feast of the Immaculate Conception.

Peter Lombard agreed with Bernard. Mary was conceived in sin, but was cleansed of it before her birth. Also in agreement were the Dominican Albert the Great and the Franciscan Bonaventure. The idea of an immaculate conception is not impossible, said the latter, but Lombard's point of view is safer and more reasonable. In agreement, too, were Alexander of Hales (another Franciscan), and no less an authority than Thomas Aquinas. All these writers accepted the augustinian view of the association of original sin and sexual intercourse, but all of them also emphasised another difficulty to which the doctrine gave rise.

Christians had always believed that the mission of Christ was to redeem the whole world, and the whole world included Mary. But if Mary were conceived without original sin, she did not need redemption, and redemption was therefore not universal. In which case, Christ came to save the whole of the human race with the exception of his mother, and that was neither the teaching of the Bible nor of the church. The doctrine of the Immaculate Conception, therefore, was unscriptural and illogical, and it had no place in the christian tradition.

Against these formidable theologians was ranged the incalculable power of popular piety and the arguments of an Oxford professor named John Duns Scotus. He was born c.1264, about a decade before the death of Aquinas, and in due course became a Franciscan. He taught at Oxford for many years but left the university c.1302 to go to Paris. Five years later he made his way to Cologne where he died suddenly in 1308. He was the first important theologian to defend the doctrine of the Immaculate Conception and to deal with the problem we outlined above: how can we reconcile Mary's original sinlessness with the universality of Christ's redemption? The essence of his argument is as follows.

Christ's principle task as mediator was to rectify the relationship between God and human beings. Since Christ was the perfect mediator, it would be expected that in at least one case he would effect a perfect mediation to demonstrate what mediation was all about. Perfect mediation involves the removal

XIII-6 The Coronation of the Virgin entered the repertory of marian iconography in the twelfth century. Mary, shown here kneeling before Christ, receives the crown from him and becomes the Queen of Heaven, his female counterpart who reigns with him in judgement. In this early thirteenth-century manuscript, the illumination is sketched in brown and red ink and woven into an initial E (*Eructavit*), marking the beginning of Psalm 44.

Coronation of the Virgin, from a Psalter, 1200–1225.
Heiligenkreuz Abbey (Austria), MS 66, f° 32.

of everything that could in any way detract from the right relationship between God and humanity, and the most difficult thing to eradicate is original sin. That, after all, is something we are born with, not something we cultivate ourselves. It is only reasonable, therefore, that the one person whom Christ selected to be the subject of his perfect mediation would be his mother, and his perfect mediation was demonstrated by preserving her not only from all sin during her life, but in her conception as well. Mary, therefore, was the living example of what mediation should be, and far from being excluded from Christ's mediatory actions, she was actually the one to be most affected by them. Duns Scotus called it the 'preredemption', for the cleansing of Mary anticipated the redemption that occurred on Calvary. What Christ had done so perfectly for his mother, he would, in course of time, also do for us. The Feast of the Immaculate Conception, therefore, was a celebration not only of the purity of the Virgin, but of the saving power of her Son.

The arguments of Duns Scotus were subtle and persuasive, but they did not terminate the controversy. At the end of the Middle Ages, the differences had still not been resolved, and in later centuries the debate would blaze up again. Between 1600 and 1800 there was an enormous literature produced on the subject and it even played a part in international politics. Not until 8 December 1854, more than five hundred years after the death of Duns Scotus, did Pope Pius IX proclaim the doctrine as an article of faith for Roman Catholics. Orthodox Christians generally do not accept it; western churches not in communion with Rome reject it; but as far as the Middle Ages are concerned, readers may make their own choice.

The heated arguments over Mary's conception stand in contrast to the general agreement on her death and assumption into heaven. The scriptures tell us nothing about the end of Mary's life, but, as usual, pious pens were eager to fill in the gaps, and there are a number of apocryphal writings pertaining to the subject that date back to the fourth century. Details vary considerably, but the general theme is that Mary is forewarned of her death, sometimes by Christ and sometimes by Gabriel,

XIII-7 The Cistercians had Mary sculpted in a keystone of the nave vault of their thirteenth-century church at Abbey Dore, in England. It was Saint Bernard who said in the twelfth century: 'She crowned him; she deserves in turn to be crowned by him'. Mary is here seated beside Christ, who holds the orb of the earth while crowning her Queen of Heaven. The vault has been dismantled and Christ's head is now missing, but this image is still testimony to the Cistercians' devotion to the Virgin, and to the widespread acceptance of the role of Mary as co-ruler of the universe.

Coronation of the Virgin, fourteenth century.
Abbey Dore, Herefordshire (England).

and makes her way to Bethlehem where she is joined by the surviving apostles. She and the apostles then travel to Jerusalem, being hindered on the way by anti-christian Jews, and when they eventually arrive in the city, Mary takes to her bed and dies. The apostles then perform the funeral rites and bury her, again with harassment from the Jews. Three days later her body is assumed into heaven and her tomb is found to be empty.

In one version of the story—a version which became very popular in the west—the description of these final events is a little more complicated. When Mary dies, her immaculate soul ascends to heaven, but her body remains on earth to be buried. Peter then suggests to the resurrected Christ that because of the intimate bond between him and his mother, he owes it to her to take her with him into heaven. Christ agrees with this, orders Michael to bring down Mary's soul from heaven, reunites it with her body, and raises her up. She is then given into the hands of the angels and is transported to heaven, soul and body.

From the seventh century onwards the general principle, if not the details, of these apocryphal narratives was widely accepted in the east, and from the eighth century it was unquestioned. John of Damascus, the voice of medieval Orthodoxy, gave it his full approval, and the Feast of the Assumption (which Orthodox normally call the Feast of the Dormition, or 'Falling Asleep') has been celebrated in the east since the year 600.

Its progress in the west was more hesitant. One sixth-century writer had no doubt that the body of Mary had been reunited with her soul and had ascended to Paradise on a cloud, but others were not so sure. One document in particular had a negative effect. It was a letter purportedly written by Saint Jerome (though the actual author was Paschasius Radbertus [c.785-c.860] whom we shall meet in Chapter XV), and although it did not actually deny the corporeal assumption of the Virgin, it made the point that since we do not really know what happened, we should not speculate on matters which God has preferred to keep secret.

Nevertheless, despite its rejection of everything in the apocryphal stories save the empty tomb, 'Jerome's' letter was extraordinarily positive in what it had to say about the Mother of God. It heaped on her the highest praise; it spoke of her superiority to the angels; it called her the Queen of Heaven; and it stressed her powers as our intercessor. Whatever honour we give to Mary is also given to the child she bore, and no-one should think that the veneration of the Mother takes anything away from the veneration of her son. In short, what the author was saying was that you don't have to accept a dubious doctrine relating to the death of Mary in order to be wholly devoted to her. So great was the authority of 'Jerome' that speculation on the corporeal assumption of the Virgin virtually ceased in the west for two and a half centuries.

Although not everyone accepted the strictures of 'Jerome', his views remained influential until the beginning of the twelfth century. At that time there appeared another treatise on the assumption, this time attributed to (but not written by) Augustine, which presented a sound theological argument in favour of the doctrine based on the unique intimacy of the relationship between Christ and his mother. Is it conceivable, asked the unknown author, that those who were so closely united in their earthly lives and in the work of redemption should not also be united in death and glory? The flesh of Jesus was the flesh of Mary, and just as the flesh of Jesus did not corrupt and turn to dust, neither did that of the one who bore him. It is unthinkable, says the author, that the sinless body of the Mother of God should be delivered to worms. If Mary received grace beyond all others in her life, will she not also receive it at death? Let her be forever with him whom she bore! Let the Mother of God be with the God whom she nourished!

This treatise, supported by popular piety, proved far more influential than that of Paschasius Radbertus, and Pseudo-Augustine ousted Pseudo-Jerome. From the twelfth century onwards, therefore, the doctrine of the corporeal assumption of the Virgin became ever more widely accepted in the west, and after it had received the approval of both Bonaventure and Thomas Aquinas, agreement was virtually universal. We might note, however, that it was not defined as an article of faith for Roman Catholics until 1 November 1950.

It is difficult to exaggerate either the importance or the popularity of the cult of the Mother of God in the Middle Ages. Much of it, of course, is understandable. All children, if they are lost or sad or hurt or in trouble, want their mothers, and

XIII-8 This is the earliest known depiction of Mary as Queen of Heaven, crowned co-adjudicatrix with Christ, and enthroned in the tympanum over the west door of Senlis cathedral in northern France. While the Christ of the Apocalypse is the dominant theme of the first gothic portals, from 1170 onwards, cathedral portals gave increased place to Mary. Here her death and assumption are shown in the two lower scenes. On the left (partly effaced) Mary lies on her deathbed, surrounded by censing angels. The doll-like image hovering over her torso is her soul, being taken to heaven by two angels. On the right, a coterie of angels lifts her lifeless body and assumes it too into heaven (for this reason, there are no relics of the Virgin Mary). The belief that she was bodily assumed first appears in late fourth-century apocrypha, and different sources assign her death to three or fifty years after the ascension, in Jerusalem. Sometimes it is said that her body was assumed on the way to burial, or that it was raised after three days.

Coronation, Death, and Assumption of the Virgin, c. 1170.
Senlis Cathedral (France).

the children of God are no different. Mary provided a feminine face for an all too masculine deity, and the compassion, love, availability, approachability, warmth, consolation, and comfort that we all like to associate with a loving mother were found in the Mother of God. But to attempt a detailed examination of

Mary's role in popular piety, her immense influence on medieval art, and her impact on medieval literature, both in Latin and the vernaculars, is not possible for us here, and we must now take leave of the Mother and return, once again, to her Son. The problems pertaining to his appearance in the flesh have already been considered in Chapters XI and XII, and it is now time to turn our attention to his appearance in other forms: in wood and paint, and in bread and wine. In other words, we must move on to examine the iconoclastic controversy in the east and the eucharistic controversy in the west, and we shall begin with the dispute over the holy icons.

XIV-1 This vivid and unmistakeable picture of the iconoclastic controversy is divided into two groups of three men, illustrating the theological conflict. To ensure a clear understanding of the scene, an inscription in the margin on the left reads: 'The holy father, together with the patriarch, refuting the iconoclast'. 'The iconoclast' is the figure seated on a throne, probably the emperor Leo V the Armenian; 'the holy father', the haloed ecclesiastic standing to the far left, is Saint Theodore of Studios; 'the patriarch', to the right of the throne (also with a halo), is Saint Nicephorus of Constantinople. On the right side are three slightly smaller figures, identified by the legend over their heads as 'the iconoclasts'. Two of them are bishops (wearing stoles with crosses) who observe with approval the third man busily whitewashing an icon of Christ, his pot of whitewash on the floor below the icon.

The Studite Psalter, c. 1066.
London, British Library, MS. add. 19352, f° 27v .
Photo: The British Library.

XIV

Incarnation and Icons

WE SAW in Chapter II that there were two main phases to the Iconoclastic Controversy. The first phase was initiated by the emperor Leo III in 726 and was brought to an end by the Empress Irene in 780. The second phase began in 814 and ended twenty-eight years later in 842. Between the two phases came the Second Council of Nicaea in 787 (the Seventh Ecumenical Council) which condemned iconoclasm and defended the use of both icons and relics.

The real turning-point in the controversy, however, was not the end of its first phase nor the beginning of the second, but the reign of the emperor Constantine V (741–75). Constantine was a fanatical iconoclast and the *bête noire* of the iconophiles; and since the iconophile party eventually won, and since most of the history of the period comes from their pens, it is understandable that they do not represent their most formidable opponent in any favorable light. It is also understandable that a great deal of what they said may be discounted. They presented a portrait, says the incomparable Edward Gibbon,

> of this spotted panther, this antichrist, this flying dragon of the serpent's seed, who surpassed the vices of Elagabalus and Nero. His reign was a long butchery of whatever was most noble, or holy, or innocent, in his empire. In person, the emperor assisted at the execution of his victims, surveyed their agonies, listened to their groans, and indulged, without satiating, his appetite for blood: a plate of noses was accepted as a grateful offering, and his domestics were often scourged or mutilated by the royal hand. . . . His lust confounded the eternal distinctions of sex and species, and he seemed to extract some unnatural delight from the objects most offensive to human sense. . . . His life was stained with the most opposite vices, and the ulcers which covered his body anticipated before his death the sentiment of hell-tortures.[1]

Cruel he may have been, but he was also a remarkable general, a wily politician, a patron of the arts, and a very good theologian. It was he who composed a series of treatises—he called them *Enquiries*—devoted to various aspects of the iconoclastic controversy, and although only two survive out of about a dozen (apart from some fragments), they represent some of the most important theological writing in defence of iconoclast policy. An iconoclast synod held in Hieria in 754 adopted the main theses presented by Constantine, and the emperor's contributions obliged the iconophiles to refine their own arguments. The chief adversary of iconoclasm in its earlier stages, John of Damascus, had died about 750, some four years before the Council of

---

1. E. Gibbon, ed. O. Smeaton, *The Decline and Fall of the Roman Empire* (London, 1910) V: 88.

Hieria, and it was left to Theodore of Studios and Nicephorus of Constantinople to take the torch from his hand and develop subtle and telling arguments which could compete successfully with those of the brilliant, if dissolute, emperor.

Let us now introduce the three main protagonists of the iconophile position. What little we know of the life of John of Damascus has already been told in Chapter XI. We may recall that when he was about forty, he retired to the monastery of Saint Sabas near Jerusalem and there, between 726 and 730, wrote his three treatises in defence of the holy icons.

As for Theodore and Nicephorus, both were born about a decade after John's death: Nicephorus in c.758 and Theodore in 759. Theodore was a Constantinopolitan whose uncle was the abbot of a well-known monastery. He soon came under his uncle's influence and decided to follow in his footsteps. He became a monk in c.780; he was ordained priest in 787; and in 794 he was appointed abbot of the monastery when his uncle resigned in his favour. Five years later, he and his monks moved to the monastery of Studios (it lay in the west of Constantinople, not far from the Golden Horn) and under Theodore's intelligent leadership, the Studios became the model for eastern monasticism. Theodore's own life, however, was by no means tranquil. His involvement in politics and theology led to his being exiled from Constantinople on more than one occasion, and when he was eventually recalled, he was still not permitted to reside in the city. He died on 11 November 826.

Nicephorus was born around the same time as Theodore and in the same city, but their lives were very different. In his earlier years Nicephorus had been a favoured member of the imperial court and had represented the emperor at the Second Council of Nicaea in 787. Some years later he retired from court, founded a monastery, and took up residence there. In 806, however, he was recalled from his seclusion and elevated to the patriarchate, but as the price of his elevation he was persuaded to agree to some dubious political manoeuvering—manoeuvering which earned him the enmity of Theodore. With the resurgence of the iconoclastic controversy in 814, Nicephorus, a staunch iconophile, was not welcome as patriarch and the following year he was banished. He retired to his monastery and spent the last fourteen years of his life (he died in 829) in prayer and study, producing two important histories and a number of treatises in defence of the holy icons. These last are lucid and sophisticated writings and Nicephorus's part in the iconoclastic controversy is too often underestimated.

What, then, were the arguments that John, Theodore, and Nicephorus had to combat? The obvious place to start is with Exodus 20:4: 'You shall not make for yourself a graven image, whether in the form of anything that is in heaven above, or that is on the earth beneath, or that is in the water under the earth. You shall not bow down to them or worship them.'[2] That this was a key text in the iconoclast arsenal is clear—all three of our iconophiles take pains to deal with it—but it raises two very important questions: (i) what does one mean by an 'image', and (ii) what does one mean by 'worship'? Let us examine these two problems in turn.

For a start, says John of Damascus, the Exodus injunction cannot possibly have applied to all images. Acting on the instructions of Moses, Bezalel made two cherubim of hammered gold for the Ark of the Covenant[3], and Moses himself made a serpent of bronze and set it on a pole as a magical antidote to snakebite.[4] In any case, in a world in which the vast majority of people could not read, images and icons were the books of the illiterate. If a pagan comes up to you and asks about the christian faith, says John, what is the best thing to do? Take him into church and show him the icons! There one can see the faith portrayed, and, as everyone knows, pictures can be far more effective than words.

The early iconoclasts were obviously aware of this difficulty, and they responded by providing a very restrictive definition of an image: in order for one thing to be the image of another, the

2. Ex 20:4 (RSV and NRSV combined).
3. Ex 37:7–9.
4. Nb 21:9.

image had to be *identical* to its prototype. In other words (using modern language), they seem to have been thinking in terms of a mirror-image or a photograph. A roughly drawn sketch of a person could not be called an image; nor could a touched-up photograph; nor could a painting by Picasso. From this it followed that no-one could ever produce a perfect likeness of Christ, partly because no-one knew exactly what he looked like, and partly because Christ was both God and man. So if someone *did* produce a so-called image or icon of Christ and then bowed down before it, they could not have been bowing down to Christ because (according to iconoclast logic) the image could not have been an image of Christ! And if it was not an image of Christ, then bowing down to it was rampant idolatry.

John of Damascus was well aware of this argument and had little difficulty in rebutting it. An image, he says,

> is a likeness and model and representation of something, showing forth in itself what it depicts. An image is not always similar in all ways to its prototype or the thing it depicts. The image is one thing and what is depicted is another: one can always see differences between them. . . . An image of a man may be an [accurate] representation of his physical characteristics, but it cannot contain his mental powers. It is not alive, and it cannot think, speak, feel, or move its limbs.[5]

It is true, says John, that the most perfect example of image-ness is the relationship between God the Father and God the Son (for Christ is the 'natural' image of the Father, consubstantial with him, and identical to him in every way save that the Father is unbegotten and the Son begotten[6]), but this does not preclude the existence of other, less perfect, images. After all, we human beings are images of God (it says so in Genesis 1:26), but no-one would be so stupid as to suggest that we are identical to God in substance, eternity, power, and glory! Similarly, artistic

5. John of Damascus, *Contra imaginum calumniatores* iii.16; ed. B. Kotter (Berlin/New York, 1975) 3: 125.

6. See *Cloud* 73.

representations are also images (though some of them may not be very good) and are even more imperfect than human beings. Nevertheless, even a poor artistic image may serve to remind us of the person portrayed and stir us to emulate his or her virtues and accomplishments. And in any case, John continues, when the faithful bow down to such images, they are not *worshipping* them but *venerating* them, and our author distinguishes very clearly between the two terms.

In general, one worships something for what it *is*; one venerates something for what it *represents*. What an icon *is* is wood and paint. To worship wood and paint is, without question, idolatry and no Christian would deny it. But the icon *represents* the person depicted upon it. Like the old representations of the roman emperors, it is an extension of their presence, and a quotation from Basil the Great appears again and again in iconophilic writings: 'The honour we show to the icon passes on to the prototype.'[7] So when we bow before an icon of Christ, we are bowing before Christ; and when we honour an icon of a saint, we honour the saint and all that he or she stands for. Icons are rather like telephones: they enable us to contact people in a different country. But when we say 'I love you' on the phone, we are not making passionate advances to a piece of electrical equipment. John has often seen people in love embracing a garment of the beloved *as if* it were the beloved, but it is the 'as if' that is important. The garment, the photograph, the image, the icon is no more than a channel for our adoration.

The case of God himself is entirely different. God is the omnipotent, omnipresent, omniscient, eternal creator of the universe, and to worship him for what he is is right and proper. Indeed, it is only God whom we should worship; to worship anything else is idolatry.

With regard to Mary, angels, and saints, John's argument is perfectly clear. Whether in paintings, statues, or mosaics they

---

7. Basil the Great, *De Spiritu sancto* xviii.45; PG 32: 149C. The quotation is actually taken out of context.

may indeed be honoured and venerated, but they must not be worshipped. But what about Christ and an icon of Christ? Christ, after all, is both God and man, and if we may worship God, may we not also worship an icon of God? John answers both No and Yes. He answers No because the essential fact still remains: an icon is wood and paint, and we do not worship wood and paint. But on the other hand, John has no wish to deny the divinity of Christ nor to suggest that Christ should not be worshipped. What we have in the case of an icon of Christ is a 'relational worship', and it is 'relational' for the reason that John has already established: worship passes through the icon to the prototype behind it. By means of the icon, the worship of the worshipper is 'related' to the Being who is worshipped. The basic principle still holds: the icon is no more than a channel for our devotion.

So far so good, but now we must face another problem. We said above that God is omnipotent, omnipresent, omniscient and eternal. True enough. But he is also invisible and without form, and it is therefore impossible (said the iconoclasts) to represent him in any way whatever. That is the reason for the proscription of 'graven images' in the book of Exodus. A depiction of God, therefore, is not only blasphemous, but impossible. How are we to deal with this?

John has no problem at all. The iconoclasts have forgotten the Incarnation and the fact that at that stupendous moment the bodiless and invisible God became embodied in visible humanity:

> In former times God, who has no body and no form, could not be depicted in any way. But now, since God has appeared in flesh and lived among human beings, I depict the God who can be seen. I do not worship matter; I worship the Creator of matter who became matter for my sake, who deigned to dwell in matter and who brought about my salvation through matter. I will never stop honouring the matter through which my salvation was brought about![8]

8. John of Damascus, *Contra imaginum calumniatores* i.16; Kotter 3: 89.

An icon of Christ, therefore, is not merely something to remind us of our Redeemer, but a true symbol of the incarnation.
As God revealed himself in the created stuff of flesh and blood, so
he may reveal himself in the created stuff of wood and paint. An
icon is a revelation of God through matter just as the Incarnation
was a revelation of God through matter, and the fact that one
was a perfect revelation while the other is imperfect does not
negate the basic principle: they are both images.

In summary, therefore, John of Damascus makes four main
points: (i) evidence for images can be found in the Old Testament itself and they are extremely useful for teaching an illiterate
population; (ii) an image need not be identical to its prototype
in order to be called an image; (iii) the true worship of God
and the veneration (or 'relational worship') of images are quite
distinct; and (iv) images of Christ bear eloquent witness to the
New Dispensation and are clear testimony to the reality and
importance of the Incarnation.

John's arguments were sufficiently persuasive to force the
iconoclast party to take steps to counter them, and the person
who took up the challenge and who was primarily responsible for
the refinement of iconoclast theology was the brilliant emperor-
theologian Constantine V. Constantine introduced four further
points and turned the controversy from a dispute over the place
of religious art to a dispute over the person of Christ.

Constantine's first move was to take up the iconoclastic definition of an image, a definition that was already restrictive,
and make it more restrictive still. As we saw above, the early
iconoclasts believed that for one thing to be the image of another,
the image had to be identical to its prototype. Constantine goes
further. For one thing to be the image of another, the image
must be identical to its prototype *in everything, including its
substance.* In other words, Constantine is restricting the use of
the term 'image' to what John of Damascus referred to as the
'natural' image. If the prototype is made of wood, the image must
be made of wood; if the prototype is flesh and blood, the image
must be flesh and blood; if the prototype is divine, the image
must be divine. A reflection in a mirror or a photograph can no

longer be considered an image. So what this means, obviously, is that we can never have an artistic 'image' of Christ since an artistic image is made of wood and paint, not of divinity and humanity, and anyone who bows down to an artistic representation of Christ must therefore be guilty of idolatry.

Constantine's second argument follows logically from this. Any image of Christ, he says, must be consubstantial with Christ himself. Its nature must be the very nature of Christ. What Christ is, it must be. Can there be such a thing? Indeed there can, says Constantine, but it is not an icon, not a statue, not a mosaic. It is the blessed eucharist itself: the bread and the wine which, after consecration, become the very body and blood of Christ! This is the only possible image of Christ, and just as it is the only true image, so it is the only true representation of the Incarnation.

Constantine's third argument is then linked to his second. All Christians were in agreement that the devout reception of the eucharist was the most important means, after baptism and chrismation, by which the grace of God was communicated to the believer, and all were agreed that this grace was essential if one was to live a christian life. Constantine goes one stage further. It is in the living of this christian life that we should strive to be images of Christ and his saints. Just as God is spirit and truth, so we should imitate him in spirit and truth, and in this way become living icons of our Creator, not in our bodies but in our souls. Constantine is here being subtle. He has agreed with the book of Genesis and with John of Damascus that human beings are images of God, but he now emphasizes that this image-ness is something that has to be carefully cultivated. We are *potentially* images of God, and the realization of our potential demands not only the grace of God, but a great deal of hard work. Do not look for the image of Christ in icons, says the emperor, look for it in your own soul! What Christian could disagree with that?

It is Constantine's fourth argument, however, that represents his most effective contribution to iconoclastic theology and which transforms the entire controversy into a christological dispute. Let us take it stage by stage. First of all, it is obvious that we cannot paint a picture of divinity. But since Christ is both divine and human, any picture of the incarnate Christ either includes the invisible divinity along with the visible humanity or it does not. There is no other alternative.

If the picture does *not* include the divinity, Christ is represented as a mere man and we have separated the natures.[9] We have depicted only his humanity and are guilty of Nestorianism (or, more accurately, of what Nestorius was thought to have said). But if the divinity is *included* with the humanity and no distinction is made between them, we have confused the natures.[10] We are then guilty of Monophysitism (or, more accurately, of what the Monophysites were thought to have said). But in both cases—either by separating the natures or by confusing the natures—we are guilty of heresy and stand condemned. Unless, of course, we agree with the iconoclasts and do away with representations of Christ altogether. How were the iconophiles to combat these arguments?

John of Damascus had died c.750, and it was his successors, Theodore of Studios and Nicephorus of Constantinople, who took upon themselves his mantle and continued his work. Some of John's ideas—the importance of icons for an illiterate population, and the distinction between worship and veneration—they simply repeated; some they elaborated; but to others they added new material and refuted the views of Constantine with theological rebuttals every bit as sophisticated as the arguments of Constantine himself. What, then, did they say?

To Constantine's first argument—that for one thing to be the image of another, it must be identical to the prototype in everything, including substance—Theodore and Nicephorus replied with an elaborated version of John's earlier argument. John's case was, in essence, supported by common sense; Theodore and Nicephorus added aristotelian logic (which we will not deal with here) and thereby added a philosophical foundation to

9. See *Cloud* 102–3.
10. See *Cloud* 101–2.

what was otherwise a fairly obvious point of view. They did not add anything new to what John had said, but they provided his arguments with a necessary scholarly scaffolding.

What, then, of Constantine's second argument, that the only true image of Christ is the eucharist? To this the iconophiles had a simple and effective reply: the eucharist is *not* an image of Christ! It is, on the contrary, Christ himself. It is his true body and blood. We are not talking about images here, we are talking about identity. Indeed, to regard the eucharist as no more than an image of Christ is rank heresy! And since the eucharist is not an image, it obviously has no place in any discussion of images. The emperor's argument was simply beside the point.

Constantine's third argument—that it is in our christian lives that we should strive to be images of God—also posed no real problem. The iconophiles had no disagreement. But the undeniable fact that we should be *living* images does not preclude the existence of other kinds of images as well. The iconoclasts' point could not be disputed, but it was quite irrelevant to the question of artistic representation. Indeed, with just a minor amendment, the iconoclast argument could be used to support the iconophile position. Everyone agrees that we should imitate God in our lives, but if an icon of Christ or his saints assists us in doing so—if it stimulates us to emulation or reminds us of saintly perfection—then who could deny its usefulness? An artistic icon may help us in realizing the potential of the living icon, and that, surely, is a good thing?

Constantine's fourth argument, however, was more difficult to deal with. He did have a point. What, after all, does an icon of Christ represent? Is it merely his humanity? Or is it humanity-confused-with-divinity? Both alternatives are heretical. Indeed, there was even a question as to whether the humanity could be represented, for how can you paint a picture of 'human-ness'? How can you draw a picture of an abstract concept? For the iconoclasts, the answer was simple: you can't.

Theodore's counter-attack to this fourth argument was two-fold: firstly he would turn the tables on the iconoclasts and use their own logic to show that it was they, not the iconophiles,

who were at fault; and secondly, he would demonstrate that
their argument, while it appeared to be sound on the surface,
was actually based on a misunderstanding.

You say (says Theodore to the iconoclasts) that Christ cannot
be portrayed. Why not? Did he not have a real physical body?
And if he did have a real physical body, why can we not depict
it? To say that Christ cannot be portrayed is to imply that he
did *not* have a real physical body, and to say that Christ did not
have a real physical body is docetism[11], a heresy that had been
condemned as early as the second century. So it is not we who
are Nestorians, says Theodore, but you who are Docetists! But
if, instead of this, you are implying that Christ's human nature
cannot be portrayed because it has been totally absorbed by the
divinity, then you are in even deeper trouble! That is to return
to the views of Eutyches[12], condemned and anathematized in
451 at the Council of Chalcedon, and it is Monophysitism of the
worst and most extreme variety. And you (says Theodore) accuse
us of being Monophysites?

Such an approach, however, is not really effective. You call
me names; I call you names. You accuse me of being Nestorian
and Monophysite; I accuse you of being Monophysite and Do-
cetist. A shouting-match like this may serve to let off steam, but
it solves nothing. Theodore and Nicephorus, therefore, turned
their attack to the underlying assumption of the iconoclast argument, and that underlying assumption involved distinguishing
between the two natures in the incarnate Christ. Which nature
was being depicted in an icon? Was it the humanity or was it the
divinity? The iconophiles answered Both and Neither! What did
they mean?

It is true (they said) that no-one can draw pictures of abstract
concepts such as divinity and humanity, but Jesus of Nazareth
was not an abstract concept. He was a real human being with
real flesh and blood who had walked and talked in Galilee and

11. See *Cloud* 92.
12. See *Cloud* 117–118.

XIV-2 The church of the Peribleptos at Mistra still has a large part of its elegant original decoration. The interior of the dome was painted with an image of Christ as Pantokrator, that is, the 'all-sovereign'. Darkly bearded, clad in tunic and *himation*, his right hand (now partly damaged) was probably raised in blessing while his left hand carries a closed book, that of the Gospels. He is surrounded by cherubim. Location of this image in the dome is particularly apt, giving the impression that Christ is entering the church from the heavenly world to establish his law on earth.

Christ Pantokrator, 1325–1350.
Mistra, Church of the Peribleptos (Greece).
Photo: James Austin.

who had suffered and died in Jerusalem. What we have in Jesus of Nazareth, therefore, is the one human *person* of the incarnate Christ, and in that one person both natures—the divinity and the humanity—coexist in a mysterious union without confusion, without change, without division, and without separation.[13] So

13. See *Cloud* 122.

when we portray Christ, we are not portraying either the divinity
or the humanity, but both together in the one indivisible person
of the God-man. The fourth argument of the iconoclasts fails,
therefore, because it is based on a misunderstanding: an icon of
Christ is a representation of the *person* of Christ, not a separate
representation of his individual *natures*, and any argument based
on natures is therefore off the point and irrelevant.

The arguments of Theodore and Nicephorus certainly persuaded the iconophiles, but it is doubtful if they had much
effect on their opponents. Battles such as this are not won by
words. One of the most important reasons for the failure of
iconoclasm was the death of its main protagonist, Constantine
V. The emperor died in 775 and was succeeded by his son, Leo
IV. But although Leo had been raised as an iconoclast, he was
by no means as fanatical as his father and was quite prepared to
compromise. And when *he* died, suddenly and unexpectedly, in
780, his widow—the Empress Irene, who was acting as regent for
her young son—reversed the imperial policy altogether and gave
her full support to the iconophilic position.

These views were given canonical approval at the Second
Council of Nicaea in 787, the Seventh Ecumenical Council,
which was convoked by the empress at the instigation of Tara-
sius, the patriarch of Constantinople. The empress invited Pope
Hadrian I to attend the council (the popes had consistently
supported the iconophile position throughout the whole course
of the controversy), and he sent two legates to represent him
and his views. He also sent a theological treatise that defended
the use of icons, pointing out, as John of Damascus had done
more than fifty years earlier, that veneration was not worship and
that the honour paid to the image passed on to its prototype. The
council, under the influence of patriarch, empress, and pope—all
staunch iconophiles—naturally decided in favour of icons and
set forth its decisions in a document which was signed by all
present, including the empress and her young son. They decreed
that images, whether painted or made of mosaic or any other
suitable material, should be set forth in churches, on vestments
and the sacred vessels, on walls and panels, in houses and by the

roadside; that they should represent our Lord and Saviour Jesus Christ, Mary the God-bearer, honoured angels, and the saints of God; that the more they are seen, the more we are drawn to emulate them; that this is to be understood as veneration, not worship; and that whoever venerates the image venerates the subject represented in that image. And if anyone teaches anything different from this, they shall be deposed (if members of the clergy) or excommunicated (if monks or members of the laity).

The iconoclastic controversy had been a messy and bloody affair. Theology, as usual, had become confused with politics and the resultant mixture was (and is) a dangerous and unstable compound. But through all the arguments and counter-arguments, through all the complexities of terminology, through all the appeals to authority and tradition, through all the name-calling and accusations, there was one essential point at issue: the reality and importance of the Incarnation. John, Theodore, and Nicephorus were insistent that in Jesus of Nazareth, the infinite and indescribable Godhead has been united with humanity in the finite and describable person of the God-man.

To say that Christ cannot be portrayed is to imply that he lacked true physical flesh, and if the flesh of Christ were unreal, then his sufferings and death were unreal; and if the sufferings and death of Christ were unreal, the whole marvellous tragedy of Calvary was a sham and a hoax and we are still in our sins. For John, Theodore, and Nicephorus, every icon of Christ was a physical testimony to the reality of the Incarnation, and not only a testimony, but a point of contact with Christ himself. Just as the power and grace of the Godhead were communicated to humankind through the created flesh of the incarnate Lord, so that grace and power can be transmitted through the created material that constitutes the icon. When we say with Basil that the honour paid to the image passes on to its prototype, it is not just a one-way process. Our honour and veneration flows in one direction; the grace of God flows in the other. Every icon of Christ is a link with the transfigured cosmos and a sacramental meeting-point of God with his creation. The eventual triumph

of the iconophiles, therefore, was not just a political victory, but
a reassertion of the one essential principle on which the entire
structure of Christianity is based: 'The Word became flesh and
dwelt among us, full of grace and truth' (Jn 1:14).

The western church had always opposed the iconoclastic position and the popes had consistently supported the iconophiles.
Medieval western theologians never had the slightest qualms
about the use of images or statues, and iconoclasm was not to
make any significant appearance in the west until the Reformation of the sixteenth century—a period which is not our concern.
Western theologians had a different problem to grapple with, a
problem that also involved the way in which Christ was present
here on earth, but not a problem relating to wood and paint.
For the west, the essential question was the way in which Christ
was present in the bread and wine of the eucharist, and to that
complicated controversy we must now turn our attention.

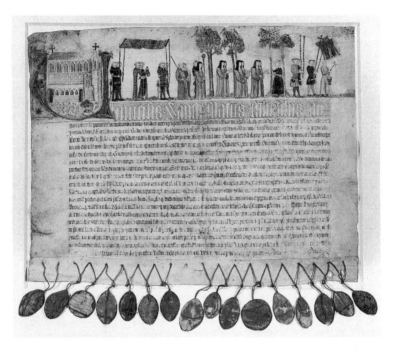

XV-1 The cistercian abbey of Herkenrode, formally attached to Clairvaux in 1217, was a celebrated place of pilgrimage in the fourteenth century because of the nuns' devotion to the Holy Sacrament. On 13 April 1363, Pope Urban V granted a plenary indulgence to all the faithful who made a pilgrimage to Herkenrode Abbey; this is the letter granting that privilege, with its sixteen official seals hanging from the bottom. The watercolor frieze at the top was made at the abbey before the parchment was sent to Avignon for certification. The procession of the Holy Sacrament is shown as it leaves the church (framed in the initial U); the sacrament is transported in a monstrance under a canopy held by four knights. The abbess is recognizable in the center by her crozier, and is preceded by four nuns, two novices, and two postulants. At the head of the procession are a young man carrying an *aspergillum* (sprinkler) and a bucket of holy water, and the banner and standard-bearers.

Letter of Indulgence in favor of Herkenrode Abbey, 13 April 1363. Saint-Trond (Belgium), Musée provincial d'art religieux, inv. KPL/sd/251. Photo: © IRPA-KIK, Brussels.

XV

The Mystery of the Eucharist

THE FIRST EUCHARISTIC controversy to trouble the western church occurred in the ninth century. Some would regard it as the first phase of a single protracted controversy. Up to that time, both eastern and western theologians had generally been prepared to accept on faith that the bread and wine on the altar became the body and blood of Christ, and they did not normally ask how the transformation took place or why the bread (if it was indeed the true body of the Redeemer) still tasted like bread and not like a piece of raw steak.[1]

1. See *Cloud* 189–194.

Problems began when a benedictine abbot named Paschasius
Radbertus composed a long treatise on the eucharist for the
instruction of certain novices. Paschasius, who was born c.785,
had entered the famous monastery of Corbie (about ten miles
east of Amiens in the north of France), and c.844 had been
elected abbot. He held the position for about nine years before
resigning as a consequence of a disciplinary dispute, and he then
devoted himself entirely to study until his death at Corbie c.860.
His most important work, the one with which we are concerned
here, was the *De corpore et sanguine Domini* (*On the Body and
Blood of the Lord*). Paschasius had written it c.831–33 for the
benefit of the novices at Corvey, the german daughter-house of
Corbie, and in 844 had prepared a revised edition which he sent
to the french king, Charles the Bald. It was the first attempt
in the history of christian theology at presenting a systematic
and comprehensive study of the eucharist, and we must now
examine its teaching and determine why it gave rise to serious
questions.

Paschasius's problem was simple. Like everyone else, he accepted the reality of the eucharistic change, but he accepted
it absolutely literally. As far as he was concerned, what was on
the altar after the consecration was the actual, physical body
of Christ, no more and no less. It was the real flesh which had
been born of Mary, which had suffered on the cross, and which
had risen from the tomb. It was now being offered up again
as a sacrifice for our redemption. Similarly, the liquid in the
chalice did not merely symbolize blood: it was the actual, physical
blood of Jesus Christ himself. The consecrated elements, in other
words, were identical with the flesh and blood of the crucified
Christ. Christ, after all, had not said: 'This *symbolizes* my body'
or 'This *represents* my body'; he had said: 'This *is* my body.' What
could be clearer than that?

There is, however, a difficulty. If the bread and wine are truly
identical with the body and blood of Christ, why don't they look
like it? The bread still looks like bread, not red meat; the wine
tastes like wine, not blood. Why is this so, and how can it be
explained?

As to the 'why', Paschasius offers two main reasons. One is what Ambrose of Milan, some five centuries earlier, had referred to as *horror cruoris*, 'the horror of blood'. God was well aware that most human beings could not tolerate getting a mouthful of raw meat at the eucharist, and therefore, by his grace, he had determined that the look and the taste of bread and wine would remain, even though they were truly the body and blood of his Son. The second reason was that if the flesh and blood of Christ actually looked like flesh and blood, where would be the need for faith? They *are* flesh and blood, says Paschasius, but only by faith can they be perceived as flesh and blood, and the eucharist is therefore both a test and a demonstration of faith.

But Paschasius has still not answered the question as to how this is possible. How can bread be the same as flesh and yet remain bread? How can one thing be two different things at the same time? Paschasius avoids the problem by taking refuge in the omnipotence of the Almighty: since God is all-powerful and can therefore do anything, this is a demonstration of his omnipotence. The Divine Judge, he says, covers the reality with a figure, he conceals it under the sacraments, he obscures it with mysteries. It is simply his will that the bread and wine look like bread and wine while they are actually flesh and blood, and beyond this there is really nothing we can say. We must remember that God is the author of the laws of nature, not their servant. On this point, Paschasius is at one with his predecessors. They, too, were content to believe and remain silent.

This emphatic realism of Paschasius, however, gives rise to problems, one of which relates to the way in which the eucharist affects us. Like everyone else, Paschasius believed that the eucharist was a channel for the grace of God and that by receiving the consecrated bread and wine we are sanctified. But how does this come about? *How* are we sanctified? For Paschasius, it is rather like taking an aspirin when we have a headache. We swallow the tablet and the headache goes away. Similarly, since the bread and wine are identical with the body of Christ, those who participate in the eucharist actually take Christ within themselves. They actually eat Christ. Then, once inside them, the perfect and sinless body of Christ begins to have an effect on them and to transform them into its own nature. Just as an aspirin drives away a headache and leaves us *feeling* better, so the body of Christ drives away sin and leaves us *being* better.

Aspirins, however, are no respecters of persons: they work for both good and wicked alike and their effectiveness is not dependent upon one's beliefs or moral qualities. It would seem, then, that if the eucharistic elements are truly the body and blood of Christ, they should have a sanctifying effect on all who partake of them, whether they be good, bad, or indifferent. Paschasius was aware of this problem, and his answer is that yes, the eucharistic body of Christ is the true body of Christ for both good and wicked, but whereas its effect on the good is to provide them with grace and bring about their sanctification, its effect on the wicked is to lead them to hell. Again, it is like aspirin: for dogs it can be beneficial; for cats, it can be lethal. It all depends on what you are. For unbelieving and unrepentant sinners, receiving the body of Christ is both blasphemous and spiritually deadly; for the righteous, it can be the best thing in this world and the next. The bread on the altar *is* the body of Christ, that is true, but it works to salvation only in those who are already united with Christ in love and faith.

Paschasius's views, though simple and logical, were seen by some of his contemporaries as being too crude and materialistic, and it is not difficult to find those who opposed him. One was a monk from his own monastery named Ratramnus (he died in 868, but the date of his birth is unknown), and just as Paschasius had written a treatise *De corpore et sanguine Domini*, so too did Ratramnus. His motivation for doing so was simple. Charles the Bald, the ruler to whom Paschasius had sent his treatise on the eucharist, seems to have had problems with some of Paschasius's ideas, and he had requested Ratramnus to answer two questions for him: firstly, did the faithful receive the body and blood of Christ in a mystery or in truth, in a figure or in reality; and secondly, was the bread on the altar the very flesh that had been born of Mary, which had suffered, died, and been buried, and which now sits at the right hand of the Father? In other words, what the emperor wanted to know was whether Paschasius's simple—perhaps naive—realism was theologically defensible. What was Ratramnus's reply?

On the first point—the matter of 'figure' as against 'reality'— Ratramnus had no doubts at all. For him, 'reality' meant clear, obvious, and straightforward facts, not obscured by shadows, symbols, images, enigmas, or anything else. On this basis, flesh is simply raw meat, and if it is not raw meat, it is not flesh. A 'figure', on the other hand, reveals the truth under a sort of veil: it shows one thing to the normal human senses, but something quite different to the minds of the faithful. An example of 'reality', says Ratramnus, is when we say that Christ was born of a virgin, suffered under Pontius Pilate, was crucified, dead, and buried. An example of a 'figure' is when Christ himself says 'I am the true vine' (Jn 15:1) or 'I am the bread of life' (Jn 6:35). So what do we have on the altar? According to Paschasius, it is the flesh that was born of Mary. If that is the case, says Ratramnus, we must be able to see the bones, nerves, muscles, and blood. Do we? Obviously not. So it cannot be flesh in 'reality', but only flesh in a 'figure'.

This is not to say that Ratramnus denies the presence of Christ in the eucharist. Indeed not. What he is doing is distinguishing between Christ's *physical* presence (as Paschasius would have us believe) and his *spiritual* presence. We might understand it better if we think of the room of someone who has recently died: a lover or wife or partner. All her things are still there— her favourite books, her photographs, small treasures carefully collected over the years—and we are still acutely conscious of her presence: not her physical presence, of course, but what we might call her spiritual or psychic presence. She is still with us in the place and in the things which once were so familiar to her.

For Ratramnus, likewise, Christ is invisibly and spiritually present in the eucharist, but he is not present in his physical flesh. It follows, therefore, that Charles's second question—do we eat the body that was born of Mary?—must be answered in the negative. No, we do not. Just as Easter Sunday is called 'the day of the Lord's resurrection', whereas we know for a fact that the

Lord rose only once and at one particular moment in history, so we refer to the eucharistic elements as 'his body' and 'his blood', even though they are not identical with the physical flesh that once walked and talked in Galilee. What we eat at the eucharist is the 'figure' of the body of Christ, a 'figure' in which Christ is spiritually, not physically present.

What, then, happens at the eucharist? What happens when we consume this 'figure' of Christ's body? The belief of Paschasius, as we have seen, was that we actually eat the physical flesh of the Saviour, and Christ begins to work on us from within. Ratramnus's view is unclear, but we cannot really blame him for that. Charles the Bald had asked only two questions, and this was not one of them. What seems most likely is that Ratramnus thought that at the eucharist, the believer, by faith, achieves a spiritual union with Christ. The actual bread and wine are digested and evacuated according to the normal processes of human metabolism, but the mind, always by faith, feeds invisibly on the Word of God who is invisibly present in the sacrament. It is by this spiritual contact that Christ communicates with us and makes us the recipients of his grace.

Paschasius and Ratramnus, therefore, represent two different approaches to the eucharist. Neither denies the effective presence of Christ in the bread and wine, but one stresses the physical aspect of his presence and the other the spiritual. But if, with some, we take these views to extremes, major difficulties occur. Paschasius's view can all too easily lead to the idea that once Christ is physically present inside you, you will be sanctified regardless of your faith, your morals, your behaviour, or your desire. Ratramnus's view can lead one to believe that the eucharistic elements are no more than symbols of Christ's body and blood, and that the eucharist is a mere commemoration of the Last Supper. It will not come as a surprise, therefore, to learn that eight hundred years later, several of the Protestant reformers claimed that Ratramnus had anticipated their doctrines.

This first eucharistic controversy faded away towards the end of the ninth century, but of the two approaches, that of Paschasius rapidly became dominant. The church, however, made no formal statement on the matter, and a number of different views of the eucharistic change continued to coexist, somewhat uneasily, for the next two centuries. Much more significant than the original controversy was its revival in the eleventh century when Berengar[2] of Tours resurrected the ideas of Ratramnus, began a long and bitter dispute, and paved the way for the formal western definition of the nature of the eucharistic change.

Berengar, born about 1000, was head of the school of Saint Martin at Tours and a flamboyant and popular teacher. In the course of the 1040s he rediscovered the treatise of Ratramnus (though he did not realize Ratramnus had written it[3]) and proceeded to use Ratramnus's ideas to attack the prevailing paschasian interpretation of the eucharist. We must note, too, that Berengar's dates—c.1000 to 1088—make him about thirty years younger than Anselm of Canterbury and place him at the very beginning of the tentative development of the scholastic method. Berengar, in other words, is going to emphasise logic and rational argument in his consideration of the facts of the faith.

So let us look at the eucharist through Berengar's eyes. What do we see? What is communicated to the human senses? Before the consecration we see bread and wine: they look like bread and wine, they taste like bread and wine, they feel like bread and wine, they *are* bread and wine. But after the consecration we see the same thing! The bread and wine still look like bread and wine, they still taste like bread and wine, they still *are* bread and wine. How, then, can we call them flesh and blood? They are not, says Berengar. The reception of the Lord's body and blood in the eucharist is a purely spiritual matter and no change at all occurs in the actual material of the eucharistic elements. Human beings, he says, are made up of body and soul: the body receives common bread; the soul receives the spiritual sustenance of the body of Christ. Christ is present, certainly, but his presence

2. His name often appears in a latinized form as Berengarius.
3. Berengar thought it had been written by John Scot Eriugena, whom we shall meet in Chapter XVII.

(as Ratramnus had said two centuries earlier) is spiritual. It is perceived only by faith, and only through faith can the eucharist be an effective channel for divine grace.

For Berengar, then, the paschasian idea that what we have on the altar is the flesh that was born of Mary was nonsense. As far as he was concerned, if one thing changed into another, the whole thing changed, subject and qualities alike. In other words, if a lump of sugar changes into a lump of coal, it is not just 'sugarness' that changes into 'coalness', but the white, sweet, soluble qualities of the sugar must change into the black, inedible, insoluble qualities of coal. So too for bread and wine. If they do change into flesh and blood, they must change *totally* into flesh and blood, and this means that after the change they must look, taste, feel, and smell like flesh and blood. If this is not the case, they have not changed; and this is not the case at the eucharist.

Furthermore, said Berengar, the realist, paschasian idea is not only ridiculous, but also blasphemous. If it were true, we would have little bits (*portiuncula*) of Jesus on all the altars of Christendom, and the flesh of the Redeemer would be chewed up and crushed by the teeth of the faithful. This would be no more than cannibalism! And apart from the absurdity of suggesting a million separate bodies of Christ, how could this be reconciled with the fact that Christ ascended to heaven in an immortal and incorruptible body and is even now seated at the right hand of the Father? How can his physical body be here on earth at the same time? Or do we (God forbid!) posit two Christs, one in heaven and one on earth? No, said Berengar, there is but one Christ and, through faith and love, we experience his spiritual and invisible presence in the mystery of the eucharist.

What Berengar has done here is take the ideas of Ratramnus, provide them with a logical and philosophical framework, and re-present them to the world of the eleventh century. But because the dominant way of thinking at that time was essentially paschasian and realist, it was inevitable that Berengar would be opposed. He was, and not just by one, but by a host of opponents, three of whom are especially important. The first was Lanfranc, born c.1005 in Italy, trained in France, and archbishop of Canterbury from 1070 to his death in 1089. The second was Guitmund, a pupil of Lanfranc, who ended his days in Italy as Cardinal and Archbishop of Aversa (nine miles north-west of Naples) from 1088 to his death c.1090–95. The third was Alger, born c.1070, a canon of Liège in Belgium, who entered the monastery of Cluny about 1121 and died there a decade later. All three wrote treatises against the ideas of Berengar, and although they differ in what they emphasize, they are united in their essential arguments.

All three begin by reasserting the teaching of the western church of the time: at the eucharist, the bread and wine are truly changed into the actual body and blood of Christ. Just as the human race fell by eating real fruit, says Guitmund, it is fitting that it be saved by eating real flesh. As Adam and Eve fell in body and soul, materially and spiritually, we too have fallen in body and soul. If we are to be redeemed both materially and spiritually, we must be united with Christ materially and spiritually. How is this to be achieved? We will let Alger take up the argument.

There can be no doubt, says Alger, that the greatest work of God was the Incarnation. When God became human, he opened up to humans the possibility of sharing in his divine nature and of becoming children of God: not by nature, of course, but by adoption. How does this possibility become actuality? By the eucharist! In that mysterious meal, the mystical body of Christ (the church) consumes the true body of Christ (the eucharist), and is thereby joined to the Father through his only-begotten Son. Only through the eucharistic body can the mystical body be united with divinity and, in the fullness of time, experience the indescribable joy of eternal and perfect blessedness. Can this be achieved by consuming a 'figure' or 'symbol' or 'representation' of Christ? Indeed it can not. There is no divinity in a symbol, and no symbol can unite us, body and soul, to God the Father.

But does this mean that all who receive the eucharist will automatically be redeemed, regardless of their faith or morals? Like Paschasius, the opponents of Berengar answer with an emphatic No. They distinguish two sorts of eucharistic reception, corporeal and spiritual, and in this way try to combine the materialistic ideas of Paschasius with the more spiritual approach of Ratramnus.

In the corporeal reception of the eucharist, what we eat is the true flesh and blood of Christ, but if one does not believe this, one's lack of faith prevents the Christ within from having any effect. It also ensures that our own wickedness in participating unworthily in so great a sacrament leads us inexorably to damnation.

The spiritual reception of the body and blood of Christ, unlike corporeal reception, is not restricted to the moment of communion. It involves a faithful and loving belief in the works and words of Christ and our attempts at putting them into practice. For Alger, it is simply the life-long imitation of Christ, but although he says that spiritual reception is more worthy than corporeal reception, he insists that the former alone is not sufficient for salvation. Corporeal reception is also essential. If, then, we receive the eucharist in faith and love, and live our lives as Christ has taught us, we are united not only with the flesh and blood of Christ on the altar—the flesh and blood which were born of Mary—but also with the eternal and incorrupt flesh and blood of the risen and ascended Lord. Both sorts of reception, corporeal and spiritual, are essential for our salvation, and since the wicked do not live faithful and christian lives, it follows that they will not be saved even if they receive the sacrament.

If, then, the bread and wine really are transformed into the true body and blood of Christ, why do they still appear to be bread and wine? The question posed by Berengar still requires an answer, and neither Lanfranc, Guitmund, nor Alger provide us with much more than did Paschasius two centuries earlier.

> We believe (writes Lanfranc) that the earthly substances on the table of the Lord are divinely sanctified through the priestly mystery, and are ineffably, incomprehensibly, and marvellously converted by the operation of supernal power into the essence (essentia) of the Lord's body. The species of the things themselves, together with certain other qualities, are preserved so that people will not be horrified at perceiving

something raw and bloody, and that by believing they may
receive the fuller rewards of faith.[4]

Once again we see the arguments of 'the horror of blood'
(*horror cruoris*) and the need for faith, and although Lanfranc
anticipates the formal doctrine of transubstantiation (a matter
we shall consider shortly), he does not use the term. It had not
yet been invented. For Lanfranc, Guitmund, and Alger, it was
enough to say that the eucharistic elements were 'transformed',
'transferred', 'converted', or 'substantially changed' into the flesh
and blood of Christ, and how this mystery occurred was ultimately a matter of faith. You either believe it or you don't.

The views of Lanfranc and his confrères were to prevail in
this second phase of the eucharistic controversy. Berengar was
condemned at Rome in 1050 (Ratramnus's treatise was burned
at the same time), but despite his condemnation, he did not
change his views. He made a half-hearted recantation at Tours
in 1054, but had to do it again (with equal reluctance) at Rome in
1059. He then returned to Tours, but soon afterwards repudiated
his recantation on the grounds that he had been forced into it.
Another retractation was demanded of him in 1079, and after
agreeing to that he lived his remaining nine years as a hermit.
He died in 1088, an old, bitter, and disappointed man.

By the first decades of the twelfth century the views of Lanfranc, Guitmund, and Alger had become the accepted views of
the western church, but they had not yet been presented in a concise and logical fashion, nor expressed in clear and unambiguous
language. Such a presentation was not long in coming. Within
about two decades Peter Lombard had produced his *Sentences*,
the standard text-book of western medieval theology, and what
he says of the eucharist in those lucid pages was to remain the
accepted view of western Christendom from the second half of
the twelfth century to the Reformation.

Lombard begins by telling us that the greek word eucharist
means 'good grace', and that in this sacrament we not only

4. Lanfranc, *De corpore et sanguine Domini* xviii; PL 150: 430BC.

experience an increase in virtue and grace, but receive entire him who is the fount and origin of all grace. He goes on to show how the eucharist was prefigured in the Old Testament, how it was instituted by Christ at the Last Supper, and why we should receive it fasting even though the disciples had been given it after eating the paschal meal. He follows this with a careful examination of the difference between the sacrament and the reality behind the sacrament, and then proceeds to explain Lanfranc's distinction between corporeal and spiritual eating. There is nothing new in this, and nothing is added to what we have already said above.

In his next section Lombard enters upon a long discussion of the eucharistic change. There are some, he says, who are so insane as to try to measure the power of God as they would measure natural things and who dare to deny that the true body of the Lord is present on the altar. Such a view, he says, is intolerable, and he calls in a number of authoritative witnesses, primarily Ambrose and Augustine, to demonstrate its heretical nature. The substance of the bread and wine is changed into the substance of the body and blood of Christ; the form or the accidents (Lombard uses both words) of the bread and wine — their taste, weight, appearance, and so on—remain unchanged. But if one persists in asking how this is possible, Lombard can only reply in the words of Lanfranc: 'It is salutary to believe the mystery of faith; it is not salutary to investigate it.'[5]

The terms Lombard uses in his discussion—substance, form, accidents—derive from the aristotelian tradition which, as we saw in our first chapter, had such a profound influence on the development of scholastic thought in the west. The substance or *substantia* of something is its essential, internal nature; its accidents[6] or qualities are its external characteristics. We

5. Peter Lombard, *Sententiae* IV.xi.2; ed. I. Brady (Grottaferrata, 1981) 2: 297 = Alger of Liège, *De sacramentis corporis et sanguinis Dominici* I.xi; *PL* 180: 767A = Lanfranc, *De corpore et sanguine Domini* x; *PL* 150: 421D. Lombard thinks he is quoting Augustine.

6. It was Guitmund of Aversa who made the term 'accidents' part of the standard eucharistic vocabulary.

XV-2 The Royal Portal of Chartres Cathedral was built during the eucharistic controversies, and this tympanum appears to have been designed to reinforce the doctrine of transubstantiation. The bottom level contains a cycle showing Christ's infancy: the annunciation to Mary, visitation with Elizabeth, nativity of Christ, and adoration of the shepherds. The central panel shows the Presentation in the Temple, while the upper register depicts Christ 'enthroned' on his mother's lap, flanked by censing angels. But when this tympanum is read vertically, a subtle emphasis is given to the eucharist in this otherwise charming and well-known story. The swaddled child at the bottom is not cradled in his mother's arms, but placed on top of the frame around her bed, in the center of the panel, as though he were being offered up in sacrifice. Directly above, the infant of the Presentation is standing on the altar in the temple, while at the top he sits enthroned in a formally frontal pose. The vertical axis and arrangement of the figures within each band emphasize the idea that the body of Christ himself is offered at the eucharistic table.

Tympanum of the Infancy portal, c. 1150.
Chartres Cathedral (France), west façade, south portal.
Photo: James Austin.

perceive these external characteristics by means of our bodily
senses—sight, smell, hearing, touch, and taste—but the bodily senses cannot penetrate to the essential, internal, abstract
nature. In the case of a slice of white bread, its substance is
'breadness' or 'breadity'; its accidents are its colour (white), its
shape (square), its taste (doughy?), its texture (chewy), its smell
(yeasty?), its weight (light), and so on. What happens at the
eucharist is that the 'breadness' or 'breadity' of the bread is
changed into the 'fleshness' or 'fleshity' of the body of Christ,
but, by God's power, the accidents or external characteristics
of the bread remain the same. They are not changed into the
accidents or external characteristics of meat. As far as all our
bodily senses are concerned, what we have before us is bread.
Internally, however, in a region to which our bodily senses cannot
penetrate, it is bread no longer.

In explaining the reasons for this change in substance, Lombard merely reiterates the old traditions. It exercises our faith and
prevents us from being overcome by *horror cruoris*. And then,
after dealing with this question, he passes on to a consideration
of further matters which are not here our concern. He discusses
whether we should receive the eucharist in two species (bread
and wine) or only one (bread *or* wine); he explains why the wine
in the chalice is mixed with water; he examines the question
of whether, at the fraction (the moment when the priest breaks
the consecrated bread), the body of Christ is torn to pieces; he
explains how the mass is a true sacrifice; and he concludes by
demonstrating that a valid eucharist cannot be celebrated by
heretics or by those who have been excommunicated.

The eucharist, says Lombard, was instituted by Christ for two
purposes: to increase virtue—that is, charity—and as a medicine for our daily infirmity. And since we sin daily, we should
receive our medication daily; because we daily fall, daily is Christ
sacrificed mystically for us. Daily he is eaten and drunk, yet
he remains ever whole and alive. This is the whole mystery of
faith, and on it depends the whole of our salvation. The grace
bestowed on us at our baptism, the grace which is strengthened
in our confirmation, becomes an ever-flowing river of grace in

the eucharist; and the union with Christ which we experience in receiving his true body and blood prefigures our blissful and unending union with him in the world to come.

Lombard, however, like Lanfranc, does not use the actual word transubstantiation (*transubstantiatio*), though it was certainly in use by his day. It seems probable that it first appeared c.1140 in a work by Rolando Bandinelli who later became Pope Alexander III. But during the course of the twelfth century the word became more and more widely accepted as the proper descriptive term for what occurs at the moment of consecration. As we explained earlier, the substance or *substantia* of the bread and wine are transformed into the substance of flesh and blood, but the accidents or external qualities remain unchanged. Transubstantiation, therefore, is quite specifically 'trans-*substance*-iation'; it is not 'trans-accidents-iation'. At the Fourth Lateran Council in 1215, the term was given official papal and conciliar recognition for the first time, and later, in the thirteenth century, it was defined and elaborated in aristotelian detail by Thomas Aquinas. For the next seven centuries, it was to remain a standard theological term in the official vocabulary of Roman Catholicism.

The conclusion of the eucharistic controversy, the reaffirmation of the reality of the eucharistic change, and the establishment of the term transubstantiation all contributed to a rapid growth in popular devotion to the eucharist. It also encouraged devotion to the reserved sacrament in churches, a tradition that dated back to a very early period.[7] The culmination of this wave of popular piety came in the middle of the thirteenth century when the visions of Saint Juliana of Liège led to the institution of a feast specifically designed to celebrate the reality of the eucharistic transformation: the Feast of Corpus Christi, the Feast of the Body of Christ.

Juliana was born in 1191 or 1192 at Retinnes, a small town near Liège, lost both her parents at the age of five, and was placed

---

7. The earliest mention of reservation is to be found in the writings of Justin Martyr, who was executed c.165.

as an orphan in an augustinian convent near Liège. There she
soon experienced mystical raptures and visions, and in a series
of these, beginning perhaps in the 1220s, she saw a full moon
shining brightly in the sky, but streaked with a dark band. The
moon, she realized, represented the church and its festivals (it
was a common symbol at the time), but what was the reason
for the disfiguration? After much pondering and prayer, she was
vouchsafed another vision in which Christ himself explained the
matter to her: the black band symbolized the absence of a feast
in the church which would celebrate the greatest mystery of all,
the mystery of transubstantiation, the moment when the bread
and wine on the altar actually became his most glorious body
and blood.

Juliana then began doing all that she could to bring about the
institution of such a feast, but met with considerable opposition.
It was not that people did not believe in the reality of the
eucharistic change, but, as they pointed out, there was already
a daily feast of the Body of Christ—the eucharist itself—and to
celebrate the mystery of transubstantiation only once a year was
surely to denigrate the most important and effective means of
grace bestowed on the church. The Dominicans, however, together with certain members of the local ecclesiastical hierarchy,
supported Juliana and, after consulting with leading theologians
from the University of Paris, they decided that the objections
were ill-founded and that there was no insurmountable barrier
to the institution of the new feast. A provisional liturgy was
composed by a local canon, and the feast was celebrated in the
diocese of Liège for the first time in 1246.

Shortly after this first celebration the bishop of Liège died,
and his successor, who opposed the feast, prevented it from being
celebrated again. Juliana herself died in 1258 without seeing its
reintroduction. The turning-point came in 1261 with the election of a new pope, Urban IV, who had earlier been archdeacon
of Liège and a supporter of Juliana and her ideas. In 1264 Urban
commanded the observance of the Feast of Corpus Christi, and
from the fourteenth century onwards it was celebrated universally throughout the western church. The liturgy of the feast,

together with a series of special hymns, was composed by no less an authority than Thomas Aquinas.

To these developments, however, there was also an unfortunate side. Since the eucharistic change was now seen as the essential reason for the mass and the subsequent elevation of the consecrated host as its central point; and since all Christians (apart from some heretics) believed that only a properly ordained priest or bishop could celebrate a valid eucharist, the western church came to see the eucharist as something done *by* the celebrant *for* the laity. The laity, in fact, were considered as mere spectators at a great drama being enacted on their behalf. Communion became an infrequent, annual event, and the mass was treated as an occasion for private devotions, private conversations, or private meetings. The first major challenge to this attitude came with the Reformation; the next with the Second Vatican Council, but these are matters well outside the scope of this present study.

The eucharistic controversies were confined to the western church. There were no greek Ratramnuses and no greek Berengars, and the eastern church accepted from the beginning both the reality of the eucharistic change and the concept of the mass as a sacrificial re-enactment of the events of Calvary. The Greeks were quite content to speak of a eucharistic 'change' or 'alteration' (*metabolē*)[8] without going into details, and Christ's presence in the eucharist was an undisputed matter of faith. It is enough to know, says John of Damascus, that the miraculous change takes place through the power of the Holy Spirit, and the precise way in which the omnipotent God works his miracles is not a matter for human inquiry or for human comprehension.

Of all the sacraments, the eucharist was generally regarded by both eastern and western Christians as the most important. It was, after all, the only one in which Christ was physically present,

8. The term 'transubstantiation' (*metousiōsis* in Greek) was not used by eastern Christians until the seventeenth century when they borrowed it from the west.

and few would have disagreed with the statement of Nicholas Cabasilas that it brought perfection to the other sacraments and that nothing could be added to it. Yet the fact remains that there *are* other sacraments and that they do play a significant role in the life of the church. It is only proper, therefore, that we should devote our next chapter to a discussion of these other mysteries and to an examination of their development and importance in the medieval christian tradition.

XVI-1 This magnificent baptismal font, made in the twelfth century for the Church of San Frediano in Lucca, is animated on the exterior by a frieze illustrating the crossing of the Red Sea by the Israelites (Ex 14-15). We see the Egyptians in pursuit, with the horses, chariots, horsemen, and army of the Pharaoh. Crossing the Red Sea marked the end of bondage for the Israelites in Egypt and was therefore regarded as a turning-point in their history. It is Saint Paul's interpretation of this event that makes it a particularly apt subject for a baptismal font: 'all were baptized unto Moses in the cloud and in the sea' (1 Cor 10:2).

Baptismal font, twelfth century.
Church of San Frediano, Lucca (Italy).
Photo: The Conway Library, Courtauld Institute of Art, London.

XVI

Channels of Grace

WHAT IS A sacrament? The english word comes from the latin *sacramentum*, which means literally 'something to be set apart' or 'something to be held sacred'. In Greek, the word is *mysterion* or 'mystery'. As far as the early fathers were concerned, a sacrament was anything that sanctified you, and that could include all sorts of things. To repeat the Creed or the Lord's Prayer with true devotion could sanctify you, and the Creed and the Lord's Prayer might therefore be regarded as sacraments. Augustine says so. His own broad definition of a sacrament was simply 'the sign of something sacred'[1], and on this basis the greatest sacrament was

1. Augustine, *De civitate Dei* 10.5; *PL* 41: 282. The canonical definition of Thomas Aquinas, produced some eight centuries later, was not very different: a

the Incarnation, a view which could be supported by quoting the Vulgate text of 1 Timothy 3:16: 'the sacrament of godliness, which was manifested in the flesh.'

In the twelfth century, the view of Hugh of Saint-Victor was similarly broad, and he listed as many as thirty sacraments, dividing them up into three groups. The first group comprised those sacraments which are essential to salvation: baptism and the eucharist; the second included those which are useful, though not essential, for salvation (being sprinkled with holy water, for example); the third contained those which could be seen as a preparation for the sacraments listed in the first two groups. It was an original and interesting analysis, though it was not to have lasting influence.

In the east the situation was little different. Theodore of Studios listed six sacraments: baptism, chrismation, eucharist, ordination, monastic tonsure, and burial. In *The Life in Christ*, Nicholas Cabasilas considers only three: baptism, chrismation, and the eucharist. And although the eastern and western churches eventually adopted the same number of sacraments (seven), they did not always agree as to which should be included. Indeed, the Greeks did not always agree even among themselves. There was never any doubt about baptism, chrismation, and the eucharist, but beyond that there was considerable variation.

Much of the problem lay in the fact that 'sacrament' was not a term clearly defined in scripture. Both Lanfranc and Alger of Liège had noted that the word appeared with numerous meanings, and it was not until the twelfth century that the now traditional number of seven came to be widely accepted. Even then, we are speaking of the western church, and even there, there was still dispute.

The first work to present a formal list of the seven sacraments which, for the west, were to become canonical was probably an anonymous treatise called the *Sententiae divinitatis* (*Sentences*

---

sacrament is 'a sign of a sacred reality inasmuch as it sanctifies people' (*Summa theologiae* 3a.60.2; Blackfriars ed. 56: 8).

on Divinity) which dates from about 1145, just about ten years before Lombard compiled his *Sentences*. The sacraments listed there are baptism, confirmation, eucharist, penance, unction, orders, and matrimony, and the text divides them up into two groups: five sacraments which are common to all Christians (baptism, confirmation, eucharist, penance, and unction); and two which are not (ordination and matrimony). In this chapter we shall confine ourselves to the five common sacraments.

But what was the reason for the number seven? It is not entirely clear, and none of the traditional definitions of a sacrament points to this specific number. One is too wide; one is too vague; and one is too limited. We have already seen that the old definition of Augustine—a sacrament is 'the sign of a sacred reality'—was too wide. What, then, of the definition that came to be accepted as standard in the Middle Ages: a sacrament is 'the visible form of invisible grace'? This definition was also attributed to Augustine, though it had not been devised by him. It seems first to have been formulated by the heretical Berengar, but by a series of misunderstandings, medieval theologians had come to attribute it to the orthodox bishop of Hippo. Whatever its origin, it is of little use in helping us decide how many sacraments there should be. The problem lies in the vague term 'visible form'. What does it mean? In baptism and the eucharist, the nature of the 'visible form' is obvious: in baptism it is water; in the eucharist it is bread and wine. But what is the 'visible form' in penance or in marriage? There was never any clear answer to this question.

A third definition was too limiting. Some theologians—the first may have been Hugh of Saint-Victor—suggested that in order for a rite to be a sacrament, it must have been instituted by Christ. But here, too, difficulties arise. Medieval churchmen had no doubt that Christ had instituted baptism and the eucharist,[2] but whether he had also instituted penance, confirmation, and unction was a matter of considerable dispute. Some said penance

2. For baptism, see Mt 28:19; for the eucharist, see Mk 14:22–25 and parallels.

XVI-2/3 These images of the seven sacraments illustrate the best-known work of William Durandus, Bishop of Mende and canon lawyer. Entitled *Rationale divinorum officiorum*, it is a compendium of liturgical knowledge with a mystical interpretation. Each of the seven sacraments is illustrated in the seven roundels woven into the rich background decoration. On the left, a baby is baptized in a font while the parents and godparents stand on either side. Confirmation is illustrated by two children receiving a bishop's blessing: and on the right, a bishop and the pastoral candidates before an altar show the bestowal of holy orders. On the facing page (left to right) are marriage, with the couple and witnesses standing before a priest; penance, illustrated by confession; eucharist, with the communicant kneeling, his mouth wide open; and extreme unction, a deathbed scene with the priest administering the sacrament.

The Seven Sacraments from the *Rationale divinorum officiorum* by William Durandus, 1385–1406.
Vienna, Österreichische Nationalbibliothek, codex 2765, f° 1ᵛ-2.
Photo: Österreichische Nationalbibliothek, Vienna.

had been instituted by John the Baptist's call to repentance; and as for unction, the consensus was that it all began with James.[3]

The truth of the matter seems to be that the origins of the number seven lie deeply rooted in traditional medieval numerology, for among both Jews and Christians, seven had always been regarded as a sacred number and a number of perfection. There were seven days of creation, Jacob served Laban for seven years, there were seven fat oxen and seven lean ones in Pharaoh's dream, Balaam had Balak build him seven altars, there were seven lamps on the lampstand in the vision of Zechariah, and the Book of Revelation is crammed to overflowing with groups of seven: churches, candlesticks, spirits, angels, seals, trumpets, bowls, and plagues. One of the most important of these groupings, noted by both east and west, was the list of the seven gifts of the Holy Spirit in Isaiah 11:2–4. Whatever the reason, seven was the number that came to be accepted, and the list that appeared in the *Sententiae divinitatis* was taken over by Peter Lombard and set out in the fourth book of his *Sentences*. From there it was adopted by Thomas Aquinas and given formal approval at the Council of Florence in 1439 and the Council of Trent in 1545–63. But if we are to signal one person as being primarily responsible for its acceptance, that person is undoubtedly Peter Lombard.

Despite the fact that it was a western formulation, the number seven also found wide acceptance in the east. But as we noted above, although the number itself proved popular, there was no agreement during the medieval period as to which sacraments should be included. It was not until the seventeenth century, when western influence on the east was at its greatest, that Orthodoxy accepted the Lombardian-Aquinian list.

When we move on to consider the purpose and operation of the sacraments, there is (happily) a large measure of agreement between east and west. Indeed, this is one of the few chapters in this book which is not dominated by controversy. While it is

---

3. Jm 5:14–15. We will discuss the matter later in this chapter.

true that there are often considerable differences in the *liturgies* associated with the sacraments, there is remarkable unanimity as to what they actually do. Let us begin with a glance at baptism and chrismation/confirmation.

In *A Cloud of Witnesses*[4] we explained that from the earliest days of the church, baptism was understood as effecting four things: firstly, Christ was accepted as one's Saviour; secondly, one became a full member of the universal church; thirdly, one's previous sins, original and otherwise, were washed away; and fourthly, one received the grace of the Holy Spirit. In the Middle Ages, these beliefs remained undisputed, though the ways in which the rites were administered had undergone certain changes. The east, for example, still insisted on total immersion in baptism (so far as was practicable), whereas from about the eighth century onwards, the west was more inclined to use *affusion*, the pouring of water on the head of the child. This was probably for reasons of health in a colder climate, not for reasons of theology, and in a few places, total immersion was still being practised in the west as late as the time of Thomas Aquinas.

We know, too, that what were originally two distinct parts of a single rite—baptismal immersion followed by anointing and the laying on of hands—became separated in the west, though in the east the older tradition was (and is) maintained. The reason for this was again no more than practicality. In the early church, the bishop and only the bishop baptised, anointed, and laid hands on those who wished to be initiated into Christianity, but after the fourth century, when Christianity had become the official state religion, the number of prospective Christians was simply too great to permit this practice to continue. What was to be done?

Western bishops solved the problem by delegating to the local priest the power to baptise, but reserved for themselves the laying on of hands. But since few bishops had the time (or

4. See *Cloud* 184–8.

the inclination) to attend every baptism, it became usual to delay what came to be called confirmation until a sufficient number of children merited an episcopal visitation or until the bishop was able to attend to the matter. In either case, it involved a delay between baptism and confirmation; and since confirmation was a necessary prerequisite for the reception of the eucharist, this too was subject to the same delay. The length of the delay was nowhere specified: it could be days, months, or even years.

The eastern bishops found a different solution. There, the entire rite—baptismal immersion and chrismation—was delegated to the local priest, and the role of the bishop was restricted to consecrating the holy oil—the chrism—before it was distributed to local clergy. In this way, there was no need for any delay between baptism and chrismation, and any child who had been baptised and chrismated was a full, communicating member of the church and was at once admitted to the eucharist. The Orthodox churches have maintained this practice to the present day.

In the west, however, the delay between baptism and the anointing and laying on of hands gave rise to certain theological problems. If immersion washed away sins and the laying on of hands communicated grace, what happened to children who died between baptism and confirmation? Did they simply go to hell, deprived of grace? The answer was that they did not, and in the fifth century the western church devised a theology to explain why they did not. Baptismal immersion itself bestowed grace upon the child, and if the child died there and then or shortly afterwards, baptismal grace was more than sufficient to ensure its immediate entry into the kingdom of heaven. But if the child survived to face the troubles and temptations of this world, additional help was necessary. That is where confirmation or 'strengthening' (*confirmatio* in Latin) comes in. The laying on of hands communicates to the child a further supply of grace to assist it in coping with life's manifold problems and, as we suggested in *A Cloud of Witnesses*, it may be likened to a booster shot which strengthens and renders fully effective a prior vaccination.[5] In some ways, says Lombard, confirmation may be regarded as a greater sacrament even than baptism, for when a child is confirmed there is bestowed upon it the seven-fold grace of the Holy Spirit in all its fullness of holiness and virtue.

Although both west and east were agreed on the essential functions of baptism, there can nevertheless be discerned between them a difference of emphasis, a difference which derives from the fact that the western church lived in the long shadow of Augustine and the eastern church did not. The origins of the difference lie in the Pelagian Controversy, a matter which we discussed in A *Cloud of Witnesses*[6], and which led the west to take a much more pessimistic view of the human condition than did the east.

Before this bitter and protracted dispute in the fifth century, there was no great difference between the approaches of east and west. Both agreed that the sin of Adam and Eve in Eden had in some way affected all their descendants. Both agreed that although we have all been contaminated by this original sin, the degree to which we have been contaminated is not insuperable. That is to say, we still possess free-will and we can still do good actions, though without grace, we cannot do enough good actions to achieve salvation. Yet even one good deed is not to be despised, for God may respond to this by making his grace available to us and thereby enabling us to do yet more good deeds and merit yet more of his grace. Thus, in cooperation with grace and only in cooperation with grace, we may slowly ascend the path that leads to salvation and the endless glory of the Beatific Vision. The eastern church always retained this optimistic view; the western church did not. Why not?

The answer is simple: because of Augustine. His whole-hearted opposition to the views of Pelagius led him inexorably to the belief that at birth we are not just partially stained with the sins of our first parents, but are totally depraved, wholly

---

5. See *Cloud* 187.
6. See *Cloud* Chapter XII.

condemned, and destined only for damnation. At birth we are 'one lump of sin'.[7] It follows, therefore, that if a baby dies before it has been baptised, it dies in sin. The sin is not its own sin, that is true (it is actually Adam's sin), but sin it is and sin must be punished. The baby's soul, therefore, must go to hell (Augustine says so), and although its eternal suffering there may not be as great as if its sins were its own, it must and will suffer. One can understand, therefore, the western stress on the importance of baptizing a child as soon as possible after birth (or even in the womb if there is a danger of still-birth), and the western emphasis on the first part of the baptismal rite: the washing off of original sin.

The eastern emphasis was different. Although the Greeks had agreed with the condemnation of Pelagius, they had not accepted the views of Augustine. Orthodoxy remained faithful to the older idea outlined above: the Fall has certainly affected us, but it has not left us in a condition of total depravity. We can still do good, though only in cooperation with grace can we be saved. It follows from this that the easterners tended to lay more stress on the positive side of the baptismal rite and to emphasize the importance of the communication of grace and the child's rebirth into the new life in Christ. The real importance of baptism was not that it cleansed one from the sin of Adam (though this was not denied), but that it was a promise of future joy, a guarantee of participation in Christ's resurrection, and the beginning of our deification. And just as we have no part to play in our physical birth, neither do we play any role in our spiritual rebirth. It is all a gift of God. By his grace we have died with Christ and have been buried in the baptismal waters; by his grace we have been raised with Christ and have come forth from our liquid tomb; by his grace we have been constituted a new creature in Christ; by his grace we are conjoined with him through Christ; and by his grace we are assured of everlasting life.

It may be suggested, therefore, that since baptism marks the beginning of our restoration and our entry into the ark of

7. See *Cloud* 147.

salvation, it is actually of more importance than the eucharist. So important, indeed, that unlike the eucharist, baptism (in an emergency) can be administered by anyone: clergy, laity, christian, or non-christian alike.[8] But despite the logic of this approach and despite occasional statements that baptism was indeed 'chief among the sacraments', there is a vast difference between the two. In baptism, we are touched by the power of the grace of God; at the eucharist we are in his very presence. The water of baptism does not *become* God, but the bread and wine of the eucharist are changed substantially into the body and blood of Christ. It is understandable, then, that the uniqueness of the eucharist would elevate it to a position of preeminence, and the resolution of the eucharistic controversies in the west in favour of the Real Presence simply confirmed this trend. As we saw in the last chapter, it was a trend that reached its apogee with the institution of the Feast of Corpus Christi. Baptism is still essential—you need to come in through the door before you can sit down at the table—but for most people, the pleasure of an invitation to dinner lies primarily in the food and wine, not in the greetings on the doorstep.

One final point before we leave the subject of baptism. As we said above, it was the view of Augustine that unbaptized infants who died in original sin would go to hell. But although this approach was logical, it was thought by many later writers to be if not unfair, at least inhumane, and the scholastic theologians of the twelfth and thirteenth centuries made a number of attempts to mitigate it. The final formulation, and the one which was to be accepted throughout the later Middle Ages, was that of Thomas Aquinas who maintained that such unfortunates do not go to hell, but to limbo. Here they experience the fullness of natural happiness, but are deprived of the supernatural happiness of the Beatific Vision. In other words, they are as happy as they could possibly be in the natural world, but they miss the indescribable

---

8. This is the western view. Orthodoxy requires that the person administering baptism must first have been baptized.

joy which comes with the vision of God. To experience that, they would need to have been baptized and cleansed from original sin. Here, however, we are anticipating ourselves, for limbo is one of the Last Things, and full discussion must be left until our final chapter.

By baptism our sins are washed away; by chrismation or confirmation, we are endowed with grace; by the regular reception of the body and blood of Christ, that grace is ever renewed and the process of our redemption and deification is continued. But still we sin. We even enjoy it. So what can we do about it? To deal with the chronic problem of human misconduct, the church developed the sacrament of penance, and, from the fourth century onwards, a great deal of material was produced on the subject.[9] Over the years, however, dramatic changes took place in the way in which penance was undergone, and the situation in the Middle Ages, both in the west and in the east, was very different from what it had been in the early church.

For about five centuries, penance was regarded as a 'second baptism', and just as one's first baptism could not be repeated, neither could one's second. Penance was public; it involved exclusion from the eucharist and a prolonged course of prayer, fasting, and almsgiving; in some cases it lasted for years; and after it was all over and one had been restored to communion, one was still required to spend the rest of one's days in chastity and continence. If you could manage it, therefore, it was wise to put off penance until the very last moment, though such a feat demanded a delicate sense of timing. You never know when you're going to have a heart-attack.

Such a penitential system was just too severe to survive, and in the late sixth century we begin to see in the west the development of a less stringent attitude to the problem of post-baptismal sin. Firstly, penitential practice began to change from public confession before a bishop to private confession to a priest; secondly, it came to be accepted that penance could be repeated;

9. See *Cloud* 188–9.

and thirdly, the demand for life-long continence as part of one's penance was quietly dropped. Public confession and penance, however, especially at Easter, were still not entirely superseded.

Accompanying this process of mitigation we see the appearance of convenient handbooks designed to assist local priests in judging the severity of sins and apportioning appropriate penances. These Penitentials, or Penitential Books, listed sins by category—murder, excess, drunkenness, fornication, and so on—and each category was subdivided into specific sins together with the length of the penance. Here are a few random examples:

> If any member of the ordained clergy is a habitual drunkard, he shall either desist or be deposed.
> If a monk gets drunk and vomits, he shall do penance for thirty days.
> If a deacon or priest does this, he shall do penance for forty days.
> If a lay Christian does this, he shall do penance for fifteen days.
> If a person vomits because he has eaten too much, he shall do penance for three days.
> If a man has intercourse with an animal, he shall do penance for ten years.
> If a man commits fornication with another man, he shall do penance for ten years.
> If a woman commits fornication with another woman, she shall do penance for three years.
> If a man has intercourse with his mother or his sister, he shall do penance for fifteen years.[10]

Such lists certainly give us a fascinating glimpse into the varieties of deviant behaviour in the Middle Ages, but whether the lengthy penances were ever carried out is unknown. What

10. These are paraphrased from the seventh-century *Penitential of Theodore.* A complete translation of this and other Penitentials may be found in J. T. McNeill & H. M. Gamer, *Medieval Handbooks of Penance* (New York, 1938; rpt. 1965).

is known is that from the first appearance of these popular Penitentials, a system was devised which enabled the penitent to substitute for a harsh and unpleasant penance such things as fasting, almsgiving, or repetition of psalms. In some cases, it was even possible to arrange for someone else to do the penance for you, but that particular solution was obviously wide-open to abuse.

In the early days of the new penitential system, absolution was given only after one had completed the penance, but as time went on it became more usual for the priest to give a conditional absolution at the time of confession, and then send the penitent away to do whatever needed to be done. Furthermore, the closer we approach the eleventh and twelfth centuries, the more the emphasis is put on confession and contrition, and the less on the severity of the penance. The monastic movement made an important contribution here, for the daily disclosure of one's thoughts and intentions to one's abbot or spiritual father had been a distinctive part of monastic life from the earliest period. Since most of those responsible for the spread of Christianity and the development of christian doctrine had had monastic training and formation, it was only natural that they would introduce to the world outside the enclosure the practices with which they had been so familiar inside.

By the second half of the eleventh century, private confession by the laity, especially before major feasts, was common in the west, though it was not until 1215 that the Fourth Lateran Council required annual confession by all western Christians. But from the mid-eleventh century onwards, the most important part of a priest's pastoral work involved hearing confessions and dealing with moral problems. It also provided them with an unrivalled knowledge of exactly what was going on in their parishes. One can therefore understand the concern of the local clergy when the ordained members of the mendicant Orders—the Franciscans and the Dominicans—began to take over this function in the thirteenth century. The laity loved the anonymity; the parish priests loathed the loss of control. One may also see how such a practice, intended originally to foster spiritual growth and

Many Mansions

encourage people to live a moral life, could be abused. The most obvious abuses were the sale of indulgences and the scandal of the pardoners.

The principle behind an indulgence is simple and wholly christian. Good deeds will be rewarded by God. If, in true charity and devotion, we decide to give money to a good cause, we may assume that God will take note of the fact. In theological terms, we accumulate merit. What could be more christian than to share this merit with others less fortunate? To offer it to those you love rather than keeping it for yourself? And since God's mercy is limited neither by time nor by space, this accumulated merit might also be used to relieve the sufferings—albeit well deserved—of souls in purgatory or even, perhaps, in hell. This idea of remission from purgatorial pain, either for oneself or for others, was central to the principle of the indulgence, but a full discussion of that matter must be left for our final chapter. An indulgence that provides a full and complete remission of the pains of purgatory is referred to as a plenary indulgence; one which provides only partial remission is a partial indulgence.

The earliest known issue of a plenary indulgence was in 1095 when Pope Urban II promised it to all who were prepared to take part in the First Crusade and brave its dangers. The idea proved popular, and in the course of the twelfth and thirteenth centuries, such indulgences were granted more and more frequently. But it is easy to see how the principle could be misused. The idea of obtaining a just reward for good deeds could easily be converted into the idea of buying salvation, and Martin Luther's attack on the plenary indulgence proclaimed in 1517 by Pope Leo IX for contributions to the rebuilding of the new Saint Peter's was understandable and justified. It reflected the repugnance felt by many theologians to what had become a lucrative and super-stitious trade. The pardoner, who went about Europe hawking indulgences to line his own pockets as well as those of his masters, was a common sight in the later Middle Ages, but many church-men were loathe to criticize such abuses with too much severity since the activities of the pardoners were a most important and effective source of revenue. Despite severe denunciations by such writers as Geoffrey Chaucer, William Langland, and John Wycliffe, the pardoners did a very good trade. Ten dollars, after all, is a small price to pay to escape the pains of purgatory or the everlasting fires of hell.

What we have said of penance so far relates primarily to the western church, and the development of the sacrament in the greek east followed a rather different course. Until the fifth century, both east and west shared a common history of the discipline, but after that they parted company. We do not find a greek equivalent of the Penitential Books, and from the sixth century onwards, the monastic emphasis on spiritual guidance rather than confession and absolution became dominant in the east. Orthodoxy always recognized the universality of sin, but it was never so besotted with the problem as was the west. Once again, Augustine must take most of the responsibility, but the satisfaction-theology of Anselm of Canterbury also played an important role. As we saw above, the east never shared the western belief in the total depravity of fallen human beings, nor did it interpret the death of Christ primarily in terms of a legal satisfaction for our sins.

The greek literature on the sacrament emphasizes repentance rather than penance[11], and almost none of the writers states that formal sacramental absolution is necessary. It may be psychologically useful, but it is not essential; and even if it is given, it need not be given through a priest. Non-ordained monks could (and can) give absolution, and Orthodoxy, then as now, emphasized that the forgiveness of sins was ultimately a matter between the penitent and God. The priest or monk was no more than a witness. This concept is reflected in the Orthodox liturgy, for in the Greek Orthodox tradition the priest who hears one's confession does not say 'I absolve you', but 'May *God* absolve you', and although we do find the 'I absolve' formula in Russian

---

11. So too does modern Roman Catholicism, but that was not the case until the Second Vatican Council.

Orthodoxy, that is simply the result of western influence and is not found before the seventeenth century.

Discussion of the last of the five common sacraments—unction—need not long detain us. The text normally cited by both eastern and western theologians as the scriptural basis for the rite is found in the Letter of James: 'Are any among you sick? They should call for the elders of the church and have them pray over them, anointing them with oil in the name of the Lord. The prayer of faith will save the sick, and the Lord will raise them up; and anyone who has committed sins will be forgiven.'[12] The Greeks took this text at face value and offered the sacrament to all who were sick; the west reserved it for those who were dying. It was also customary in the east to have more than one priest involved—the ideal number was seven, though five or three was (and is) common—and the sacrament had two purposes: the healing of the body and the cleansing of the soul. If those who were sick recovered, all well and good. If they died, they died with their sins forgiven and at peace with their Maker.

Lombard's brief discussion provides us with the western view of the sacrament. He defines it as 'the anointing of the sick, which is done at the end [of life] with oil consecrated by a bishop'[13]; he traces its institution to the passage from the letter of James quoted above; and, as usual, he distinguishes between the sacrament itself and the reality behind the sacrament. The outward sign is the actual anointing; the inward grace is the remission of sins and the increase of virtues. He concludes with a discussion as to whether the sacrament can be repeated, and decides, reasonably, that it can. But despite Lombard's statement that bodily recovery is perfectly possible, the west did not normally expect it and generally referred to the sacrament as *extreme* unction, thus implying the imminence of death.[14] In Latin, *extremus* can be

---

12. Jm 5:14–15 (NRSV).

13. Peter Lombard, *Sententiae* IX.xxiii.1; ed. I. Brady (Grottaferrata, 1981) 2: 390.

14. Again, the Second Vatican Council brought about changes in this matter, but this is not the place to discuss them.

translated 'last' or 'at the end'. Orthodoxy simply refers to the sacrament as the *euchelaion*, 'the oil of prayer'.

Let us suppose, then, that as a medieval Christian, eastern or western, you have been baptized and chrismated or confirmed. You have attended the eucharist in complete faith all your years. You have regularly received the body and blood of Christ. You have attempted to imitate him in your life and work. You have made regular confession of your sins and have received either absolution or the guidance of your spiritual father. You are now on your deathbed and have been anointed with holy oil. The time of death approaches. The veils descend. And slowly and gently (let us hope) you take your leave of this troubled planet and begin your journey to an unknown destination. Where are you going? If you are an easterner, you can be fairly sure you are making your way to heaven. But if you are a westerner, you have no guarantee at all. Why not? Because Augustine and his successors have repeatedly reminded you of what it says in Romans 9:22–23: that God has made some of us vessels of wrath intended for destruction, and some of us vessels of mercy which he has prepared beforehand for glory. In other words, you have to take account of predestination, and it is now time for us to consider the problems and controversies relating to that dubious doctrine.

XVII-1 The Last Judgment was a common subject for the tympanum over the western door in a romanesque church. At Conques Abbey on the pilgrimage road to Compostella, the sculptor has established an architectural frame in which the various actions of Judgment Day have been tidily arranged. Christ sits formally at the top center, indicating with semaphoric gesture the two options available to mortals below. At his feet, angels lift the lids off sarcophagi while the dead climb sleepily out. At his right hand, the worthy are received into their heavenly reward (under the arcade, for example, Abraham holds two little souls to his bosom). Heaven is serene and organized; its inhabitants are well-clothed, all have shoes, some are smiling. Hell, while perhaps a less desirable permanent condition, was certainly more fun to illustrate, and is charged with acts of torture, ropes and threatening tools, devils, snakes, and repulsive beasts, convoluted positions, crowds and general chaos, culminating in fire and brimstone at the bottom right.

Last Judgment, twelfth century.
Conques (France), Pilgrimage church of Sainte-Foy.
Photo: James Austin.

XVII

Vessels of Wrath
and Vessels of Mercy

A PREOCCUPATION with the problems of predestination was almost entirely a western phenomenon. The reason for this is not far to seek. At the root of the matter, yet again, lie the ideas of Augustine of Hippo, and although the scriptures seem to make reference to some sort of predestination, it was the doctrines of Augustine which made it a major concern.

The scriptures offer evidence of predestination both in the gospels and in the letters. In Matthew 20:23, for example, Jesus tells his disciples that the decision as to who will sit on his right or left in heaven is not up to him. 'It is for those (he says) for whom it has been prepared by my Father.' More explicit is the

pauline teaching in Romans 8:28–30, where we are told that
God knows in advance those who are called according to his
purpose, and that these he predestines to be conformed to the
image of his Son. 'And those whom he predestined he also called;
and those whom he called he also justified; and those whom he
justified he also glorified' (Rm 8: 30). In Romans, too, we find the
reference, mentioned at the end of the last chapter, to 'vessels
of wrath, made for destruction', which God has endured with
much patience, and 'vessels of mercy, which he has prepared
in advance for glory' (Rm 9:22–23). But against these ideas we
must place the statement in 1 Timothy 2:4 that God wants
everyone to be saved and to come to the knowledge of the truth.
If God had made up his mind on the matter, the controversy
over predestination might never have occurred.

Augustine, however, was not in the least ambivalent, and had
no doubt at all that predestination is a necessary part of the
divine plan. His logic is impeccable, though his conclusions are
uncomfortable. In his view, since human beings have inherited
the whole of the sin of Adam and Eve, they are born 100%
depraved and incapable of performing even a single good act
by their own volition.[1] At birth we are *una massa peccati*, 'one
sinful lump'; and because we are *una massa peccati*, we are also
una massa damnati, 'one damned or condemned lump.' How,
then, can we be saved? Only by grace. So how can we get grace?
Here lies the problem.

Because we are incapable of performing any good actions by
our own power, we can never earn or deserve grace. It's like telling
a person who is totally blind that you will pay for the operation
that will restore their sight provided they first read the top line
of the optician's chart. They can't even see the chart, much less
the top line. So if we do not deserve grace and cannot earn it,
what can we do to gain it? The answer, obviously, is nothing at all.
The matter is entirely in the hands of God. He alone will decide
to whom he will make his grace available, and those to whom it

1. See *Cloud* 147–8.

is made available may be saved. Those to whom it is not made available can only go to hell. Since they cannot do a single good action by their own volition, they have nowhere else to go. Such, in a nutshell, is Augustine's doctrine of predestination.

Many of us would not consider this doctrine to be particularly fair, but that is not the view of Augustine. It *must* be fair because God is fair. He is, by definition, a just God and cannot do anything that is not just. The problem is that we cannot possibly understand how his mind works—the finite cannot comprehend the infinite—and when Augustine is questioned on this matter, he normally takes refuge in the statement that God's judgments are inscrutable. Whether this is any consolation to those condemned to everlasting torment I do not know.

Augustine's doctrine of predestination is referred to as Single Predestination. This means that there is but one single act of predestination, and that by this one act God predestines some of us to receive grace. What happens to the rest of us is not stated. By Double Predestination, we maintain *two* acts of predestination: on the one hand, God predestines some of us to receive grace and go to heaven; on the other, he predestines the rest not to receive his grace and go to hell. But although the end result is the same, there is a certain difference between the two approaches. It is one thing to watch a man walking blindly towards the edge of a cliff and do nothing to stop him from falling over; it is another to go up to him, put your hands in the middle of his back, and give him a good push. In the one case, the law may not condemn you; in the other, you are guilty of first-degree murder. In actual fact, neither approach could be called particularly christian, and one of the major problems that arises out of augustinian predestination is how we can defend the Almighty from the accusation that he is either a cold-blooded killer, or, like Rhett Butler, he just doesn't give a damn.

It is often stated, presumably by those who have never read Augustine, that he himself does not teach Double Predestination. This is not true. It may not be his usual teaching, but we do find him saying that some people are 'predestined to condemnation'[2], or that they are 'predestined to go into eternal fire with the devil'.[3] It was such harsh statements as these that enabled Gottschalk of Orbais, whom we shall meet in a moment, to maintain that in his own teachings he was doing no more than reiterating the ideas of the bishop of Hippo.

We saw in A Cloud of Witnesses that Augustine's ideas were not without their critics, even in the west.[4] In the fifth and sixth centuries we see the development of what would later be called Semi-Pelagianism[5], a viewpoint much the same as that held by the west before Augustine and by the east both before and after his time. According to Semi-Pelagianism, we have been seriously, *but not wholly*, contaminated by original sin, and because the contamination is not total, we can still choose to do some good actions. God may then respond to these good actions by making his grace available, and enabling us to cooperate with this grace in attaining salvation. Semi-Pelagianism, however, was condemned at the Council of Orange in 529, and from that time onwards the doctrines of Augustine were accepted as the norm in the latin west.

The first major controversy to centre on predestination occurred in the ninth century when a reluctant benedictine monk named Gottschalk began preaching the extreme views of Augustine and openly advocating Double Predestination. Gottschalk (c.805-c.868) had been forced by his parents to enter the famous benedictine abbey of Fulda[6], but was never happy in the monastic life. He fled from the monastery and initially obtained a dispensation from his monastic vows, but because of the opposition of the abbot of Fulda, this dispensation was revoked and Gottschalk was forced to return, if not to Fulda, at least to another benedictine house. He was assigned to the abbey of

2. Augustine, In evangelium Johannis, tractatus 111.5; PL 35: 1929.
3. Augustine, De civitate Dei, 21.24.1; PL 41: 737. There are at least three other similar passages.
4. See Cloud 150–51.
5. It could just as easily be called 'Semi-Augustinianism'.
6. Fulda lies about fifty miles north-east of Frankfurt in modern Germany.

Orbais near Soissons. Here he devoted himself to study, especially the study of Augustine, and it was here that he developed the doctrines which were to cause such a furore.

According to Gottschalk, no-one born in original sin can do any good at all. No-one therefore can be saved without grace. But since God and God alone decides to whom he will make his grace available, he does not will the salvation of everyone, and Christ died only for the predestined. It follows, therefore, that those who are not predestined for salvation are predestined for hell. Such, said Gottschalk, is the teaching of Augustine; such is the teaching of the church.

But if this is so, how can we explain the statement in 1 Timothy 2:4 that God wants everyone to be saved? Gottschalk once again finds his inspiration in Augustine and solves the problem by combining 1 Timothy 2:4 with Romans 9:18. The verse in Timothy tells us that God 'wills that everyone should be saved'; the verse in Romans tells us that 'he has mercy on whom he wills'. The word for 'wills' is identical in both verses, and what this means, says Gottschalk, is that God 'wills' salvation not for everyone, but for those whom he 'wills' shall be saved: in other words, those he has predestined to glory.

There were those who agreed with Gottschalk. Ratramnus of Corbie, whom we met in Chapter XV, was one. But there were others who were implacably opposed, and the most influential of these was the archbishop of Reims, Hincmar (c.806–882). Hincmar was an ecclesiastical politician and canon lawyer rather than a speculative theologian, but he succeeded in pin-pointing the three essential problems of Double Predestination, and offered his own solution to the question.

The problems, said Hincmar, are as follows. Firstly, Double Predestination denies the teaching of scripture. It denies 1 Timothy 2:4, which states that God wants everyone to be saved; and it denies such passages as 2 Corinthians 5:14–15[7], which declare

---

7. 2 Cor 5:14–15: 'For the love of Christ urges us on, because we are convinced that one has died for all; therefore all have died. And he died for all, so that

that Christ died for all. Secondly, if we say that God predestines some people to go to hell, what we are saying, effectively, is that God creates some people so that they will sin and, as a consequence, suffer everlasting pain. Such a view makes God the author of evil and it cannot be reconciled with a belief in a God who is infinitely loving and perfectly good. Thirdly, if we say that some people are to be saved and the rest are to be condemned, what place is there in this for free-will? Hincmar, therefore, accuses Gottschalk of denying free-will and of reducing a human being to the status of an automaton.

Hincmar's solution, which was based on Ambrose and a sixth-century treatise attributed to Augustine but not written by him, was to make a distinction between foreknowledge and predestination. The two are not the same. To know something in advance is not necessarily to make it happen. If you see someone pick up a glass and then drop it, you know in advance that it is going to hit the floor and break. But you are not responsible for the damage. But if *you* pick up the glass and deliberately let it fall, you both foreknow and predestine its destruction on the floor. The analogy we introduced above—watching a man walk over a cliff as distinct from actually pushing him—illustrates the same thing.

God, says Hincmar, knew everything in advance. When the worlds came into being, he knew exactly what would happen at all times and in all places, from events of the greatest moment (such as the Incarnation) to those of the slightest consequence (such as my making this splling erorr on this computer). He therefore knew in advance what everyone would do and whether they would be good or wicked, but he does not force them to do good nor does he compel them to be wicked. That is up to them. Then, for those whom God knows will be good, he predestines heaven, and for those whom he knows will be wicked, he predestines hell.

---

those who live might live no longer for themselves, but for him who died and was raised for them' (NRSV).

Hincmar's scheme certainly has advantages. Firstly, it does not deny the universality of the saving will of God, nor does it deny that Christ died for all. God does indeed want everyone to be saved, but not everyone will cooperate with him in fulfilling his desire. Christ has indeed died for everyone, but not everyone will take advantage of it. Secondly, Hincmar's scheme does not make God the author of evil. God does not force us to act wickedly. That is our own choice. But if we *do* act wickedly, then we must pay the price. Thirdly, Hincmar does not deny free-will. We are not compelled to be either good or wicked. It's entirely up to us. And although God knows in advance what choices we will make, he predestines only the *consequences* of those choices, he does not predestine the choices themselves.

On the other hand, there are also two major problems, and Hincmar's opponents were not slow in drawing attention to them. Firstly, to say that God predestines only the consequences of our actions may support one passage in scripture, but it denies others. Romans 9:18 states specifically that God has mercy on whom he wills, and he hardens the heart of whom he wills. It is *God* who does this, not us. He selects some and has mercy on them; he selects others and hardens their hearts. He makes some vessels of mercy and he makes others vessels of wrath. This is an unambiguous and incontrovertible statement that God directly affects human beings: he does not leave them to their own devices and predestine only their eventual reward or punishment. Since this is the teaching of Saint Paul, it must also be the teaching of the church. But it was not the teaching of Hincmar.

Secondly, Hincmar's idea that we use our free-will to choose either good or evil and that God foreknows what we will choose is contrary to the established teaching of Augustine. It also teeters on the brink of Semi-Pelagianism and, as we saw above, Semi-Pelagianism had been condemned by the western church in 529. The whole point of Augustine's teaching is that because we are born *una massa peccati*, 'one lump of sin', we can *never* choose good unless we are first given grace; and since the only way we can get grace is by God's free gift, whether we get it or not is entirely up to him. For Hincmar to say that 'God foreknows those who will do good' is absurd. *No-one* can do good without grace, and those who receive grace are those whom God has predestined to receive it.

Hincmar's opponents had a point. He does not, in fact, accept that as a result of original sin we can do no good at all. The Fall had a severe effect, Hincmar had no doubt of that, but in his view it did not wholly annihilate our ability for good actions. Our free-will has been rendered 'weak and feeble' as far as our capacity for doing good is concerned, but Hincmar does not agree either with Augustine or with Gottschalk that of our own power we can only fall. Is this Semi-Pelagianism? Yes, it is. Is it heretical? According to the decisions of the Council of Orange: Yes, it is.

Hincmar's attempt at solving the problem of predestination did not work. It looked persuasive on the surface, but it was not a satisfactory answer to the question. Another and radically different solution was suggested by a scholar whom Hincmar himself had commissioned to prepare a decisive reply to the teachings of Gottschalk: John Scotus Eriugena[8] (c.810-c.877). He had been born in Ireland—both 'Eriugena' and 'Scotus' mean 'Irishman'—but had made his way to northern France, gained the patronage of Charles the Bald, and established schools at one or more of Charles's palaces. He was remarkable in being fluent in Greek, a most unusual accomplishment for a westerner at the time, and his fascination with greek ideas and greek philosophy led him to produce a distinctive and intriguing philosophy. He was the most original thinker of the ninth century.

Eriugena's attack on Gottschalk (whom he called a heretic, madman, and blasphemer) was utterly novel and reflects the degree to which he had been influenced by Later Platonism.[9] For him, God was the Neo-Platonic One: incomprehensible, indescribable, unsearchable, unknowable, un-everything-able, but overwhelmingly and supremely ONE. God is and has but one will, one love, one power, one wisdom, and so on, and in his

8. Or Erigena. Both spellings are common.
9. See *Cloud* 23–5.

unspeakable unity, to be, to will, to love, to know, to have, to do are all the same thing. Similarly, in that absolute Oneness, there is no past or present or future, there is only the Eternal Now. What does this imply for our discussion of foreknowledge and predestination?

First of all, since God is one and has only one will, one power, and the like, so there is only one predestination. Double predestination is a theological impossibility. God does not have two minds. Secondly, since God's willing, loving, knowing, and so on are all identical with his being, it follows that predestining and foreknowing are likewise identical. There can be no difference between them. But thirdly, if God is an Eternal Now, how can we speak of predestination and foreknowledge at all? Both terms imply a distinction between present and future, and present and future are all one in God. God may destine, but not *pre*destine; he may know, but not *fore*know. And since God's destining and knowing are identical, the whole problem can be resolved into a single incontrovertible statement: 'God is'!

But let us go further. Platonism taught that evil did not exist as a positive entity. It was simply the absence of good, something entirely negative. This was a well-known principle and had been accepted by many writers, including Augustine. It is like saying that darkness has no reality in itself, but is merely the absence of light. But if evil or sin has no positive existence, how can it be predestined? You cannot make someone do something that does not exist. No, says Eriugena, sin is not something foreordained by God, but the result of human beings abusing their God-given free-will. What we call 'doing evil' is actually 'not doing good', and the more we do evil, or do not do good, the more we separate ourselves from God. It is this separation from the divine source of all joy and blessedness that is our real punishment.

If, then, our punishment comes from within ourselves, what need is there for a physical hell? You're right, says Eriugena, there isn't one, and he presents two arguments to prove his case. The first is based once again on his belief that evil has no positive existence in its own right, for if evil has no positive existence, the idea of a totally evil place is an impossibility. Something wholly negative cannot exist. If you ask a woman what she has in her purse and she replies 'Nothing', you cannot then ask her to take out the Nothing and hand it round for inspection.

Eriugena's second argument is founded on the perfect beauty of the universe, for when God had finished his work on the sixth day of creation, he 'saw everything that he had made, and behold, it was very good' (Gen 1:31). How, then, could something so beautiful be marred by something as ugly as hell? Eriugena's own analogy is of a wonderful palace, richly and magnificently built, perfectly proportioned and beautifully adorned. God has built it both for his children (the good) and for his slaves (the wicked), but whereas the children enjoy it to the full, it provokes the slaves to envy and hence to suffering. They cultivate their own punishment and they make their own hell.

The reaction to Eriugena's treatise can easily be imagined. He had side-stepped the issue of predestination rather than solving it; he had denied the real existence of evil; and he had done away with hell. How could priests and prelates keep people on the straight and narrow if it had nothing with which to threaten them? Hincmar, who had commissioned the work, found himself in a most embarrassing position and could only get out of it by claiming that the treatise was a forgery. Others simply condemned it, and the controversy over predestination became a sort of theological free-for-all. The same arguments were reiterated again and again, and each side became ever more strident in its denunciation of the other.

Inevitably, the controversy became mixed up with politics, and synod followed synod with no final resolution being achieved. Hincmar called synods at Quiercy in 849 and 853 and, as we might expect, they condemned Gottschalk. Two years later, in 855, the Council of Valence supported Gottschalk and rejected the ideas of Hincmar. The council also condemned the treatise of Eriugena, as also did the Council of Langres in 859. Finally, a half-hearted reconciliation was achieved at the Council of Tuzey in 860, and the controversy gradually fizzled out in the later decades of the ninth century. It was not that it had been solved, but simply that both sides had exhausted all their arguments and were weary of the whole business. As for Gottschalk, whose ultra-augustinian ideas had precipitated the whole affair, the Synod of Quiercy in 849 deprived him of his priesthood and condemned him to life imprisonment in the abbey of Hautvillers in the diocese of Reims. Here he continued his feud with Hincmar, accusing him now of entertaining erroneous ideas about the Trinity, and in his last years he seems to have become more and more irrational and out of touch with reality. He died, unstable, unreconciled, and unrepentant, about 868.

Throughout the tenth and much of the eleventh century, the problem of predestination lay dormant. There seemed nothing else to say. But with the development of scholasticism and the appearance, beginning with Lombard, of various attempts at a logical and comprehensive presentation of the entire christian tradition, the matter had to be re-examined and some sort of understanding achieved. The same problems, however, still remained. On the one hand, the scriptures seemed to contradict themselves; and on the other, hard-line Augustinianism appeared to leave no effective place for human free-will. What was to be done?

Just as Gottschalk and Hincmar had represented two different approaches to the question—one emphasizing predestination rather than foreknowledge and the other foreknowledge rather than predestination—so we see the same two trends in the writers of the scholastic period. The two approaches are often referred to as 'predestination before (*ante*) foreseen merits' (*ante praevisa merita*), and 'predestination after (*post*) foreseen merits' (*post praevisa merita*).

The theory of predestination *ante praevisa merita* is firmly rooted in the doctrines of Augustine and it reflects the old ideas of Gottschalk. It was also the view of Thomas Aquinas and, following him, of the Dominicans. Central to it is the belief in the total depravity of human beings and their inability to do any good whatsoever without the aid of grace. According to this theory, God, from all eternity and for inscrutable reasons known only to himself, has decreed that certain people will achieve salvation. This has nothing whatever to do with them or their actions, nor has it anything to do with God foreseeing their goodness or wickedness. It is simply something determined by the Almighty, and there is nothing that we or they can do about it.

Having decided that this group, and this group alone, will be saved, God then provides its members with the graces necessary to attain their predestined end. In other words, God first assigns the goal, and then provides the means by which the goal may be achieved; but in the order in which things actually occur, the means merit the goal. Imagine a group of starving people. If they do not get food, they will die. Someone then appears with food enough for all, but decides, for obscure reasons, that it shall be given to only three people. These three are given the food, they eat it, and they survive. They may then say, in all honesty, that the reason they survived was because they ate the food. The real reason, however, was that they were the only ones selected to receive it in the first place.

The question of how many people had been chosen by God to belong to this fortunate group was unclear. Augustine suggested that the number of the predestined would be equal to the number of the angels who fell with Lucifer[10], but since no-one knew exactly how many were involved in the celestial rebellion, this suggestion was not a great deal of practical help. Others thought the number of the predestined would equal the number of *good* angels, and yet others, the optimists, considered the number to be that of all angels, good and bad alike. But once again, our lack of precise information on the population of heaven precludes any specificity on this matter. The best answer, says Thomas Aquinas, is to say that God alone knows the number of his elect; but, he adds in a gloomy and augustinian aside, it undoubtedly includes only a minority of the human race.

The chief problem with this theory is not so much that it turns God into an all-powerful despot making arbitrary decisions (for God is, by definition, fair and just), but that it comes all too close to Double Predestination. We do not actually *say* that God

10. See *Cloud* 148.

predestines to hell those whom he has not chosen, but we certainly imply it. Hincmar's objections to Double Predestination remain valid. And if we remember the analogy we used earlier, a God who stands back and watches someone walk over a cliff is not, in my view, much better than a God who helps them on their way with a push. The end result is the same.

What, then, of the other attempt at a solution: predestination *post praevisa merita*, predestination *after* foreseen merits? How does this deal with the problem? Here we are closer to Hincmar than to Gottschalk, for in this scheme, God's foreknowledge is of fundamental importance. But whereas for Hincmar, God predestined only the consequences of one's actions, in predestination *post praevisa merita*, he predestines the grace that leads to these consequences. Aquinas's teacher, Albert the Great, preferred this point of view, as also did Alexander of Hales. It has two main advantages. It does not envisage a God who makes arbitrary decisions, and it does not maintain that he first predestines certain people to glory and then provides them with the means of getting there. In other words, this second scheme is both more humane and more logical.

It begins with a reassertion of the universal saving will of God. God, in theory, predestines everyone to glory. As the letter to Timothy says, he wants all of us to be saved. He therefore makes his grace available to all, but he knows in advance (for he is all-knowing and in him there is no past or future) that not all will take advantage of it. So to those whom he foreknows will cooperate with his grace and do good, he makes this grace available. They, and they alone, are predestined to achieve salvation, and the others, by their own choice and not by God's decree, must go to hell.

Imagine that I have a number of bottles of the best wine in the world—the 1945 Mouton-Rothschild, for example—and, for pure love, wish to give them to my friends.[11] But if some of my

11. I should perhaps add that I cannot envisage any circumstances in which I would actually give away a bottle of 1945 Mouton-Rothschild. Sharing it is a different matter.

friends are teetotal, there is no point in my giving them the wine.
It is not that I love them less, but to give them something that I
know in advance they will not use is simply a waste. The situation
is just the same with God and his grace. His love is infinite and
universal, and it is grief and suffering to him that there are those
whom he knows will not take advantage of his gifts. But if they
will not, they will not, and there is therefore no point in making
those gifts available to them. It is no more than common sense.

As we said above, this scheme certainly has advantages. God's
decisions are based on our actions, and rather than being predestined to glory and then given grace, we are predestined to grace
and therefore attain glory. There is, however, a difficulty. If we
follow Augustine and maintain that as a consequence of original
sin we are *una massa peccati*, how can we, of our own free-will,
cooperate with God's grace in the first place? Remember what
Augustine said: of our own power we can only fall. And if we
go on to say that the only ones who will cooperate with God's
grace are those whom God has predestined to do so, then we
are right back with Thomas Aquinas and predestination *ante
praevisa merita*!

Other western theologians were aware of these difficulties and
made valiant, though unsuccessful, attempts to solve them. Both
Anselm of Canterbury and Bernard of Clairvaux wrote treatises
endeavouring to harmonize freedom of choice with the need for
grace, but if, with Bernard, we can conclude only that freedom of
choice is certainly free, but free only to sin, we have not got very
far. In the thirteenth century, the scholastic theologians took up
the matter, and they too presented long and complex analyses
of the nature of free-will in an attempt to show how, despite
Augustine, there were certain ways in which the term 'free' could
still meaningfully be applied. But to examine their arguments
would lead us deep into the realms of scholastic philosophy
and aristotelian terminology, and that is not our purpose in
this present volume. In any case, none of their attempts was
particularly satisfactory.

A different solution to the problem was suggested by a later
spanish Jesuit named Luis de Molina. He was born in 1535,

entered the Society of Jesus in 1553, and taught at the universities of Coimbra and Evora. He then settled in Lisbon and, in 1588, published his *Concordia liberi arbitrii cum gratiae donis*, the *Harmonization of Free-Will with the Gifts of Grace*. Two years later he retired to Cuença and remained there until 1600 when he was appointed professor at the newly-founded jesuit school of moral theology in Madrid. He had just taken up the position when he died on 12 October of that year. Molina is really outside the scope of this present study, but a simplified version of his teachings which was adopted by many of his followers provides us with a neat solution to the problems we have encountered.

The basis of his argument is not difficult to understand, for it involves no more than a simple extension of the concept of God's omniscience. God, Molina maintained, knows not only what *will* happen, but what *might* have happened had circumstances been different. In other words, God not only knew in advance about the birth of Adolf Hitler and the horrors of the holocaust, but he also knew what would have happened had Hitler been aborted. Similarly, God not only foreknew Thomas Aquinas, but he also foreknew how christian theology would have been different had Aquinas been born Thomasina.

It is a straightforward projection of this principle to say that God not only foreknows what each one of us *will* do with our lives, but what we *would* have done *if* we had had perfect free-will, unaffected by original sin. So to those whom God foreknew would have cooperated with his grace and done good actions if they had been able to do so, he makes his grace available; to those who would not, he does not. In this way, we retain the principle that it is we, not God, who render ourselves fit for heaven or hell, and avoid the problems that result from the doctrine of the total depravity of human beings as a consequence of original sin.

If one insists on being augustinian, the molinist interpretation of predestination *post praevisa merita* is perhaps the most satisfactory solution to the problem, though the Dominicans and other followers of Thomas Aquinas never agreed with it. Nor has the latin church ever specified which of the two approaches—

predestination *ante praevisa merita* or predestination *post praevisa merita*—was to be accepted. For western Christians, the problem of predestination remained unsolved.

For the eastern church, the situation was entirely different. The Greeks had never accepted the augustinian doctrine that human beings were 'one lump of sin', and had never maintained that as a consequence of original sin we can do no good at all. There was no doubt, they maintained, that our free-will has been seriously affected by the Fall, but we have not wholly lost the ability to choose the good and do it. The omniscient God knows in advance those who will do good, and to them he makes his grace available. Then, in cooperation with this grace, those so selected may do enough good to achieve salvation. Such is the teaching of John of Damascus, and it was actually his ideas, translated into Latin in the course of the twelfth century, which played an important role in inspiring such writers as Albert the Great and Alexander of Hales to present their own western version of his doctrine. In short, the byzantine answer to the problem of predestination was essentially the same as that which western theologians referred to as predestination *post praevisa merita*.

We are left with only one final question. Whatever belief we may have about predestination, there is no doubt that we will die; and whatever our ultimate destination, it can do no harm to get some inkling of what we might expect. There are four possible alternatives—limbo, purgatory, heaven, or hell—and we may now, in our final chapter, inquire of the medieval theologians what these places might be like.

XVIII-1 This early representation of purgatory is one of the most striking features of the carved altarpiece of Narbonne Cathedral (southern France). A deep interest in the pains of purgatory—and a yet deeper interest in how to avoid them—spread rapidly in the area after 1336. In that year Pope Benedict XII decreed that purgatorial torments begin immediately after death, but it was believed that such torments could be avoided by doing good works, especially by making donations to worthy causes. The grim Purgatory of Narbonne reminded people of what could happen if they were insufficiently generous. The tortures depicted here were inspired by a popular medieval text called *Saint Patrick's Purgatory*, which contains a description of the pains of purgatory as revealed by Christ to Saint Patrick. This scene shows the seventh torment, that of the cauldron, where demons force six sinful souls to bathe in boiling liquids and molten metal. Their faces and bodies demonstrate their agonies; one tries to climb over the edge to escape the torture. The river on which the cauldron is floating evokes the eighth torment: a fetid and icy stream in which sinners suffer unendurable cold. The cauldron would have been easily recognizable to people of this region as the type of barrel used for pressing grapes, and no doubt made a particularly strong impression in this grape-producing region where wine was (and still is) one of the staples of the economy.

Purgatory, second half of the fourteenth century.
Narbonne, Cathedral of Saint-Just-Saint-Pasteur, chapel of Notre-Dame-de-Bethléem.
Photo: Jean-Marc Colombier, Ville de Narbonne.

XVIII

Last Things

BEFORE WE VENTURE into the pastures of paradise or the horrors of hell, let us say a few words about the events which precede them: judgment and resurrection. The earliest christian fathers were uncertain about what happened in the moments after death, but by the fourth century the prevailing opinion was that some sort of judgment took place immediately, and that as a result of this the soul, in accordance with its merits, was assigned to a region of pain or pleasure until the Second Coming, the Last Trump, and the general resurrection.[1] At that time the dead would be raised in new and incorruptible bodies and would

1. See *Cloud* 199–201.

be subjected to a final, general judgment which would normally confirm what had been decided earlier. The possession of these resurrected bodies would then serve to intensify the pains or pleasures they had hitherto experienced: those in hell would suffer greater torment; those in heaven would enjoy greater felicity.

This, in general, was the view held by Augustine of Hippo, but in one area, and despite his immense authority, Augustine's ideas were not accepted by the church. According to Augustine, the righteous dead did not, in fact, enjoy the full glory of the vision of God straightaway, but went first to a place of temporary happiness which Augustine, following Luke 16:23, called 'the bosom of Abraham'. Only at the general resurrection, when they had been reunited with their bodies, could they enjoy the vision to the full and perceive God, as the angels perceive him, in all his wonder and glory.

Gregory the Great, the most important transmitter of the ideas of Augustine to the Middle Ages, did not agree with this. He maintained that the souls of the blessed entered the presence of God immediately after death, and that the resurrection of the body at the end of time would only enhance their delight. There is no intermediate place of partial happiness, and if the joy experienced in the resurrection body does indeed differ in quality from that experienced by the soul immediately after one's decease, the difference is not something we can express in human terms. It was this gregorian view which, in general, was accepted by all medieval christians, both eastern and western, though the east did not derive it from Gregory and the west did not state it officially until the fourteenth century.

The western statement was, as usual, a consequence of controversy. Despite the authority of Gregory and the prevailing opinion of the times, Pope John XXII, bishop of Rome from 1316 to 1334, had a different idea, and he expressed his views in a series of four sermons delivered in the winter of 1331–32. John had been reading the works of Bernard of Clairvaux and had found there a slightly elaborated version of the old augustinian suggestion that the grace of the Beatific Vision was not bestowed upon the blessed immediately after death, but was delayed until the general resurrection. Until that time, they would contemplate only the humanity of Christ, not his full divinity. The pope, we should note, had expressed these ideas not as the official teaching of the church, but only as his own personal opinions; yet that did nothing to prevent the eruption of a major theological scandal. A number of Franciscans supported John; the Dominicans, together with a majority of churchmen, were just as vehemently opposed. Some called for a general council and the deposition of the pope, but this proved unnecessary when John, who was already in his eighties, fell mortally ill. On his deathbed, he made a qualified retraction of his position, and declared that, in his opinion, the souls of the blessed contemplated God face-to-face immediately after death *so far as their condition permitted.* The truth of the matter was presumably made clear to the pope shortly afterwards, but he did not communicate the information to those who watched over his body.

John's half-hearted retraction did little to quell the controversy, and his successor, Benedict XII, found it necessary to settle the matter once and for all by issuing a papal decree in January 1336. This document, unlike John's sermons, was intended to represent the official voice of the church, and in it Benedict stated (i) that those deemed worthy to behold the divine essence did indeed see God face-to-face; (ii) that this vision took place immediately after death or (should it be required) after the cleansing pains of purgatory; and (iii) that when the blessed experienced this vision, they received from it not some partial fulfilment, but the very plenitude of joy and delight. But in making this statement, Benedict was doing little more than reiterating what had commonly been believed for several centuries.

It seems, then, that the vast majority of medieval Christians expected an individual and particular judgment of the soul immediately after death, then an indeterminate period of suffering or joy, and finally a bodily resurrection which would be followed by a general and irrevocable judgment. But what was the nature of the resurrection body? What were its qualities, and how did it differ from the body we have at present? The matter was of

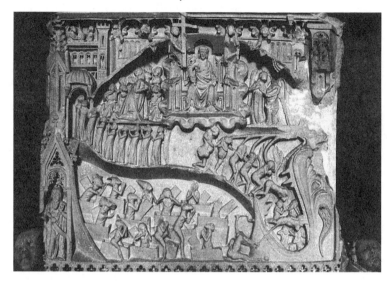

XVIII-2 This illustration of the Last Judgment occurs as the epilogue to a story of ill-fated lovers sculpted on one end of the stone sarcophagus of Dona Inés de Castro (c.1325–1355), a young galician lady-in-waiting to Constanza, wife of the infante Pedro. Pedro fell in love with Inés (perhaps even before the death of his wife in 1345), but his father, the king of Portugal, forbade the liaison and ordered Inés (who was by that time living with Pedro) executed in 1355. After his father's death two years later, Pedro became king. Still in love and revolted by the death of his beloved, he had her executioners condemned and declared himself married posthumously to Inés, making her his queen. The legitimacy of the marriage was rejected by the pope in 1361. Her remains had meanwhile been transported to the royal cistercian abbey of Alcobaça where Pedro had a double tomb made, for her and for himself. He never remarried. The Last Judgment shows Christ enthroned at the top, presiding over the divine tribunal, while the Virgin kneels in supplication with angels and apostles. Trumpets sound from the balcony, while souls climb out of their tombs and stream upwards toward the canopy of heaven or downwards to the yawning hell-mouth. In a tiny double window at the upper right, the lovers pray.

Last Judgment from the tomb of Inés de Castro, c. 1360.
Alcobaça Abbey, Portugal.

interest to both eastern and western theologians, but it is the western scholastics, following in the footsteps of Augustine, who provide us with the most detailed information.

There are three characteristics, they tell us, which are common to the resurrected bodies of the good and the wicked alike: identity (the body is one's own and no-one else's), entirety (there are no bits missing), and immortality. The bodies of the blessed, however, possess four further qualities which the wicked do not share. The first is impassability, which places them beyond the reach of pain. The second is luminosity, by which the bodies of the saints shine like the sun. The third is agility, by which the body is enabled to move from place to place with the speed of thought. And the fourth is 'subtlety'[2], by which the resurrected body is wholly subject to the perfected will of the soul and so spiritualized that it can act as if it were itself spirit. It is not limited by physical walls or material boundaries. With these ideas the greek writers were in general agreement, though they did not express themselves with the same scholastic precision or in the same vocabulary.

So much, then, for resurrection and judgment. Where do we go from there? What awaits us when we have passed beyond the walls of this world and have made our case before the just Judge? According to the eastern theologians, there are but two possibilities: heaven or hell. The west, however, added two further alternatives: limbo and purgatory, and we will begin our investigation by examining the doctrine of limbo.

The term limbo is an anglicized form of the Latin word *limbus*, 'a threshold, border', and it normally refers to the *limbus infantium* or 'limbo of the infants'. In Chapter XVI we saw that the main reason for positing its existence was to deal with the problem of children who died before being baptized and who were therefore stained with original sin, but not with sins they had committed themselves. Augustine maintained, quite logically, that since they were contaminated by sin, and since sin must always be punished, they would go to hell. They would suffer the least of torments, that is true, but the fact remained that they would still suffer.

2. *Subtilitas* in Latin. We could also translate it as 'fineness' or 'refinedness'.

In this matter as in so much else, Augustine's ideas were both novel and idiosyncratic, and most of those who preceded him had held different and more humane views. Gregory of Nazianzus, for example, agreed that because of the stain of original sin such children could not be admitted to the full joy of the Beatific Vision, but neither would they be punished. He therefore posited some sort of neutral or intermediate condition, though he did not give it a name. Ambrose, Augustine's teacher, saw original sin more as an inclination to evil than as actual guilt, and stated that those who were stained by original sin alone need have no fear on the day of judgment.

In the west, however, the all-pervasive influence of Augustine led such reputable theologians as Anselm of Canterbury to reiterate his views, and it seems that Abelard, who was so original in so many ways, was one of the first to challenge them. According to Abelard, it was contrary to divine justice that unbaptized children, who had never deliberately intended to defy God and who were stained with no sins of their own, should suffer real physical torment; and Augustine's qualification that those torments would be minimal was, in his opinion, no solution to the problem. On the other hand, Abelard could not deny that sin was present, and he agreed that the presence of sin, original or otherwise, precluded such infants from experiencing the Beatific Vision. What they suffered, therefore, was not the positive pain of physical torture, but the negative *poena damni*, 'pain of loss': the pain of being deprived of that vision which alone could provide the fullness of joy and blessedness.

Despite the fact that Abelard was condemned for almost everything else he said, this was one idea of his which, for a time, proved acceptable. It was taken up and popularized by Peter Lombard and given quasi-official approval in a letter of Pope Innocent III. But the fact remains that 'pain of loss' is still pain. Indeed, we shall see later that most theologians, eastern as well as western, considered that 'pain of loss' was the worst of all the pains endured by the damned in hell. Was it right, then, that unbaptized infants, through no fault of their own, should suffer in this way? Was it right, in fact, that they should suffer at all?

The first westerner to make a complete break with the old augustinian tradition was Thomas Aquinas. No, said he, it is not right that they should suffer, and although it remains true that the inheritance of original sin prevents them from enjoying the Beatific Vision, they are themselves unaware of this, and what the eye doesn't see, the heart doesn't grieve. It follows, then, that such children enjoy the highest natural happiness, being joined to God by a love of him proportionate to their capacity, and the fact that they are missing the supernatural joy of the vision of God is, for them, irrelevant. This more humane view of Aquinas proved understandably popular, and limbo became part of the official teaching of the western church. With very few exceptions, it remained unchallenged until the Reformation.

Our discussion of limbo has so far has been restricted to the *limbus infantium*, the 'limbo of the infants', which resolved the vexing problem of the fate of unbaptized children. There was, however, another form of limbo which solved a different though related problem: what had happened to all those men and women who, though also unbaptized, had lived good and righteous lives, but who had died after the Fall yet before the Redemption?

It was a commonly held belief of medieval writers that the sin of Adam and Eve had created a breach between God and humanity, and that as a consequence of this, the gates of heaven had been shut. They would not be opened again until the atonement, when Christ, through his death and his victory over death, healed the breach between God and human beings and reunited the Creator with his creation. At that time, in the days between his crucifixion and resurrection, he descended into hell, 'preached to the spirits in prison' (1 P 3:19), and liberated them; and since the gates of heaven were open once again, these spirits could at last enter upon their promised reward.

The 'prison' in which these spirits had been confined was referred to as the *limbus patrum* or 'limbo of the fathers'. We may imagine it as a sort of international airport departures lounge where the righteous dead had waited for centuries for the flight to heaven; but unlike the majority of such lounges, the *limbus patrum*, like the *limbus infantium*, was a place of positive, though temporary, happiness. When Christ rose from the dead, however, the entrances to heaven were unbarred, and there was no further need for the *limbus patrum*. It may therefore now be regarded as no more than a curiosity of theological history.

Far more important than limbo was purgatory. Indeed, we might not be wrong in saying that purgatory was even more important than heaven or hell, and it not only played a significant theological role in the medieval west, but an important economic and political role as well. The concept had a long history. It can be traced back as far as the third century of the christian era,[3] but its real development went hand-in-hand with the evolution of the sacrament of penance.

We saw in Chapter XVI that by about the year 1000 it was common practice for a priest to give conditional absolution to a penitent at the time of confession, but that the absolution took effect only after the penance had been completed. What happened, then, to penitents who died before they could perform their allotted penance? Did they go to heaven or to hell? And what happened to those who had not gone to confession at all? What happened to those who, having committed some trivial sin, had died before they had had the time, or perhaps the inclination, to confess their misdemeanour to a priest and thereby receive absolution? Were they destined for everlasting torment? The answer was that they were not. They went to purgatory, a place of temporary punishment where they could expiate their sins and then, cleansed and purified, move on to the blissful experience of the Beatific Vision. But for a full appreciation of this western doctrine, we need to make some preliminary observations on the difference between mortal and venial sins (for not all sins can be expiated in purgatory), and the distinction between guilt and punishment.

A mortal sin is not defined simply by the act involved, but by a combination of the act and the attitude of the actor. It must involve a 'grave matter' (murder, for example, or adultery),

---

3. See *Cloud* 200.

and it must be committed with the full consent of the will and with a clear knowledge of its guilt. In other words, you cannot commit mortal sin unknowingly or accidentally. But if you do commit it, you are deliberately and wilfully rejecting God and you completely block off the communication of his grace; and where there is no grace, there can be no salvation. You have nowhere to go but hell. Only by confession and absolution can the communication of grace be restored and the possibility of salvation regained.

Venial sin is any sin less than this. It may certainly be very serious, but it does not involve a complete blockage of grace; and because some grace can still get through, a sinner who dies in venial sin goes not to hell, but to purgatory. In short, the general teaching of the medieval church in the west (and also the teaching of modern Roman Catholicism) is that the only way to get to hell is to die in a state of unconfessed mortal sin. Other than that, you go to purgatory.

As to the matter of guilt and punishment, it is like a young boy breaking a window. His parents may forgive him for having committed the deed, but they will still stop his allowance until he has paid for the damage. Similarly, the guilt of sins may be forgiven, but, like the cost of the window, there is still something to pay. Sinning produces a sort of dislocation in the order of the universe, and order must be restored before we can move on. Purgatory, therefore, serves to purge us from the punishment (not the guilt) due to venial sins or confessed mortal sins, and only after we have paid the penalty can we enter the perfection of heaven.

How painful are the pains of purgatory? Very painful indeed! The principal agent of this pain is real and material fire, and according to Augustine, the pain caused by this fire is greater than any pain that can be suffered here on earth. Gregory the Great agreed with him and so did Thomas Aquinas and Bonaventure. Thomas makes things worse by reminding us that we must also take into consideration the 'pain of loss' which we mentioned earlier. On the other hand, the souls in purgatory know that however dreadful the punishment, it is only temporary, and that after it is all over they will enter heaven. It's like going to the dentist: it may not be nice, but it won't last for ever. This, we are told, makes the pain somewhat more bearable (Pope Benedict XII said so officially in 1336), but it is still true that we are dealing with a very unpleasant period. The next question, therefore, is obvious: how can we avoid it?

From a very early period, the church had taught that prayers and masses for the dead could be of benefit to them. The idea occurs as early as Tertullian and Cyprian—in other words, by the late second or early third century. Augustine, similarly, tells us that prayers for the faithful, giving alms on their behalf, and the 'holy sacrifice of the altar', can aid those who have died and move the Almighty to deal with them with mercy and kindness. By the Middle Ages, the principle was universally accepted, but from the time of Gregory the Great, the number of prayers that had to be said, the quantity of alms that had to be distributed, and the number of masses that needed to be celebrated had all alike been subject to inflation.

Gregory himself reports a vision in which one particular monk had been released from purgatory after the celebration of thirty masses on his behalf on thirty consecutive days, and this series of thirty—the so-called Gregorian Masses—came to be widely accepted as a means of releasing one's loved ones from purgatorial fire. By the fourteenth century, it was not unusual to find wealthy merchants asking for thousands of masses, sometimes hundreds of thousands, to be said for their souls and making very large bequests to churches, chapels, or monastic houses to ensure that this was done. Almsgiving, similarly, could range from straightforward donations of money or land to the establishment of entire monasteries; and the continual attempts by the wealthy, particularly the sinfully wealthy, to pressure God into releasing them from future torment at the earliest possible moment proved a major source of revenue for the late medieval church.

Indulgences, too, were a most important source of income, for we saw in Chapter XVI how the basic principle of the indulgence—that good deeds may be rewarded by God—had been distorted in the medieval west. Aquinas, with his usual clarity, had stated that although the primary purpose of an indulgence was to benefit the individual who had gained it, there was no reason why this benefit should not be applied to souls in purgatory; and although there was some dispute among the later scholastics as to the precise effects of this application, popular piety was in no doubt at all. Prayers, alms, masses, or indulgences—together with the money to pay for them—could get you or your dear departed out of purgatory, and that was all you needed to know.

The concept of purgatory and its subsequent development was almost entirely a western phenomenon. It was not and is not the teaching of Orthodoxy, and, as we shall see, the Orthodox rejection of the idea had certain political consequences. The east had no objection in principle to petitioning God on behalf of those who had died, and the *Liturgy of Saint John Chrysostom*, the most commonly used of the Orthodox liturgies, contains a prayer for 'those who have fallen asleep in the faith'. But in the view of the greek theologians, a distinct intermediate state is nowhere specified in scripture, and the usual verses cited by westerners to prove its existence—1 Corinthians 3:12–15, which speaks of some as being 'saved, but only as through fire'—were thought to be vague and unclear. On the contrary, said the Greeks, Christ himself tells us that when Lazarus died, he went straight to Abraham's bosom, and as far as the eastern church was concerned, Abraham's bosom was not some sort of augustinian intermediate condition, but paradise itself.

The Greeks, therefore, preferred to think only in terms of heaven and hell, and those few eastern theologians who accepted the possibility of purgatory did not conceive of it in the same way as their western counterparts. They rejected any idea of material fire, and they did not accept the distinction between guilt and punishment. If God forgave you your sins, he forgave the whole of your sins, not just the guilt; and the idea of having been forgiven, but still having to suffer, was, for the east, as illogical as it was unjust.

It is not surprising, therefore, to learn that at those councils that attempted (unsuccessfully) to reconcile the eastern and western churches—the Council of Lyons in 1274 and the Council of Florence in 1439[4]—the question of purgatory was one of the stumbling-blocks. It is true that the westerners were able to force the east to accept it (though they had to avoid any mention of fire and did not distinguish between guilt and punishment), but after the failure of these councils to achieve any lasting reunion, the Orthodox churches returned to their earlier view. There is no clear evidence, they said, in either scripture or tradition for any intermediate state, and the fate of the soul after death is a matter best left to God.

Let us suppose now that we have sinned so deliberately and so spectacularly that there is no hope left. We have cut ourselves off entirely from the grace of God and have been consigned, justly, to hell. What will it be like? The scriptures mention some of its more obvious characteristics—darkness, weeping and wailing, gnashing of teeth, unquenchable fire, and the worm that does not die—but in the Middle Ages in the west there developed a large visionary literature on the subject in which all manner of people—men and women, clerics and laity, monks and nuns— testified to experiences in which they had been given guided tours of paradise and hell.

A typical example is the so-called *Apocalypse (or Vision) of Saint Paul*. It was originally written in Greek and probably dates from the second half of the fourth century, but it was soon translated into Latin and various vernacular languages and enjoyed great popularity in the Middle Ages. Dante quotes it in his *Inferno*. Paul, we are told, was taken up into the third heaven, just as the scriptures relate[5], and once he was there he was given the opportunity not only of seeing the wonders of paradise, but also of viewing the torments of the damned. Having accepted this offer with what some might regard as untoward alacrity, Paul is escorted by an angelic guide in the direction of the setting sun, and after a lengthy journey he and the angel eventually arrive

4. Both Councils were discussed at the end of Chapter X.
5. See 2 Cor 12:2.

at the boundless ocean which encircles the whole earth. Beyond this ocean is hell.

First of all, Paul sees men and women sunk to various depths in a river of fire. Some are immersed to their knees, some to their navels, some to their lips, and some to their hair. The angel then explains to Paul the particular sins for which they are being punished. Those immersed up to their lips, for example, are those who go to church, but once there indulge in the sin of slander. Then we come upon an old man who is being strangled by demons, but the demons have also hooked up his intestines on a trident and are dragging them out of his mouth. This, Paul is told, is a priest who celebrated the eucharist, but who was also guilty of gluttony and fornication. Not far away is a former bishop who is up to his knees in the fiery river and whose face is being continually smashed by stones. In his life he had failed to have compassion on widows and orphans. Next we see a sinful deacon who, like the bishop, is immersed up to his knees, but his hands are all bloody and worms are crawling out of his mouth.

And so it goes on. There are souls being devoured by worms; souls eating their own tongues; souls with their hands and feet cut off; souls hung up by their eyebrows; souls in pits of brimstone and boiling tar; souls being torn to pieces by animals; and souls being mangled by dragons. Other similar visions add further details. We find souls nailed to the ground with red-hot nails; souls tied down by their hair and exposed to the continual bites of snakes and venomous reptiles; souls immersed in pits of molten metal; souls tormented by ice and cold; souls lying on a burning pavement and being eaten by worms; souls being beaten by demons with fiery scourges; souls being lashed with flails; souls being attacked by flame-spitting vipers; souls hung on the spines of great thorn-trees; souls boiled in oil or pitch; souls forced to climb burning ladders; and on it goes. The authors of these visions vie with each other in devising ever more inventive ways of inflicting pain, and the wide circulation of the manuscripts that contained these tales testifies to their great popularity. The greeks, for the most part, were much less specific.

When we turn from these popular descriptions to the concerns of the western theologians, we find less of a sadistic concern with the bloody details of punishment, and a greater interest in such questions as the location of hell, or how a physical body can endure eternal pain, or how material fire can affect immaterial bodies, or whether the punishment is really eternal. Much of what the theologians have to say is based on the speculations of Augustine in the twenty-first book of his monumental treatise *The City of God (De civitate Dei)*. Original and inventive thinkers like John Scotus Eriugena, who (as we saw in Chapter XVII) denied the existence of hell, had virtually no following.

As to the location of hell, and despite some hesitation on the part of Augustine and Gregory the Great, the medieval writers generally accepted that it was somewhere under the earth, and they were agreed that those who were so unfortunate as to be consigned there were there forever. As to pain, it was twofold. The damned suffered everlasting sensory pain as a consequence of the material fire, but they also suffered the *poena damni*, the 'pain of loss', as a consequence of their eternal separation from God. It is the 'pain of loss' which the scholastics considered to be the greater torture and they tended to see it as the very essence of eternal punishment: it meant an utter loss of faith, and an endless void of despair and abject hopelessness. For those in hell there is no pleasure and no respite: nothing to hope for, nothing to look forward to; only everlasting darkness and ceaseless suffering.

According to the *Apocalypse of Paul*, the apostle, with support from Michael and other angels, succeeded in persuading Christ to grant the damned a relaxation from their torments every Sunday, but the church was not prepared to entertain this view. Nor was it prepared to consider the suggestion of a few other humane theologians that the prayers of the faithful might benefit not just the souls in purgatory, but also those in hell. No, says Thomas Aquinas (who is following Augustine), when we say that the damned suffer eternal torment and everlasting pain, we mean precisely what we say.

Let us now leave these depressing matters and turn our attention to the happier prospect of heaven and the Beatific Vision.

XVIII-3 This miniature of the heavenly throne comes from the most famous of all manuscripts illuminated in the south of France, the *Beatus Apocalypse* from the abbey of Saint-Sever. It contains not the Book of Revelation itself, but a commentary on it composed between 776–784 by the spanish monk, Beatus, abbot of Liébana. The work was adopted by the spanish church and copied century after century. The illustrations were probably intended as a visual aid to memorizing the text, but they contributed as much to the success of the book as did the text itself; they were reproduced continually from the tenth to the early thirteenth centuries. The copies were not slavish imitations of the originals, but imaginative interpretations, and their fame went beyond the borders of Spain. The manuscript shown here was made during the eleventh century in Gascony (southwestern France), and is one of the most magnificent of the series. This splendid illustration of the beatific vision was inspired by chapter four of the Book of Revelation: a rainbow surrounds the throne, twenty-four seated elders, four six-winged beasts full of eyes front and back. These beasts, also called the Tetramorph, here represent the four writers of the gospels, each with a book in hand: the Lion (Mark), the Calf (Luke), the Man (Matthew), the Eagle (John). The outer edges of the scene are filled with the heavenly host. The elders, although not all clothed in white, are seated on chairs of wildly different colours and designs.

The Beatus Apocalypse of Saint-Sever: Christ between the four beasts and twenty-four Elders. Gascony (France), 1028–1072.
Paris, Bibliothèque nationale, ms lat 8878, f° 121ᵛ–122.
Photo: Bibliothèque Nationale, Paris.

The visionary literature that provides us with graphic accounts of hell also offers descriptions of heaven, but since it is always more difficult to portray good than evil, these descriptions tend to be somewhat bland and uninspiring. They are, in any case, more bound to the biblical text, for whereas the scriptures describe hell in fairly general terms—outer darkness, fire, and so on—the book of Genesis gives us a detailed account of the First Paradise and the book of Revelation provides us with a ground-plan of the New Jerusalem.

If, once again, we consult the *Apocalypse of Paul*, we find that the heavenly city of Christ is constructed entirely of gold and is surrounded by twelve walls, each dominated by a tower, and each one separated from the next by a celestial *stade*.[6] How long is a celestial *stade*, asks Paul? As great as the distance between heaven and earth, explains the angel, and adds (unnecessarily) that heaven is very large. There are twelve gates in the great walls, and beyond them are four rivers: a river of honey, a river of milk, a river of wine, and a river of oil.

At the river of honey, Paul meets the major and minor prophets and those who, like them, have done God's will rather than their own. At the river of milk, he sees the children whom Herod slew at the Massacre of the Innocents[7], along with those who have kept themselves chaste and pure. At the river of wine he finds the patriarchs and all who have given hospitality to strangers. And at the river of oil he sees people rejoicing and singing psalms: these are they who have dedicated themselves entirely to God.

The angel then conducts Paul into the middle of the city, close to the twelfth wall, and he sees there golden thrones and figures sitting on them, crowned with golden diadems and adorned with jewels. Beyond these thrones are yet others, intended for the unlearned who, in their innocence, have fulfilled all the commandments of God. Then, in the very heart of the city, Paul sees a great and high altar, and by the side of it a man holding

6. An ordinary, non-celestial *stade* or *stadion* is about six hundred feet.
7. See Mt 2:16.

in his hands a psaltery and harp. This is David, and he is singing 'Hallelujah!' in such a voice that the towers of heaven tremble and the foundations of the celestial city are shaken.

For Paul, this vision of David represents the end of his journey. The angel now leads him down from heaven and they begin their tour of hell which we have described above. Other medieval visionaries, however, did not stop at this point, and many of them claimed to have seen Christ, Mary, and even God on his throne surrounded by choirs of angels. Such visions as these are important reflections of popular conceptions of heaven, and probably differ little from popular ideas nowadays. For many Christians today, heaven is no more than a magnified version of the earth, with all its terrestrial glories but none of its problems. There are no taxes in heaven, no police, no diseases, no hangovers, no pollution, and (according to Thomas Aquinas, poor man) no animals. When you get there, you can expect to see Joe or Jane waiting to meet you within the golden (or pearly) gates. They will be dressed in white nightshirts with golden belts, and they will lead you into a realm of everlasting light where you will praise God forever. How this is done is not clear, but it may involve clouds and harps. People are just as gullible nowadays as they were in the Middle Ages.

The concerns of the medieval theologians differed somewhat from those of the medieval visionaries, for they were not primarily concerned with supplying detailed descriptions of the New Jerusalem. In the east, they tended to dwell on the culmination of the process of deification when human beings, by God's grace, would participate in the uncreated energies of God, and share in his love, perfection, bliss, and immortality. And after Symeon the New Theologian and the rise of hesychasm, much of what they had to say concentrated on the rapturous vision of the Divine Light.

Western theologians tended to echo Augustine's discussion in the twenty-second book of his *De civitate Dei*. The twenty-first book had already supplied them with much of their information on hell. Augustine spends most of his time dealing with the problem of bodily resurrection, but he also makes it clear that heaven is a place of eternal bliss. It is an everlasting sabbath where the blessed see God face-to-face, and, through this vision, achieve their greatest joy. The wills of the blessed are eternally fixed on God, and because of this, there is no place for sin. They have an everlasting desire for God, yet that desire is always satisfied. Augustine calls it 'insatiable satiety.' There is no disharmony here, no wickedness, no weariness, no sorrow or suffering, no pain, no loss, nothing to interfere with the endless rapture of eternal beatitude. For Augustine and the theologians who followed him, the reward of virtue is not to be thought of in terms of the quasi-material delights of a celestified earth such as we find in the *Apocalypse of Paul* and the other medieval visions: the reward of virtue is the God who gave that virtue, together with the promise of himself, the greatest and best of all possible promises.

Not all of this joy is reserved for the life to come. Some of it we can know here and now, for as we have seen in earlier chapters, the purpose of the monastic life and of christian spirituality was not just to lead one to the endless vision of God in the next world, but also (by God's grace) to achieve a foretaste of that experience here below. Nor was it just a matter for monks and nuns. According to the eastern writers (and especially Symeon the New Theologian), all of us can gain a glimpse of the divine glory if we would but try. The essential plan of the path had been laid out long ago by Pseudo-Dionysius: we begin with purgation; we move on to illumination; we find the culmination in union. Union with what? According to Gregory Palamas, union with the uncreated energies of God; a union which would lead to our transformation not into God, but into 'what God is'; a union which can reveal to us by experience what we cannot comprehend intellectually.

How this experience differs from the Beatific Vision we cannot say. The one is eternal, the other temporary, that is true; but if there is also a difference in quality between them, it is not a difference which is susceptible to logical analysis. The Beatific Vision is indescribable and the mystical experience is likewise indescribable. Any difference between them, therefore, is also indescribable, and we cannot describe that which is, by definition, beyond description.

The true nature of the last things may also defy description, but that has never stopped people from making the attempt. Mystics and visionaries of all ages, both eastern and western, have maintained that what they experienced could not be communicated in words, but few of them could resist trying. In any case, for the medieval church, descriptions of the joys of heaven and the horrors of hell, expressed as graphically as possible in either words or pictures, were useful tools for controlling the populace. The Last Judgment was a common theme in western art in the Middle Ages, and we have already seen how the desire to escape the pains of purgatory provided a major source of ecclesiastical revenue.

Whether the medieval descriptions of heaven and hell are accurate is not something we can know at present. That we will know is not in doubt, for longevity is not synonymous with immortality, and even the best of us must die. Unfortunately, that knowledge, once acquired, cannot easily be shared, for according to christian belief, one person alone returned from those shadowed realms, and he said little about them. The christian hope, therefore, remains a hope, a hope which is founded on the promises of a merciful and compassionate God, and a hope which, despite our present sufferings and travail, we may hope to see fulfilled. According to William of Saint-Thierry, we were created in order to see God, and the vision that is promised us is no more than the natural and God-given realization of our human potential. In the beginning, we were created in the image and likeness of God; in the meantime, we have lost that likeness through sin; in the end, we may regain it. Whether or not we do so, said Pelagius, is entirely up to us.

Index

Numbers in **bold** refer to illustrations

CISTERCIAN PUBLICATIONS
Texts and Studies in the Monastic Tradition

TEXTS IN ENGLISH TRANSLATION

THE CISTERCIAN MONASTIC TRADITION

Aelred of Rievaulx

- Dialogue on the Soul
- The Historical Works
- Liturgical Sermons, I
- The Lives of the Northern Saints
- Spiritual Friendship
- Treatises I: Jesus at the Age of Twelve; Rule for a Recluse; Pastoral Prayer
- Walter Daniel: The Life of Aelred of Rievaulx

Bernard of Clairvaux

- Apologia to Abbot William (Cistercians and Cluniacs)
- Five Books on Consideration: Advice to a Pope
- Homilies in Praise of the Blessed Virgin Mary
- In Praise of the New Knighthood
- Letters
- Life and Death of Saint Malachy the Irishman
- On Baptism and the Office of Bishops
- On Grace and Free Choice
- On Loving God
- Parables and Sentences
- Sermons for the Summer Season
- Sermons on Conversion
- Sermons on the Song of Songs, I-IV
- The Steps of Humility and Pride

Gertude the Great of Helfta

- Spiritual Exercises
- The Herald of God's Loving-Kindness, Books 1 and 2
- The Herald of God's Loving-Kindness, Book 3

William of Saint Thierry

- The Enigma of Faith
- Exposition on the Epistle to the Romans
- Exposition on the Song of Songs
- The Golden Epistle
- The Mirror of Faith
- The Nature and Dignity of Love
- On Contemplating God, Prayer, Meditations

Gilbert of Hoyland

- Sermons on the Song of Songs, I-III
- Treatises, Sermons, and Epistles

John of Ford

- Sermons on the Final Verses of the Song of Songs, I-VII

Other Cistercian Writers

- Adam of Perseigne, Letters, I
- Alan of Lille: The Art of Preaching
- Amadeus of Lausanne: Homilies in Praise of Blessed Mary
- Baldwin of Ford: Commendation of Faith
- Geoffrey of Auxerre: On the Apocalypse
- Guerric of Igny: Liturgical Sermones, I-II
- Helinand of Froidmont: Verses on Death
- Idung of Prüfening: Cistercians and Cluniacs. The Case of Cîteaux
- In The School of Love. An Anthology of Early Cistercian Texts
- Isaac of Stella: Sermons on the Christian Year, I-[II]
- The Letters of Armand-Jean de Rancé, Abbot of la Trappe
- The Life of Beatrice of Nazareth
- Mary Most Holy: Meditating with the Early Cistercians
- Ogier of Locedio: Homilies [on Mary and the Last Supper]
- Serlo of Wilton & Serlo of Savigny: Seven Unpublished Works (Latin-English)
- Sky-blue the Sapphire, Crimson the Rose: The Spirituality of John of Ford
- Stephen of Lexington: Letters from Ireland
- Stephen of Sawley: Treatises
- Three Treatises on Man: A Cistercian Anthropology / Bernard McGinn

EARLY AND EASTERN MONASTICISM

- Besa: The Life of Shenoute of Atripe
- Cyril of Scythopolis: The Lives of the Monks of Palestine
- Dorotheos of Gaza: Discourses and Sayings
- Evagrius Ponticus: Praktikos and Chapters on Prayer
- Handmaids of the Lord: Lives of Holy Women in Late Antiquity and the Early Middle Ages / Joan Petersen
- Harlots of the Desert. A Study of Repentance / Benedicta Ward
- Isaiah of Scete: Ascetic Discourses

- John Moschos: The Spiritual Meadow
- The Life of Antony (translated from Coptic and Greek)
- The Lives of the Desert Fathers. The *Historia monachorum in Aegypto*
- The Spiritually Beneficial Tales of Paul, Bishop of Monembasia
- Symeon the New Theologian: The Practical and Theological Chapters, and The Three Theological Discourses
- Theodoret of Cyrrhus: A History of the Monks of Syria
- Stewards of the Poor. [Three biographies from fifth-century Edessa]
- The Syriac Book of Steps *[Liber graduum]*
- The Syriac Fathers on Prayer and the Spiritual Life / Sebastian Brock

LATIN MONASTICISM

- Achard of Saint Victor: Works
- Anselm of Canterbury: Letters, I–III
- Bede the Venerable: Commentary on the Acts of the Apostles
- Bede the Venerable: Commentary on the Seven Catholic Epistles
- Bede the Venerable: Homilies on the Gospels, I–II
- Bede the Venerable: Excerpts from the Works of Saint Augustine on the Letters of the Blessed Apostle Paul
- The Celtic Monk [An Anthology]
- Gregory the Great: Forty Gospel Homilies
- Guigo II: The Ladder of Monks and Twelve Meditations / Colledge, Walsh edd.
- Halfway to Heaven
- The Life of the Jura Fathers
- The Maxims of Stephen of Muret
- Peter of Celle: Selected Works
- The Letters of Armand-Jean de Rancé, I–II
- The Rule of the Master
- The Rule of Saint Augustine
- Saint Mary of Egypt. Three Medieval Lives in Verse

STUDIES IN MONASTICISM / CISTERCIAN STUDIES

Cistercian Studies and Reflections

- Aelred of Rievaulx. A Study / Aelred Squire
- Athirst for God. Spiritual Desire in Bernard of Clairvaux's Sermons on the Song of Songs / Michael Casey
- Beatrice of Nazareth in her Context, I–II: Towards Unification with God / Roger DeGanck
- Bernard of Clairvaux. Man. Monk. Mystic / Michael Casey
- The Cistercian Way / André Louf
- Dom Gabriel Sortais. An Amazing Abbot in Turbulent Times / Guy Oury
- The Finances of the Cistercian Order in the Fourteenth Century / Peter King
- Fountains Abbey and Its Benefactors / Joan Wardrop
- A Gathering of Friends. Learning and Spirituality in John of Ford
- Hidden Springs: Cistercian Monastic Women, 2 volumes
- Image of Likeness. The Augustinian Spirituality of William of St Thierry / D. N. Bell
- Index of Authors and Works in Cistercian Libraries in Great Britain / D. N. Bell

- Index of Cistercian Authors and Works in Medieval Library catalogues in Great Britain / D. N. Bell
- The Mystical Theology of Saint Bernard / Etienne Gilson
- The New Monastery. Texts and Studies on the Earliest Cistercians
- Monastic Odyssey [Cistercian Nuns & the French Revolution]
- Nicolas Cotheret's Annals of Cîteaux / Louis J. Lekai
- Pater Bernhardus. Martin Luther and Bernard of Clairvaux / Franz Posset
- Rancé and the Trappist Legacy / A. J. Krailsheimer
- A Second Look at Saint Bernard / Jean Leclercq
- The Spiritual Teachings of St Bernard of Clairvaux / John R. Sommerfeldt
- Studies in Medieval Cistercian History
- Three Founders of Cîteaux / Jean-Baptiste Van Damme
- Understanding Rancé. Spirituality of the Abbot of La Trappe in Context / D. N. Bell
- William, Abbot of Saint Thierry
- Women and Saint Bernard of Clairvaux / Jean Leclercq

Cistercian Art, Architecture, and Music

- Cistercian Abbeys of Britain [illustrated]
- Cistercian Europe / Terryl N. Kinder
- Cistercians in Medieval Art / James France
- SS. Vincenzo e Anastasio at Tre Fontane Near Rome / J. Barclay Lloyd
- Studies in Medieval Art and Architecture, II–VI / Meredith P. Lillich, ed.
- Treasures Old and New. Nine Centuries on Cistercian Music [CD, cassette]
- Cistercian Chants for the Feast of the Visitation [CD]

Monastic Heritage

- Community and Abbot in the Rule of St Benedict, I–II / Adalbert de Vogüé
- Distant Echoes: Medieval Religious Women, I / Shank, Nichols, edd.
- The Freedom of Obedience / A Carthusian
- Halfway to Heaven [The Carthusian Tradition] / Robin Lockhart
- The Hermit Monks of Grandmont / Carole A. Hutchison
- A Life Pleasing to God: Saint Basil's Monastic Rules / Augustine Holmes
- Manjava Skete [Ruthenian tradition] / Sophia Seynk
- Monastic Practices / Charles Cummings
- Peace Weavers. Medieval Religious Women, II / Shank, Nichols, edd.
- Reading Saint Benedict / Adalbert de Vogüé
- The Rule of St Benedict. A Doctrinal and Spiritual Commentary / Adalbert de Vogüé
- Stones Laid Before the Lord [Monastic Architecture] / Anselme Dimier
- What Nuns Read [Libraries of Medieval English Nunneries] / D. N. Bell

Monastic Liturgy

- From Advent to Pentecost / A Carthusian
- The Hymn Collection from the Abbey of the Paraclete, 2 volumes
- The Molesme Summer Season Breviary, 4 volumes
- The Old French Ordinary and Breviary of the Abbey of the Paraclete, 5 volumes
- The Paraclete Statutes: *Institutiones nostrae*
- The Twelfth Century Cistercian Hymnal, 2 volumes
- The Twelfth Century Cistercian Psalter [NYP]
- Two Early Cistercian *Libelli Missarum*

MODERN MONASTICISM
Thomas Merton

- Cassian and the Fathers: Initiation into the Monastic Tradition
- The Climate of Monastic Prayer
- The Legacy of Thomas Merton
- The Message of Thomas Merton
- The Monastic Journey of Thomas Merton
- Thomas Merton Monk
- Thomas Merton on Saint Bernard
- Thomas Merton: Prophet of Renewal / John Eudes Bamberger
- Toward An Integrated Humanity [Essays on Thomas Merton]

Contemporary Monastics

- Centered on Christ. A Guide to Monastic Profession / Augustine Roberts
- Inside the Psalms. Reflections for Novices / Maureen McCabe
- Passing from Self to God. A Cistercian Retreat / Robert Thomas
- Pathway of Peace. Cistercian Wisdom according to Saint Bernard / Charles Dumont
- Poor Therefore Rich / A Carthusian
- The Way of Silent Love / A Carthusian

CHRISTIAN SPIRITUALITY PAST AND PRESENT

Past

- A Cloud of Witnesses. The Development of Christian Doctrine [to 500] / D. N. Bell
- Eros and Allegory: Medieval Exegesis of the Song of Songs / Denys Turner
- High King of Heaven. Aspects of Early English Spirituality / Benedicta Ward
- In the Unity of the Holy Spirit. Conference on the Rule of Benedict

- The Life of St Mary Magdalene and of Her Sister St Martha [Magdalene legend]
- The Luminous Eye. The Spiritual World Vision of St Ephrem / Sebastian Brock
- Many Mansions. Medieval Theological Development East and West / D. N. Bell
- The Name of Jesus / Irénée Hausherr
- Penthos. The Doctrine of Compunction in the Christian East / Irénée Hausherr

CISTERCIAN PUBLICATIONS Titles Listing

- Prayer. The Spirituality of the Christian East II / Tomás Spidlík
- Russian Mystics / Serge Bolshakoff, Introduction by Thomas Merton
- Silent Herald of Unity. The Life of Maria Gabrielle Sagheddu [Patron of Ecumenism] / Martha Driscoll
- The Spirituality of the Christian East / Tomás Spidlík
- The Spirituality of the Medieval Latin West / André Vauchez
- The Spiritual World of Isaac the Syrian / Hilarion Alfeyev
- The Venerable Bede / Benedicta Ward

Present

- Bearers of the Spirit: Spiritual Fatherhood in the Romanian Orthodox Tradition
- The Call of Wild Geese / Matthew Kelty
- The Contemplative Path. Rediscovering a Lost Tradition
- Drinking from the Hidden Fountain / Tomás Spidlík

- Entirely for God. The Life of Michael Iwene Tansi / Elizabeth Isichei
- Grace Can Do More. Spiritual Accompaniment / André Louf
- Interior Prayer / A Carthusian
- A Hand On My Shoulder. Memoirs of John Willem Gran, I–II
- The Hermitage Within / A Monk
- How Far to Follow. The Martyrs of Atlas / Bernardo Olivera
- Memoirs. From Grace to Grace / Jean Leclercq
- Mercy in Weakness / André Louf
- No Moment Too Small / Norvene Vest
- The Prayer of Love and Silence / A Carthusian
- Praying the Word / Enzo Bianchi
- Praying with Benedict / Korneel Vermeiren
- Sermons in a Monastery / Matthew Kelty
- Tuning In To Grace / André Louf
- Words To Live By. Journeys in Ancient and Modern Egyptian Monasticism / Tim Vivian

EDITORIAL OFFICES

Cistercian Publications • WMU Station
1903 West Michigan Avenue
Kalamazoo, MI 49008-5415   USA
tel 269 387 8920   fax 269 387 8390
e-mail cistpub@wmich.edu

CUSTOMER SERVICE—NORTH AMERICA: USA AND CANADA

Cistercian Publications at Liturgical Press
Saint John's Abbey
Collegeville, MN 56321-7500 USA
tel 800 436 8431   fax 320 363 3299
e-mail sales@litpress.org

CUSTOMER SERVICE—EUROPE: UK, IRELAND, AND EUROPE

Cistercian Publications at Columba Book Service
55A Spruce Avenue
Stillorgan Industrial Park
Blackrock, Co. Dublin, Ireland
tel 353 1 294 2560   fax 353 1 294 2564
e-mail sales@columba.ie

WEBSITE

www.cistercianpublications.org

Cistercian Publications is a non-profit corporation.